An A to Z of
Lourdes

First published in Great Britain by
New City

Unit 17
Sovereign Park
Coronation Rd
London NW10 7QP
© New City, London 2011

Translated by Claudine MacLullich

Graphic and Cover Design by
Hildebrando Moguiê

British Cataloguing in Publication Data:
A catalogue reference for this book is available
from the British Library

ISBN 978-1-905039-13-5

Typeset in Great Britain by
New City, London

Printed and bound in Malta by Gutenberg Press

Photo cover and photos incorporated in the text:
© Sanctuaires Notre-Dame de Lourdes/EURL Basilique Rosaire et Nino Bucca

An A to Z of Lourdes

Edited by Nino Bucca O.M.I.

New City
London

Contents

List of Entries	5
Preface	7
Introduction	9
Entries	11
Credits	217

List of Entries

Accueil Marie Saint-Frai	11
see also *Saint-Frai*	
Accueil Notre-Dame	12
AMIL : see *Bureau Medical*	
Annals of Our Lady of Lourdes	13
Apparitions	14
Apparitions (theology)	17
Aquero	18
Architecture	19
Archives	20
Augustin-Marie : see *Cohen*	
'Ave Maria' (the Lourdes hymn)	21
Bartrès	23
Basilca of St Pius X	26
Basilica of the Immaculate Conception	24
Basilica of the Rosary	25
Baths	27
Bernadette	28
see also Church; Museum; Diary	
Bétharram	31
Bigorre	32
Billère, Rosper-Marie	33
Billet, Bernard	34
Boissarie, Gustave	34
Boly : see *Mill of Boly*	
Bookshop	36
Brathomme, Henry	37
Bureau Medical	37
Cachot	39
Castérot, Louise	41
Castle	42
Centenary	43
Chaplains	44
Children of Mary : see *Enfants de Marie*	
Choquet, Georges	46
Church	47
see also *Parish*	
Church of St Bernadette	48
Cinema	49
Cité Saint-Pierre	51
Cohen, Hermann	52
Courtin, Jean-Baptiste	53
Cros, Léonard-Marie	54
Crowned Virgin	55
Crypt	55
Dance Theatre	57
De Lavaur : see *Marie-Antoine*	
De Saint-Maclou, Dunot	57
Désirat, Antoine	58
Diary of Bernadette	59
Diocese	59
Disabilities : see *Service*	
Donze, Henri	60
Dozous, Pierre-Romain	62
Dufo, Brice	63
Dutour, Vital	63
Ecumenism	65
Enfants de Marie	66
Espèlugues	66
Estrade, Jean-Baptiste	67
Eucharist	68
Eucharistic Procession	70
European Marian Network	71
Ex-Voto : see *Thanksgiving Plaques*	
Festival of Sacred Music	73
Garaison	75
Garicoits, Michel	76
Gave	76
Gerlier, Pierre Paul-Marie	77
Grotto	79
Grotto Estate	80
Hospice	81
Hospitalité	82
Hymn : see *'Ave Maria'*	
Images	85
Immaculate Conception	86
see also *Basilica; Missionaries;*	
Oblates; Statue	
Information Forum	88
Internationality	89
Internet	90
Jacomet, Dominique	91
John Paul II	93
John XXIII	92
Jourdan, César-Victor	94
Lacadé, Anselme	97
Lagues, Marie	98
Langénieux, Benoît	99
Lasserre, Henri	100
Laurence, Bertrand	100
Laurentin, René	102
Leo XIII	104
Light	104
Literature	106
Liturgical Music	109
Liturgy	109

Lourdes Magazine	112	Prayer	162
Magazine : see Lourdes Magazine		Presbytery	164
Marian Network : see European Marian Network		Press see also Media; Radio	165
Marian Procession	113	Procession : see Eucharistic Procession; Marian Procession	
Marie Saint-Frai : see Accueil; Saint-Frai			
Marie-Antoine	114	Prominent Women	166
Mariology of Lourdes	115	Pyrenees	167
Mary	117	Radio	169
Massy, Oscar	118	see also Press; Media	
Media	119	Ravier, André	169
see also Press; Radio		Rectors	170
Message	120	Religion see Popular Religion	
Mill of Boly	123	Rock	171
Miracles	124	Roncalli see John XXIII	
Miracles of Lourdes	125	Rosary	172
Missionaries of the Immaculate Conception	126	see also Basilica	
Montini : see Paul VI		Sahuquet, Jean	175
Museum (Treasure)	130	Saint-Frai, Marie	176
Museum of Bernadette	128	see also Accueil	
Music: see Festival of Sacred Music; Liturgical Music; Organs		Saint-Maclau : see De Saint-Maclau	
		Saint-Pierre : see Cité	
Napoleon III	131	Salus Infirmorum	177
Nevers	132	Schoepfer, François-Xavier	178
see also Sisters		Science and Lourdes	179
Notre-Dame : see Accueil, Hospitalité		Sempé, Rémi	180
Oblates of Mary Immaculate	135	Service for people with disabilities	182
Organs	137	Shrines	183
Outreach of Lourdes in the World	138	Sick Pilgrims	185
Pacelli : see Pius XII		Signs	186
Parish Church	141	Sisters of Nevers	187
Pastoral Ministry	142	Sisters of Saint-Joseph of Tarbes	189
Paul VI	143	Society and Lourdes	190
Pavilions	145	Soubirous, François	191
Penance	146	Spring of the Grotto	192
Peyramale, Dominique	149	Stations of the Cross	193
Photography	150	Statue of the Immaculate Conception	194
Pichenot, Pierre-Athanase	151	Tarbes :see Diocese; Sisters	
Pictures : see Images; Photography		Thanksgiving Plaques	197
Pilgrimage (theology)	151	Théas, Pierre-Marie	198
Pilgrimages to Lourdes	152	Town	199
Pius IX	154	Treasure Museum : see Museum	
Pius X	155	Veuillot, Louis	203
see also Basilica		VIPs	204
Pius XI	156	Virgin : see Crowned Virgin	
Pius XII	156	Water	207
Ploërmel Brothers	158	Wojtyla : see John Paul II	
Poirier, Alexandre	160	Women : see Prominent Women	
Pomian, Bertrand-Marie	160	Young people	211
Popular religion	162		

Preface

Welcome to the history of Lourdes.

In these pages you will find every aspect of the Shrine covered and listed in alphabetical order. There are many biographical notes, as the Lourdes experience has a long history: so many things have happened there over the last 150 years! Hence we could not just limit it to the early protagonists. So, for example, you will be able to read about my fellow bishops and predecessors. Other articles explain the many traditions of Lourdes, from its origins to the present time. I would include, among these traditions, the Ave Maria of Lourdes. Do you know its history? Here you can learn all about it.

But this book does not just present historical or technical information. It also helps to penetrate the spirit of Lourdes. What is the message of Lourdes? What does the Lady mean when she speaks of 'penance'? Why is she called the Immaculate Conception?

We owe a debt of gratitude to Fr Nino Bucca, first for having conceived this enterprise, and then for having brought it to fruition. Fr Bucca served as chaplain at the Shrine for quite a few years. He was therefore well qualified to select the subjects and to write many of the texts. This little encyclopaedia, launched more than ten years after its conception, will help Lourdes to leave a deep and lasting impact on its many visitors.

I feel certain that, even for Lourdes 'experts', this book will prove useful. As to the others, it will almost be a necessity.

Jacques Perrier
Bishop of Tarbes and Lourdes

Introduction

Lourdes has left an indelible mark on many people, including myself. As a young seminarian I offered my services to the Shrine. Years later, meeting up again with the people involved at that time it seemed that our shared experience had taken place just the day before, but thirty years have passed since then!

Dominique, now a doctor and father of seven children, had kept the printed sheets of the prayer vigils and of the songs as a souvenir of a time of discovery and joy, of a shared awareness and of prayer.

Yves and Christine had to travel hundreds of miles to come to our reunion. But they, like many of the others, were able to relive, through a simple glance or word, the experience we had shared so many years ago, and felt that they had come home. They felt free to recall the past, talk about their dreams and, above all, let themselves be enveloped by the Grotto.

Lourdes is a place of rebirth. A young girl I met there, not yet 18, radiated such joy, that she distributed hope all around her. She said to me: 'Here it is enough just to come inside the compound and stroll on the grass, to find your heart refreshed.' Yet at Lourdes there is suffering of a magnitude never imagined before in such concentration. Here I have experienced so much simple holiness; so much heroic faithfulness lived out on a daily basis.

By now, Lourdes has its own history. More than 150 years have passed since the apparitions. Going around the different places and observing everything more attentively than usual, I started to realise how much gratitude was contained in a tombstone, how much sweat and effort a building must have cost, how many long reflections lay behind a statue, how much pain was expressed in the church and how many ardent invocations had been uttered at the foot of an altar. Everything deserves respect!

When I agreed to co-ordinate the contributions to this little dictionary, I could never have imagined to what extent it would plunge me back into the atmosphere of Lourdes, a place I visited regularly over the last thirty years, nine of which I spent in the actual Shrine as co-ordinator for the Italian pilgrims. It allowed me to meet up again with many old friends, who never hesitated to help me whenever necessary. I also met many new ones, who proved to be equally generous.

The publishers planned a book which would address not those 'in the know', but rather the ordinary pilgrims, having in mind a famous phrase of Bernadette's to Fr Cros: 'That which shall be written in the simplest of terms will be the best.' I tried to be faithful to this principle, without sacrificing quality. In the process, personally, I learnt a lot.

Since this book consists of a series of entries appearing in alphabetical order, we were faced with the problem of possible repetitions in those which dealt with similar themes or with the connection between one entry and another. However, with conciseness in mind, we succeeded on the whole in avoiding repetition, except in cases where any change would have rendered the text incomplete.

I wish to thank the people in charge of the Shrine and of the various services affiliated to it for the welcome they have given me, among whom Jacques Perrier, Bishop of Tarbes and Lourdes, who reviewed the manuscript in person, offering a number of relevant and precious suggestions.

I also wish to express my profound gratitude to Mr Gerard Altuzarra, ex-director of personnel and a special friend, who not only contributed some entries but also put me in touch with other authors whom I would not otherwise have met. My sincere thanks also to Fr André Doze who wrote the greatest number of articles and who kept me on the right track with his competence and friendship. And how could I not mention Fr Michel de Roton, ex-rector of the Shrines, who could not hide his joy at the possibility of writing once again about Lourdes, and Fr André Cabes, my first contact with the Shrine.

Above all I would like this to be an act of love for aquero, as Bernadette called the young woman, luminously dressed, who appeared at the cave of Massabielle, and for all those with whom I had such deep conversations.

Nino Bucca O.M.I.

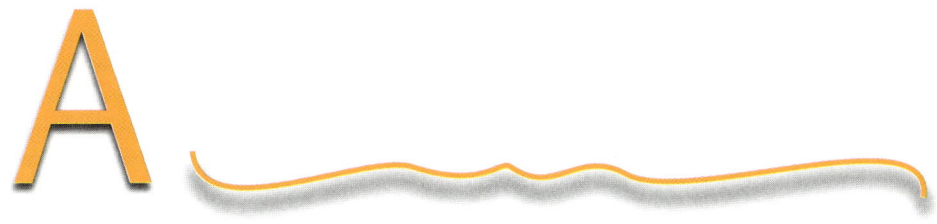

ACCUEIL MARIE SAINT-FRAI

As the war of 1870 came to an end, the Sisters of Saint-Frai, known then as the Daughters of Our Lady of Sorrows, had a difficult task to keep up with the influx of sick pilgrims making their way to Lourdes. Their founders, Mother Saint Jean-Baptiste and Fr Ribes, were responsible for the first basic buildings where the sick could be welcomed and cared for.

In 1873 plans for a large hospital were approved by Bishop Pichenot, and the foundation stone was laid by his successor, Bishop Langénieux, on 7 April 1874. Not having a penny, the Sisters set out to seek funds as the building began

to take shape. Time and again Mother Jean-Baptiste, under pressure from the contractors, had to send the sisters out in painful and humiliating conditions. Finally in 1878, when the first national pilgrimage took place, they managed to welcome and look after a total of 300 sick pilgrims. In 1900 Mgr Schoepfer blessed the two great dining halls and in 1913 another large wing was added and spacious lifts installed. It was not until 1938, that, after extensive building work and the generous help of grateful benefactors, the Sisters of Saint-Frai were able to see the original ambitious plans of 1874 fully realized.

The building stands as 'a monument to human compassion and divine charity; every stone paid for by the hidden contribution of sacrifice and dedication of people too many to count' (G. Bernoville). Although remarkably modernised by the end of the 20th century, the original spirit of its founders is still very much present there.

ACCUEIL NOTRE-DAME

Accueil means place of welcome. The very first *Accueil* was the *Accueil Marie Saint-Frai* (400 beds), situated close to the Shrine. Inaugurated in 1878, it expressed the vocation of Lourdes to welcome the sick.

In 1910, the original '*Abri du Pelerin*' (pilgrim's shelter), built in 1877 on the left bank of the Gave, was extended and renamed as the *Accueil Notre-Dame* (700 beds).

In 1975, the *Accueil Saint-Bernadette* (400 beds) was added to the right bank of the river making the total capacity of the *Accueils* 1,500 beds.

When the two oldest buildings finally became obsolete, *Accueil Saint-Frai* was completely refurbished and *Accueil Notre-Dame* (now known as the old Notre-Dame) was built on the site of the former *Accueil Saint Bernadette*. Eventually part of it was pulled down in order to construct a road alongside the river whilst the remaining part was converted into the chapel of reconciliation, medical centre and dispensary, hospitality offices and meeting rooms. Meanwhile the design of the future *Accueil Notre-Dame* was being undertaken by GERCAM.

After three years of careful study, its unique structure was finally worked out. It was to be neither a hospital nor a hotel, but a combination of the two, as well as a place for quiet meditation, festivities, prayer and joyful celebrations. As well as overlooking the Shrine, it had to offer comfort and security and safeguard the privacy of its guests.

All of these requirements on paper were faithfully converted into reality by the architects, Grésy, father and son. Within 14 months the *Accueil* was successfully completed and its doors opened in 1997. We see a picture of it here. Together with the St Pius X Basilica it is a living tribute to twentieth century architecture. With its 1,000 beds, 8 restaurants, 2 chapels and huge reception area for arrivals and departures, the new *Accueil* is well equipped to respond to the special

needs of all its visitors. Its state-of-the-art facilities and attractive design (two wings of the building mirror the two ramps of the Rosary Basilica), the way in which it is integrated into its surroundings and its proximity to the Grotto, are all benefits of inestimable value to the sick and disabled who now have their own special place at Lourdes worthy of welcoming them.

ANNALS OF OUR LADY OF LOURDES

Coming from Garaison, where they were founded, the Missionaries of the Immaculate Conception settled in Lourdes at Bishop Laurence's request in May 1866 with a view to starting a ministry in the new Shrine. From the month of April 1868, Fr Duboé, right hand man of Fr Sempé, the Superior, planned to start a regular publication (called *Annales de Notre Dame de Lourdes*) to provide details on the life of the Shrine and to inform the public on the apparitions.

This decision infuriated the journalist and writer Henri Lasserre, who had been sponsored by Fr Peyramale to write a book on Lourdes. Up to then, his relationship with the priests of the Grotto had been excellent, but the *Annales de Notre-Dame* seemed to rob him of the honour of being the first to publicise the events. He started work on his book which was published a few months later, in 1869, and on 3rd November 1869 began to attack the new chaplains by means of a dreadful pamphlet accusing them of all kinds of malice. From 1877 to 1882, he was to launch the *Echo des Pelerins* in order to discredit the *Annales.* This sad quarrel was to continue, unfortunately, until the death of the writer, in 1900.

The *Annales de Notre-Dame* were published until 1944 and constitute an irreplaceable collection for the study of the events. They have also been catalogued and are available to researchers.

APPARITIONS

Times were hard that winter of 1858: unemployment, starvation and an epidemic took their toll. Millers by trade, the Soubirous family had lost everything and with nowhere else to go, the *cachot* was now their home. With no wood for the fire, Bernadette, the eldest, set out to collect dead wood. Accompanied by her sister and a friend, they made their way to Massabielle, an infamous place by the river where everything was about to begin.

A 1st APPARITION
Thursday 11 February:
The Sign of the Cross
There was a sound like a gust of wind and a soft light. Then: 'I saw a lady dressed in white, with a blue sash…' Transfixed, Bernadette made the sign of the cross with the Lady and prayed the rosary. The Lady then vanished without having spoken.

2nd APPARITION
Sunday 14 February: The Smile
Bernadette felt drawn to return to the Grotto, 'in order to see whether I had been mistaken.' As she knelt and prayed the Lady appeared. Bernadette threw some holy water… The Lady smiled but did not speak.

3rd APPARITION
Thursday 18 February:
'Would you be so kind…?'

One of the stained-glass windows depicting the apparitions, in the Basilica of the Immaculate Conception.

Lent has just begun. Bernadette, unable to read or write herself, held a pen and paper up to the Lady asking her to write he name. 'It is not necessary,' the Lady told her, and then she added 'Would you be so kind as to come here every day for fifteen days? I cannot promise you happiness in this life, only in the next.'

4th APPARITION
Friday 19 February
Bernadette returned to the Grotto carrying a candle, accompanied by her mother and aunt.

5th APPARITION
Saturday 20 February
Thirty people followed Bernadette to the Grotto to witness her ecstasy. They marvelled at her calmness, joy and fervour.

6th APPARITION
Sunday 21 February
Over a hundred people gathered at the Grotto before dawn to see Bernadette. The police kept watch. Inspector Jacomet later questioned her roughly as to who she had seen, but Bernadette simply referred to her vision as *aquero* which is Bigordian dialect for *cela*, meaning 'she' or 'that one'.

NO APPARITION
Monday 22 February
Bernadette was forbidden to go to the Grotto, but by the afternoon her parents had changed their minds. The Lady did not appear. 'I do not know how I have failed her.' Bernadette was full of sadness. Everyone else was busy gossiping.

7th APPARITION
Tuesday 23 February
At 5.30 a.m. 150 people were already waiting at the Grotto, including the tax collector and sceptic, Mr Estrade. After witnessing Bernadette in ecstasy, he went home filled with enthusiasm, which he did his best to convey to others.

8th APPARITION
Wednesday 24 February:
Prayer and Penance
300 people... Bernadette entered into ecstasy, but her face betrayed an unspeakable sadness, surely due to the Lady's words: 'Penance: pray to God for the conversion of sinners; go and kiss the ground as penance for sinners.'

9th APPARITION
Thursday 25 February: Acts of penance and the discovery of the spring
Bernadette's radiant ecstasy was witnessed by more than 300 people, including important personalities. Then they saw her crawl on her knees, eat grass, and scratch at the ground below the Grotto, her face all muddy... 'She's mad ... a piece of filth.'

Bernadette was only doing what the Lady had asked her to do – acts of penance for the sake of sinners. 'Go and drink from the spring and wash yourself with the water.' The Lady pointed to the very back of the Grotto. It took Bernadette some time to find the spring. 'I had to spit out the water three times because it was so dirty. The fourth time I managed to drink some.'

NO APPARITION
Friday 26 February
600 people waited for Bernadette at the Grotto. She prayed the Rosary and carried out the same acts of penance but the Lady did not appear. 'How have I offended her...?'

10th APPARITION
Saturday 27 February
The Lady reappeared, asking Bernadette for the same acts of penance: to drink the water and kiss the ground.

11th APPARITION
Sunday 28 February
More than 1,000 people had gath-

ered. Bernadette repeated the same gestures of penance requested by the Lady: some of the crowd followed her example, others laughed at her. Jacomet interrogated, and then released her.

12th APPARITION
Monday 1st March: Penance and the first miracle
By midnight there was already a crowd of 1,500 people at the Grotto, but the atmosphere was peaceful and recollected. Bernadette repeated the same gestures of penance. The first miracle: Catherine Latapie bathed her crippled arm in the spring and was cured immediately.

13th APPARITION
Tuesday 2 March:
Procession and Chapel
The Lady entrusted Bernadette with a mission: 'Go and tell the priests that I would like processions to be held here, and that they must build a chapel.' Accompanied by her aunts, Bernadette conveyed this message to the Curé Peyramale, who was extremely unwilling to carry out the request. 'Who is this Lady? Tell her to give her name and also a sign: ask her to make the rosebush flower in the middle of winter!'

14th APPARITION
Wednesday 3 March
Bernadette arrived at 7 a.m. There were 3,000 people waiting for her, but the vision failed to appear. Bernadette was sent to school, but by the afternoon she felt the powerful call to return to the Grotto where the Lady repeated her request.

15th APPARITION
Thursday 4 March
The most long-awaited day of all: the last of the fifteen days of apparitions and also market day. More than 7,000 people had gathered, but at the end the Lady still had not given her name.

16th APPARITION
25 March 1858:
The Lady gives her name
The Feast of the Annunciation. Three times Bernadette asked the Lady her name. At the fourth request the Lady raised her eyes towards heaven and placed her hands together in prayer, saying the words: 'I am the Immaculate Conception.' Bernadette hurried to the curé repeating these words over and over to herself as she did not understand them. Deeply moved the curé at once recognised the truth of faith, declared 4 years earlier by Pope Pius IX, in 1854.

17th APPARITION
Wednesday 7 April:
the Miracle of the Candle
Easter Wednesday. Bernadette felt drawn to the Grotto where she entered into a long and silent ecstasy. She held a lit candle in her hands. About 1,000 people were present, including Dr Dozous who had come in the name of 'science'. The candle flame danced around her fingers, but did not burn her. After the ecstasy, the Doctor examined her hands but 'Nothing!'

18th APPARITION
16 July 1858: Beyond the Barricades
For several weeks the town had been in a state of agitation. In

gin, in order to confuse her. When he read his report back to her, she said: 'You have changed what I said.' She held firm in the discussion, to the point that he became exasperated and made the tassel of his bonnet twirl, to Bernadette's great amusement.

In the second version, we see the term *aquero* appear, in the real version of Bernadette: '*That one* told me,' '*that one* asked me.' It is only on the following 25 March that, at Mr Estrade's and his sister's home, Bernadette will finally know who *aquero* was when the meaning of Mary's words heard that morning was explained to her: 'I am the Immaculate Conception.'

*Dialect spoken in the ancient county of Bigorre, the capital of which was Tarbes.

ARCHITECTURE

At the time of building the Basilica of the Immaculate Conception in 1861, there were two main currents of thought amongst intellectuals; those who still believed in religious creativity (that religion and religious ideas could inspire artistic creativity), and those who rejected such ideas in favour of purely modern scientific theories. A rediscovery of the Middle Ages was also prevalent. The archaeologist Alexandre Lenoir, writer Prosper Mérimée, and architects Lassus and Violet-le-Duc, were studying and restoring Mediaeval works of art which had been ransacked by the revolutionaries of 1789. They classified three main art forms characteristic of this Mediae-

val era: Roman-Byzantine, Gothic and Flamboyant. Two periods in particular attracted them: 11th century Roman, and 13th century Gothic, because of their particular harmony.

Hippolyte Durand, architect of the Basilica of the Immaculate Conception, was inspired by the French Middle Ages. Léopold Hardy, architect of the Rosary Basilica, drew his inspiration from the Roman-Byzantine churches based on the Greek cross complete with domes. The interior mosaic décor was reminiscent of the churches of early Christendom.

As regards the St Pius X Basilica, in 1958 architect Pierre Vago used the most innovative of building techniques, namely concrete, setting a precedent for overtly modern structures not found in any religious building to date. Partly underground, this huge space, however, did not in any way upset the harmony of the two earlier basilicas, built one above the other.

Lourdes has always sought to welcome and shelter its pilgrims in all types of inclement weather and during the night. The porch of the Basilica of the Immaculate Conception, for example, was specifically designed with this in mind. When it became too small, it was replaced (in 1877) by a neo-Gothic building on the bank of the River Gave, but as the number of sick and disabled pilgrims continued to grow so too did the need for still more new and better buildings to welcome and shelter them. Old ones were pulled down or used for other purposes such as the office for the examining of medical evidence (1883), and accommodation for volunteers.

ARCHIVES

The Shrine archives contain a series of original documents relating to the period of the apparitions. They include letters, such as those written by Fr. Peyramale, parish priest of Lourdes, dating from 15 March 1858, to Bishop Laurence of Tarbes; and letters from Adélaide Monlaur, a young woman of 23, who wrote to her cousin detailing the precise events of Lourdes from 8 March 1858 onwards. Among the original documents is the interview of Bernadette by Inspector Jacomet on 21 February 1858.

The Jesuit priest, Fr Cros, later commissioned to write the history of Lourdes, researched in great detail many records written down by various witnesses at the time of the apparitions, including that of the High Commissioner of Hautes-Pyrénées, which contains, for example, the reports of Inspector Jacomet to the High Commissioner. Fr Cros also interviewed witnesses of the apparitions and asked the early pilgrims to write an account of their first pilgrimage. These original letters constitute a considerable amount of material and provide evidence about the period from 1858 to 1878. His extensive research forms part of the Shrine archives.

In 1958, several documents which had been lost, such as the report of the commission of enquiry set up by Bishop Laurence on 28 July 1858, and Inspector Jacomet's notebook, were providentially handed over to Bishop Théas. This coincided with the work of the two historians, Fr Laurentin and Dom Bernard Billet, who were in the process of publishing the original documents relating to the period 1858 – 1866.

The Shrine archives also hold the replies from the dioceses and religious congregations on the occasion of Bishop Laurence's public pronouncement in recognition of the apparitions of the Mother of God to Bernadette Soubirous. There are also letters from benefactors, from people who have been cured, as well as correspondence from architects: Hippolyte Durand for the Basilica of the Immaculate Conception; Léopold Hardy for the Rosary Basilica and Pierre Vago for the St Pius X Basilica. These documents allow us to follow the evolution of the three great building projects.

From 1970 onwards, the archives have recorded the development of the various ministries at the Shrine, such as the *hospitalités* and the services to young people, and everything that happened at the large manifestations such as the Eucharistic Congress (1981) and the two visits of Pope John Paul II in 1983 and 2004.

AVE MARIA, THE LOURDES HYMN

Few hymns have known as much success in the Catholic world as the *Ave Maria* of Lourdes. But what is its origin?

The tune of the chorus is supposed to have originated, according to M Cramoussel (chapel master of the cathedral of Albi at the beginning of the 20th century), from an old song in dialect, which the Bigordian grandmothers used to sing to their grandchildren in the middle of the 19th century, at the same time as the apparitions of Lourdes. As for the tune of the verses, it comes from the '*Choix des plus beaux air de cantiques arrangés a deux parties*' by Fr Lambillotte (Paris, 1842).

The old text of the *Ave Maria* is by Fr Gaignet, priest at Saint-Sulpice. Its story is worth telling. Around 1872, this priest from the Vendée who, almost certainly, had occasion to accompany the pilgrims of his diocese, wrote 8 verses to the above tune, calling the finished work *Salut d'Arrivée* – arrival greeting. This text was quickly judged too short and Fr Gaignet was asked to produce a longer version. The new text, bearing the title '*Chapelet de Notre-Dame de Lourdes*' comprised sixty verses. Why sixty? Because, at the time, it was believed that the rosary of the Virgin Mary, during the apparitions, consisted of six decades instead of five, due to an incorrect interpretation of the statue of the Grotto. This new text was sung for the first time on 27th May 1873. It spread like wild fire.

But, although the Vendéan text fulfilled its purpose for almost a century, it was judged outdated in 1968 by the directors of pilgrimages who wished to revise the manual of the pilgrim. Bishop Théas, on the advice of Canon Lesbordes, Chapel Master of the Shrines, ordered a new text from Maurice le Bas.

The new text of the *Ave Maria* had to be at the same time: a) faithful to the account of the apparitions, b) evocative of the message of Lourdes and c) respectful of the very demanding rhythm of the ultra short verses.

This text was established thanks to a close collaboration between a historian, a musician and a poet. Following rigorously the chronological account of the apparitions day by day, it uses a language which, although mostly clear and direct, is also not devoid of poetry. This text is significantly dated 11 February 1969. Canon Lesbordes, having died a few days before, was therefore not able to see it, at least not in its edited version. Let us not forget that it was he who arranged the rich harmonisation of this tune, a harmonisation which had an important role in the success of the *Ave Maria* throughout the world.

In conclusion, what can we say about this hymn? Should the fact that it is so popular mask any critical comment? Well, there is a fault inherent in the Latin chorus: the incorrect emphasis of the word Ave (on the second syllable). Thus some, namely the New York pilgrims, prefer leaving out the first note (the so) and bring forward the emphasis. In the literary sense this is better but, musically, it is unfortunate. No doubt, popular success should be accepted with its weaknesses.

Finally, let us recall a description – a little romantic but not without inspiration – of the *Ave Maria* song such as M. Cramaussel heard it sung at the beginning of the 20th century: '*The tune of the* Ave Maria *lends itself admirably to its avowed goal. Its execution by the crowds, its untiring and ceaseless repetition, its powerful harmony without dissonance, make it the ideal song and, on the days of the great pilgrimages, sung by thousand of voices, it rolls in sonorous waves to the neighbouring mountains where it expires and from where, sometimes, it rebounds in successive echoes like breaking ocean waves and spreads over the plain'.*

A

BARTRÈS

To the north west of Lourdes, on a little hill, is situated the village of Bartrès. Linked to Bernadette's childhood, it has become a place of pilgrimage. Pilgrims are attracted by its elevated setting, 3 kilometres from Lourdes, and by the magnificent views over the Pyrenees. In the attractive church they contemplate a very beautiful 17th century art work which tells the story of St John the Baptist and which Bernadette also used to contemplate, while dreaming of making her first communion.

She stayed twice at Bartrès. Nine months after her birth, her mother had been burnt by a candle which had fallen on her blouse. She could no longer feed her little girl. Fortunately, she knew the Lagues-Arravant family in Bartrès who often used to come to the mill of Boly. The Lagues had just lost their first-born and the farmer's wife agreed to feed Bernadette for five francs per month.

A healthy baby, she tried her

The sheepfold at Bartrès.

first steps in the farmyard, trying to catch the hens that pecked around her little clogs. The farmer's wife became very attached to her and even accepted to keep her, past the weaning stage, free of charge.

During that time, in the mill of Boly, little Jean Soubirous had been born and had gone to paradise at just two months old on 10 April 1845. In her sorrow, Louise wanted to see her daughter again. The carer brought her back, in floods of tears. She would never forget her and, taking advantage of the Lourdes market, would go and give her a hug from time to time.

Bernadette's second stay at Bartrès came at the end of June 1857. The Soubirous had to leave the mill of Boly and their attempt at starting again in Arcizac had failed. They ended up in that very insalubrious place called the *cachot* (jail). Louise was advised to move her daughter away as a matter of urgency. Bernadette again found herself on the road to Bartrès. She was thirteen and was going to help the Lagues family and become a shepherdess. The Lagues were happy to have her back.

The sheep shed which she used in the company of Pigou, her faithful dog, has been kept intact. She did her work, said her Rosary and enjoyed the beautiful scenery. The parish priest tried to teach her the rudiments of the catechism as she had never been to school and had not made her first communion. Unfortunately, the priest left the village to enter a monastery and it was left to Marie Lagues to introduce her to the basic concepts of faith.

Bernadette returned to Lourdes, happy to be among her own again, despite the hovel in which they lived. This was on 21 January 1858. Three weeks later, the apparitions began.

BASILICA OF THE IMMACULATE CONCEPTION

When Bishop Laurence declared the authenticity of the apparitions in January 1862, he had already purchased the plot of land containing the Grotto of Massabielle and instructed the architect, Hippolyte Durand, to submit plans for the building of the chapel requested by Our Lady.

The first plans were submitted in December 1861, but they had to be revised several times before the bishop could get them authorised almost a year later in October 1862.

The architect, Hippolyte Durand,

The basilica under construction.

The inauguration of this great 'chapel', dedicated to the Immaculate Conception, took place on 15 August 1871, in the wake of France's deep political crisis, a crisis which led to the birth of the first national pilgrimage to Lourdes. Known as the Pilgrimage of Banners, it took place on 6 October 1872. 300, 000 pilgrims travelled to Lourdes to ask for Our Lady's healing grace for France. An organ was presented as a gift, and banners filled the newly built Shrine, commemorating the first of the large-scale pilgrimages. In 1874, Pope Pius IX raised the status of the 'chapel' to that of minor basilica, and appointed Cardinal Guibert, Archbishop of Paris, to be his representative at the consecration ceremony on 2 July, 1876. Visitors to the Basilica may obtain indulgences.

was inspired by the pilgrimage churches of the Middle Ages, whose side chapels radiated outwards from a central point, but he had enormous obstacles to overcome: the site on which he was to build a structure 51 m long, 21 m wide and 19 m high, was almost a crevasse, with a steep drop both to the east and to the north, and mountains to the south. To compensate for both the uneven level and shape of the site, he inserted a crypt below.

The high altar of the basilica is situated directly above the Grotto. Unfortunately, Bishop Laurence did not live to see the completion of the chapel, but his work was carried on by Mgr Pichenot.

BASILICA OF THE ROSARY

By 1872, there was already talk of building another church, to be named after the Rosary, as Our Lady never appeared to Bernadette without her rosary. The first gift of money arrived from the organisers of the great national pilgrimage of 1872 who were Dominicans.

Plans were submitted in February 1875 by Bishop Langénieux to Pius IX who approved and blessed them, but the project never went ahead. Instead, it was the architect Léopold Hardy who finally took up the challenge of Fr Sempé's programme of building work. He placed a church designed to hold 1,500 people at the foot of the

Basilica of the Immaculate Conception.

Following the form of the Greek cross, one branch made up the nave, whilst the other three each had five altars corresponding to the 15 mysteries of the rosary. Outside, the church is encircled by ramps intended for processions leading to the Basilica of the Immaculate Conception. The foundation stone was laid on 16 July 1883, the 25th anniversary of the Apparitions, by Cardinal Desprez, Archbishop of Toulouse, and papal legate of Pope Leo XIII.

Léopold Hardy faced many challenges. He had to create a large enough area in which to lay the foundations for the future basilica without undermining the solidity of the existing basilica and he had to arrest the flow of the River Gave and River Merlasse, both particularly powerful at this point.

The church was blessed in 1889 in the presence of a cardinal, three archbishops, eight bishops, 1,500 priests and 30,000 pilgrims. Every altar was decorated with roses: white for the joyful mysteries, red for the sorrowful and yellow for the glorious. A very large sculpture of St Dominic receiving a rosary from the hands of the Virgin Mary, donated by Léopold Hardy, features on the tympanum above the entrance. Consecrated as a church by Cardinal Langénieux on 6 October 1901 it was later raised to the status of minor basilica on 24 September 1926.

BASILICA OF ST PIUS X

Architects of the St Pius X Basilica were: Pierre Vago (1910-2002), son of Joseph Vago, one of the architects who designed the League of Nations building in Geneva; Le Donné (1899 –1983), pupil of Auguste Perret, and Pinsard (1906 – 1988), painter and architect, a collaborator of Lurçat. The building work was carried out by the firm Campenon-Bernard at a cost of FF 1,347m, fully paid for by donations from pilgrims. Construction work lasted 22 months. The church was consecrated on 25 March 1958 by Cardinal Roncalli, a few months before his election as pope.

This underground church covers an area of 14,500 m square. In the form of an ellipse - a two-dimen-

sional shape like a stretched circle with slightly longer flatter sides, 200m long, and 80m wide, at the narrowest point. Built of concrete, it holds over 20,000 people and is dedicated to Pius X who was pope from 1903 to 1914 and was canonized in 1954. Amongst other things, in 1906 he encouraged frequent Holy Communion and Holy Communion for children. A reliquary containing his hand can be found in front of the Blessed Sacrament altar of the Pax Christi Chapel, a chapel that commemorates the site of the original peace monument which had to be pulled down in order to make way for the building of this third basilica. The relics of St André Bobola, St Pierre Chanel and of Blessed Jean-Gabriel Perboyre are embedded in the main altar.

The church was designated a minor basilica by Pius XII, on 16 May 1958 At the request of the architects, no sculpture or image was allowed to interfere with the harmony of this great curved structure, although gradually the 'gemmail', (images made of coloured glass lit from behind) were introduced, inspired by the work of a young mentally handicapped painter, Meb, whose painting of the disciples' boat, was completed for the first pilgrimage of Faith and Light in 1971. Since the Jubilee of 2000, many tapestries depicting the saints can also be seen. Above all, the basilica lends itself in a special way to celebrations of the liturgy on a very large scale, of which the Eucharistic Congress in 1981 is a spectacular example.

BATHS

Go and drink at the spring and wash yourself!

Our Lady's words to Bernadette inspired the building of the Baths in whose waters so many pilgrims come to immerse themselves. Built initially only on the east side of the Grotto, in 1958 more were added on the west side. The baths are the special responsibility of the *Notre-Dame Hospitalité*, the central co-ordinating body that welcomes everyone to Lourdes. Since the beginning, their waters have been a source of prayer, freshness and joy for millions of pilgrims.

With John the Baptist as their obvious Patron Saint, the baths are made up of many individual units. Everyone is welcome, the well and the sick alike. In order to accompany each pilgrim safely through

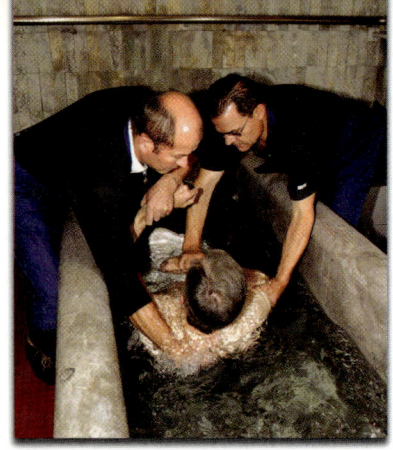

this strong moment of grace, there is a team of trained volunteers known as 'hospitaliers'. To avoid health risks, the waters are checked continuously, and remarkably, no accidents have ever occurred.

There are 17 baths in total (10 for ladies, 5 for men and 2 for children). They are open everyday both in winter and in summer. They are always busy. In 2005, 386,688 pilgrims bathed in the waters, of whom two thirds were women.

The water flows constantly from beside the Grotto throughout the rest of the Shrine. There are taps available for those wishing to drink the water, and recently, on the right hand bank of the Gave, a special waterside walk has been created to recall the different wells that appear in the Bible.

BERNADETTE

Everything we know about the apparitions and the message of Lourdes comes from Bernadette herself. So, who is she? We can see her life as made up of three stages: (i) the 'unnoticed' years of her childhood (ii) her 'public life' during the time of the apparitions and her time of witness; and finally (iii) her 'hidden' life as a nun in Nevers.

The 'unnoticed' years

When we speak of the apparitions, Bernadette is often presented as a poor, sick and ignorant child, living in the *cachot* in the most miserable conditions. That is so, but it had not always been the case. Bernadette was born on 7 January 1844, at the Boly Mill, the first and therefore the eldest child of François and Louise Castérot, who had married for love, which was unusual for that era. Bernadette grew up in a family who loved one another and prayed together. The first ten years of her life were spent in this atmosphere, making her an exceptionally solid and well-balanced child. She never lost these qualities even as their life deteriorated into abject poverty. She was then just 14, small for her age, and suffering from asthma. She was not just anyone, however. She was a true Bigordian, very practical with good common sense as 'firm as the stones on the Lourdes roads'. She was lively, spontaneous, willing and sharp-witted and, as Inspector Jacomet was to discover to his cost, she was incapable of deceit. She possessed self-esteem, something her mother superior was well aware of: 'Her character was very direct. She had great sensitivity.' Her shortcomings saddened her and she fought them tirelessly.

She had a strong personality, but was completely uneducated. She never went to school: she had to work as a maid in her Aunt Bernarde's guest house. She knew no catechism and had a very poor memory for abstract formulas. At 14, she could neither read nor write, which set her apart from the

other children. But she was determined to overcome this and make her First Holy Communion, which she did finally on 3 June 1858. How did she learn her catechism? From Our Lady, at the Grotto!

Bernadette's 'public' life

Then came the apparitions. It was while she was carrying out a simple menial chore - going to collect wood - that Bernadette was confronted with 'the mystery'. A noise 'like a gust of wind', a light, and a presence. How did she react? With great normality and discernment. Thinking that she must have been mistaken, she looked around her, rubbed her eyes, tried to understand the situation. She checked with her companions, 'Did you see anything?' Then she turned to God, and began to pray her Rosary. She turned towards the Church by seeking advice in confession from Fr Pomian, the curate: 'I saw something white which looked like a lady,' she said. When interrogated by Inspector Jacomet, like the apostles before the Sanhedrin (Acts 4, 13), she replied to his questions with surprising certainty and wisdom for a girl who had never been to school: 'I did not say the 'Virgin Mary', Sir, I only said 'she' (*aquero* in dialect]. You have changed everything I have told you.' She related what she had seen with astonishing detachment and freedom: 'I have only been asked to tell you what I saw, not to make you believe it.' She described the vision very precisely, without adding or taking away anything. Only once, when frightened by the roughness of Fr Peyramale did she ever add a word of her own: 'Father, the lady is still asking for a chapel – no matter how small!' Later, when Bishop Langénieux pronounced the authenticity of the apparitions, he referred to the 'simplicity, candour, and humility of this child... she does not exaggerate anything, her ingenuity is disarming... and whenever she is questioned, her answers are always clear, precise and uttered with conviction.' Equally unaffected by threats or bribes, 'Bernadette's sincerity is undeniable: she never wished to deceive anyone.' But could she have deceived herself? - the bishop asked himself - the victim of a hallucination. But then he remembered her calmness, her common sense, her complete lack of boasting and the very fact that she had not made them happen, they happened unexpectedly, and twice during the fortnight she had gone to the Grotto but Our Lady had not appeared.

These conclusions, however, were only reached after Bernadette had faced endless questioning and interviews by admirers, journalists and others, not to mention those who were simply curious. She had

The room where Bernadette was born.

to appear before many civil and religious enquiry commissions. Thus she was catapulted from obscurity to the very centre of public attention. She was battered by a 'media storm'. Imagine the patience, composure and good humour that were needed in order to withstand it all and to still remain faithful to her story.

She never accepted any gifts: 'I prefer to remain poor.' She did not bless any Rosaries handed to her: 'I am not a priest.' Nor did she sell any medals: 'I am not a shopkeeper.' When she saw pictures of herself being sold for 10 sous she exclaimed: '10 sous - that is all I am worth!'

Circumstances could not permit her to continue her life at the *cachot*: she needed protecting agreed Fr Peyramale and Mayor Lacadé who had her admitted as a destitute sick person at the Hospice run by the Sisters of Nevers. She arrived there, aged 16, on 15 July 1860. She learnt to read and write and sent letters home whenever there was a baptism or First Communion or a funeral. She even wrote a letter to the pope. She visited her family who had been given a new home. She cared for the sick, whilst seeking to understand her vocation: unqualified and without a dowry, how could she become a nun? Finally, she entered Nevers, 'because they did not try to persuade me.' From that moment she understood that her mission at Lourdes had finished. Like John the Baptist, she had to decrease in order to let Mary increase.

The 'hidden' life of Nevers
She herself used the expression 'I have come here to hide myself.' At Lourdes she was the visionary. In Nevers she was Sister Marie-Bernarde. It has often been mentioned that the sisters were quite severe towards her, but one has to remember that Bernadette was an unusual case: she had to be removed from people's curiosity, in order to protect her and the rest of the community.

The day after she arrived, Bernadette gave her account of the apparitions to the religious community: after that she was forbidden to speak of it. She was kept at the mother house, although she would have dearly loved to take care of the sick. On the day of her profession she was not entrusted with any particular job or responsibility, so the Bishop, through his own inspiration, gave her the 'job of praying'. 'Pray for sinners,' the Lady had said. She would certainly be faithful to that. My weapons, she wrote to the pope, are prayer and sacrifice.

Through her own illness she was often confined to the infirmary and to 'endless interviews in the parlour'. 'Those poor bishops,' she would say, 'they would do better to stay at home. Lourdes is so far away... I will never return to the Grotto. Everyone would follow me instead of the Blessed Virgin.' But every day her soul made its pilgrimage there.

Although she did not speak of Lourdes, she lived it. 'You must be the first to live its message,' said Fr Douce, her confessor. Shortly afterwards she fell ill. She fulfilled her task of prayer by accepting with perfect love the crosses she had to bear 'for the sake of sinners'. 'After all, they are my brothers and sisters', she said. During long sleepless nights, uniting herself to every Mass being offered throughout the world, she offered herself as a 'living crucifix, in the immense conflict between dark and light, associated with Mary to the mystery of the redemption, her eyes always fixed on the crucifix: 'It is there that I draw my strength.'

She died in Nevers, on 16 April 1879, at the age of 35. The Church proclaimed her a saint on 8 December 1933, not for having been chosen as the one to whom the apparitions were revealed, but for the way in which she responded to them.

BÉTHARRAM

The Marian Shrine of Bétharram, on the banks of the Gave just 15 km from Lourdes, had been the great Shrine of Our Lady for centuries before the apparitions of Lourdes. Bernadette went there on pilgrimage with her parents. It was there that she acquired the little Rosary from which she never wanted to be separated, despite many offers to change it. It cost just a few pence and she bought it two days before the first apparition. During the apparition of 1 March a pious lady from Lourdes wanted Bernadette to use her Rosary, but the Virgin Mary asked Bernadette to keep using her own! All those who were firm supporters of the events at Lourdes were also fervent devotees of Bétharram.

The name Bétharram means 'beautiful branch' because there is a legend which tells that the Virgin Mary saved a young girl from drowning in the river by holding a branch out to her. This story is just one of the many which gave the Shrine its reputation. The original church was burnt down by Protestants in 1559. The present church was consecrated in 1660.

Michel Garicoïts, a saint of great renown in the area, had built up the reputation of the place at the time of Bernadette, and it was to Bétharram that Bernadette sent her first account of the apparitions, written in her own hand, on 28 May 1861.

It goes without saying that the shopkeepers and hoteliers of Lestelle-Bétharram had become rather concerned by these new events. 'Our Lady of Lourdes will

The shrine at Bétharram.

bring down Bétharram!' they said. But Fr Garicoïts prophesied, to the joy of all, that 'Our Lady of Lourdes will help make Bétharram better known!'

BIGORRE

Bigorre is a geographical region standing in the upper basin of the River Adour and is part of the Pyrenees. It belongs to the department of Hautes-Pyrénénees with, on the ocean side, Béarn, and further away still, the Basque country, all very much tourist areas, known locally as the 'three Bs'. The highest peak in the French Pyrenees, Vignemale (3,300 m), together with the unique location of Gavarnie, the pride of the region and a very wealthy area, and elsewhere places with great natural resources like the waters of Cauterets or Barèges, have been popular for hundreds of years. The ski runs attract many visitors, especially from nearby Spain.

Further north, the rich plain of Tarbes is an important centre for agriculture and livestock farming. Tarbes horses are highly valued, and rightly so, as are the haricot beans and onions that grow in the region. The three great plains in the mountain area are ideal for rearing sheep and for pasture.

From the 10th century the Bigorre region made up the county of Bigorre: Count Bernard 1st had given his allegiance to Our Lady of Puy in 1062 and had endowed the church with an annuity. Coming under the French crown in 1307, the county was founded on the Maison du Foix in 1425 and was directly controlled by the monarchy under King Henry IV, who was born nearby, at Pau, in 1607. However, in 1097 the mountain folk had acquired certain privileges, known as *les fors de Bigorre* – the oldest known in France – which they held on to and defended through thick and thin down the centuries. And this was the region in which Our Lady chose to appear.

BILLÈRE, ROSPER-MARIE (bishop)

Bishop Prosper-Marie Billère (1817-1899) was one of the gems of Bigorre, because like Bishop Laurentin he had grown up there. His birth place was close to Bagnères-de-Bigorre. His many years as bishop were very fruitful as far as the Shrine was concerned, not least for the completion of the Rosary Basilica.

Born into a very small parish, he became a priest in 1843 and taught at the seminary. His first parish was small, but he was then made a canon and given the much larger parish of Bagnères in 1871. He succeeded Bishop Jourdan in 1882, much to the delight of the Bigordian people. In July 1883, he celebrated two solemn occasions alongside Fr Sempé: the 25th anniversary of the apparitions and the laying of the foundation stone of the future Rosary Basilica. Fr Sempé had been working on the plans for over ten years, with many advisers. Needing once again to cut into the mountain side, they predicted high labour costs. Six years later a special *triduum* of celebration took place on 6, 7 and 8 August to mark the blessing of the completed Rosary Basilica by Archbishop Gouzot of Auch, in the presence of numerous bishops and a very large crowd. This was followed just a few days later by the funeral of Fr Sempé, also celebrated on a grand scale.

Bishop Billère had many excellent initiatives: the creation of the office for medical examinations (1884); the founding of the association of welcome of Our Lady of

Lourdes (*Hospitalité de Notre-Dame de Lourdes*) with Count Combettes de Luc; the building of the baths (1890); the printing press (1894) and the excavation of the mountain side to create the Way of the Cross, another huge undertaking. There was also the interior of the Rosary Basilica to consider: the mosaics and other décor, the installation of the great organ and the blessing of the high altar (1897).

On the liturgical front, Bishop Billère authorised the procession of the Blessed Sacrament and the blessing of the sick in 1887, as well as launching the office and mass of the apparitions in 1892. Through his personal intervention, the parish priest of Lourdes was awarded 300,000 francs to complete the building of the parish church of Lourdes, which Fr Peyramale had previously been forced to abandon, due to lack of funds. Bishop Billère died at his home in Lourdes in 1899 at the age of 82, having valiantly worked for the glory of her whom he used to call 'the young lady of his diocese'.

BILLET, BERNARD
(historian of Lourdes)

Dom Bernard Billet, of the Abbey of Notre-Dame of Tournay, in the High Pyrenees, was a first class collaborator for Canon Laurentin with regard to the scientific study of the events in Lourdes.

Born in 1919, Bernard Billet was attracted to the Grotto from an early age. At the age of 24 he entered the Benedictine abbey of Madivan, in the Atlantic Pyrenees. This abbey was relocated, a few years later, to Tournay in the High Pyrenees and became *Notre-Dame de Tournay*. The young monk followed with great interest the works of Fr Laurentin, who was considered by Bishop Théas as the 'theologian of Lourdes'. He participated in the research of the *Documents Authentiques* and his signature appears, alongside Fr Laurentin's, in the last three volumes.

In 1961, Fr Laurentin founded the review *Recherches sur Lourdes, hier et aujourd'hui* (Research on Lourdes, yesterday and today). This was a quarterly bulletin designed to 'continue' the work of the *Documents Authentiques*. The first five numbers are the work of Fr Laurentin. Dom Bernard Billet became its editor-in-chief until 1984, when the bulletin ceased publication.

Since 1973, the *Bulletin de*

A young Bernard Billet at the Grotto with Bishop Théas.

l'Hospitalite de Notre-Dame de Lourdes has been published jointly with the former bulletin and continued until 1999.

Dom Bernard has also participated in the considerable work set up by Mgr Henry Branthomme, entitled *Histoire des Sanctuaires de Lourdes* (1947-1988). This work, written mostly by Mme Chantal Touvet, follows on mainly from the research conducted by Canon Jean-Baptiste Courtin from Rennes and published in 1947 as *Lourdes, le domaine de Notre-Dame, de 1858 à 1947*.

BOISSARIE, GUSTAVE
(doctor)

Dr Gustave Boissarie (1836-1917) played a crucial role in the recognition of Lourdes, from the medical point of view, at the end of the 19th century and at the beginning of the 20th. The street where he lived in Lourdes bears his name as does the quay where cars used to park along the Gave. Born in Sarlat in 1836, he pursued his studies at the famous college there, run by the Jesuits. Later, he left for Paris to study medicine. He practised his profession in that little town in the Dordogne from 1862 to 1883.

He visited Lourdes, out of curiosity, in 1865, on his way from the Couterets where he had been staying, but he was not very interested in religion at the time. In 1872, following the serious illness of his eldest son, he returned in a completely different frame of mind.

It was in 1886 that he was introduced to the president of the *Bureau Medical*, who was very impressed by him and saw him as his successor. Fr Sempé, always anxious to attract people of high quality, asked him to come and assist the doctor already in post, and a fruitful collaboration began between the two men. Dr Boissarie observed, reflected and wrote articles in the *Annales de Notre-Dame de Lourdes*. This collection was published in book form in 1891 entitled *Lourdes: Histoire Medicale,* a deep reflection on everything touching medical science at Lourdes, from 1858 to 1891.

This study, 450 pages long, constituted an important event which attracted the attention of a great number of doctors to Lourdes and created a growing interest in the Shrine. As it happened, Dr Boissarie did succeed Dr Dunot de Saint-Maclou as Head of the *Bureau des Constatations* (office for reports and findings). This was a crucial period given the violent anti-clerical climate of the time.

The role of the doctors, in terms of the healings, is considerable. The bishops, bound by highly restrictive legislation regarding miracles dating from the 13th century, dared not intervene. A hundred years later, Dr Maugispan said: 'Dr Bois-

sarie, a cultured and sensible man, dared to write, in 1894, without risk of being contradicted or criticised: "*The miracle grows and develops each year. One can no longer count the number of those who give accounts of the apparitions.*"' In fact, the doctors assumed the role of the church leaders, who seemed prepared to leave them to themselves, to consider their analysis as sufficient, contented themselves with it and... remained silent.

In August 1892, Emile Zola paid Dr Boissarie a flying visit. He was very selective in what he wanted to see and took no account of any serious medical observations. From this visit he wrote his famous book *Lourdes,* which caused scandal, as he makes people who had been miraculously healed suffer relapses. Dr Boissarie used this situation to proclaim the truth in a famous conference in Paris, in front of a large audience. On 24 November 1894 he demonstrated what the Virgin Mary had done, as opposed to what Zola had told, despite the latter's promise to be objective.

It is estimated that, between the year 1890, when records started, and the year 1913, 6313 doctors, of whom 1457 were from abroad, came to Lourdes.

In 1904, Bishop Schoepfer of Tarbes organised a pilgrimage to Rome which put Dr Boissarie in the spotlight, as the latter presented the wonders observed in Lourdes from the medical point of view. The last years of his life were spent in a fervent and inspirational apostolate. He passed away in his eightieth year on 27 June 1917.

BOOKSHOP

Inaugurated in the spring of 2006, *la nouvelle librairie des Sanctuaires de Lourdes* (the new bookshop of the Lourdes Shrines), has become in the words of its director, 'the house of the message of Lourdes'. Since the second pilgrimage by Pope John-Paul II to Lourdes in 2004, the hall of the centre for pastoral activities has seen the progressive extension of the bookshop, a place where there is a continuous flow of pilgrims. The same manager co-ordinates the bookshop, the Lourdes Magazine, the publishing house NDL and the Shrines press, forming together a group of well-integrated services. The bookshop team, made up of professionals, organizes book-signing sessions, inviting authors to meet pilgrims. A three-year effort of modernization and updating has in effect trebled the output of the operation, under the name of *EURL Basilique du Rosaire*, the legal entity authorized for the exercise of commercial activities. 'A book can change a life' is the motto of the current *Librairie de la Grotte* where all the main names of the publishing house spend some time. The Italian writer Vittorio Messori, Fr René Laurentin, and many others are there during the season of pilgrimages, enabling fruitful conversations to take place in this international bookshop, the main objective of which is to give everyone access to the Gospel. Indeed, the Bible is one of the most sought after works, together with its authorized commentaries such as the work of Benedict XVI on Jesus of Nazareth, published in 2007.

BRANTHOMME, HENRY
(historian of Lourdes)

Born in 1907, Mgr Henry Branthomme was profoundly affected by the First World War, as his eldest brother was killed in 1917. Ordained in 1932, he left France for a long voyage in the South Seas before reaching Manila to attend the International Eucharistic Congress there. Not only did his health improve on this occasion but his mind was opened to cultures and religions which were previously alien to him. He became passionate about their history from which he starts to grasp some insights into the mentality of the nomadic people in ancient history.

During the Second World War he was taken prisoner and remained in captivity for 15 months. Due to poor health, he was sent back to France where Cardinal Grente, Archbisop of Le Mans, appointed him chaplain to the *Anciens Prisonniers de guerre de la Sarthe* (the ex-prisoners of war of la Sarthe). Having successfully organised a first gathering for the returning prisoners of war at Notre-Dame du Chene, he was made director of pilgrimages in Le Mans. Henceforth, for 40 years, Fr Branthomme travelled across Europe, in discovery of the important places of faith, such as Santiago de Compostella and Rome, but also the Middle East and Turkey, in the footsteps of the apostle Paul and of the first martyrs. However, Lourdes was his most regular and favourite destination. His knowledge of Lourdes and his love of the Holy Virgin encouraged him to undertake, at the end of his life, a study of the history of the Shrine devoted to the buildings of the pilgrimage and to the life that took place there from 1947 to 1988, against the background of what was happening in the world and in the universal Church.

In 1958, the centenary year of Our Lady of Lourdes, M. Branthomme became secretary of the National Association of the Diocesan Directors of Pilgrimages of France, organising congresses in the great Shrines of France, and creating special relations with other countries which soon joined the association. He also edited many manuals for the use of pilgrimages, inviting reflection on the pilgrim's condition and on their goals. To this end, he founded an office for historical and pastoral studies dedicated to the phenomenon of pilgrimage. This lead to writing three authoritative books with Professor Chelini: *Les Chemins de Dieu, l' histoire des pèlerinages chrétiens des origines a nos jours'* (the ways of God, the history of Christian pilgrimages from their origin to the present time) in 1982, and '*Histoire des pèlerinages non chrétiens, entre magie et sacre: le chemin des dieux*' (history of non-Christian pilgrimages, between the magic and the sacred: the way of the gods), in 1987, and *Les Pèlerinages du Monde'* (pilgrimages of the world), published a few days before his death, on 19th October 2004.

BUREAU MEDICAL

The task of the *Bureau Medical des Constatations* is to authenticate the statements – voluntary and spontaneous – of people testifying that they have received the grace of healing through the intercession of Our Lady of Lourdes. The bureau was established in 1883 by Baron Dunot de Saint-Maclou (who was a graduate in medicine from the Catholic University of Louvain) to respond to the accumulation of inexplicable cures occurring at the Massabielle Grotto and elsewhere.

In 1925, due to the influx of doctors to the *Bureau Medical*, Dr Vallet founded an association which quickly became international: the *Association Medicale Internationale de Lourdes (AMIL)*. In 1927, he decided to establish the *Bulletin de l'Association* which has been published ever since.

Since then, a dozen doctors have held the permanent post of head of the *Bureau Medical*, with the task of receiving pilgrims, in particular those who declare themselves cured, as well as the health professionals who visit Lourdes. More and more the role of the doctor at the AMIL consists of informing the media and giving talks in Lourdes and all over the world (a hundred per year on average).

The AMIL brings together all the health professionals, doctors, pharmacists, dentists, nurses and medical auxiliaries (around 20,000 of the latter of 75 different nationalities) who come to Lourdes to give their services freely and accompany the sick.

The bulletin of AMIL, *Fons Vitae,* a quarterly published in five languages (French, Italian, English, Spanish and German) looks at the question of miraculous healings: both practical (medico-spiritual observations) and theoretical (reflections on the link between science and faith) from an anthropology of the person in all its dimensions (body, soul, spirit), which is necessary to evaluate the question of miracles.

It is interesting to note that two Italian members of AMIL were canonised by John-Paul II: Professor Giuseppe Fossati in 1987 and the paediatrician Gianna Molla in 1994.

C

CACHOT (jail)

After leaving the *Moulin de Boly* (Boly mill) the Soubirous were looking for work. Francois was a hired hand and was paid less than the fee for the hire of a horse (FR 1.20 as against FR 1.55 for a horse), and consequently hardly able to feed his family of four children. They

lived in destitution, aggravated by the risk of cholera which was raging in Lourdes in the autumn of 1855. Bernadette, still fragile, contracted asthma, a condition which would never leave her. Her maternal grandmother, on her death, left a legacy and the family decided to take on another mill. Alas, being illiterate and ignorant of business methods, they allowed themselves to be duped and were unable to make the first payment. They found themselves, again, with nothing.

Bernadette went to work as a waitress in the inn owned by her aunt and godmother, Bernarde. The Soubirous, evicted from their miserable dwelling, ended up in Lourdes, in the *cachot*, formerly a prison and one which had been judged insalubrious for prisoners. Their cousin Sajous, who let it to the destitute seasonal Spanish workers who came to Lourdes to earn a little money, accepted them as tenants.

Consisting of one single room, approximately 4 metres square, there was only space enough for two beds, which were shared by six persons, and the few possessions

C they had brought in a small cart. Very quickly the Soubirous became victims of the famine which was rife in the region. Their state of poverty led to Francois being accused of having stolen two sacks of flour and being put in prison. 'It was his wretched state that made me believe that he could be the culprit,' his accuser admitted.

By contrast, a neighbour was to make the following judgement at the time of the apparitions: 'They are poor, as poor as our Lord was on earth...' In spite of these successive tribulations, the family were always noted for their unity. 'Never a quarrel,' their cousin testified, 'I heard only the murmur of prayer.' Little by little the *cachot* would become a symbolic place, connected to that cave, that black hole in the rock, where Bernadette would look upon a young woman radiating light. On 11 February, her sister Toinette and a friend were going to gather bits and pieces to sell to the rag-and-bone man and so earn a few pennies to buy vegetables to put in the soup at lunch time. Bernadette decided to go with them. Bernadette refused to stop in a field on the way for fear that they could be accused of stealing. They made their way to where the canal joins the River Gave, a place which faced the black hole of Massabielle.

In time, this place would radiate a brightness which would illuminate the darkness of the *cachot*. Those who came later to visit the place of the apparitions could not fail also to want to make the detour to that 'foul and dark hovel'. The event at the Grotto was an encounter which consisted not only of a message from Heaven but also brought us into an exchange of love, full of grace, by means of a particular form of recognition.

We speak of the apparition of Mary to Bernadette, but we ought to speak of the apparition of Bernadette to Mary. The Virgin 'recognized' this little one who resembled her, whereas, in Lourdes, Bernadette was invisible. When, at last, she was able to attend catechism class, someone pointed out to the curate of the parish, 'You know that you have Bernadette in your group,' to which he replied, 'I had to call the register and she got up, when her name was called, I recognized Bernadette Soubirous.' He had not noticed her. She had not appeared to him!

The *cachot* reveals, still today, the hidden face of Lourdes. Bernadette wanted to return to it in January 1858, even though she was staying again with the person who had been her wet nurse. She had to come back to that poor room with the barred window to make herself available to Heaven which would open itself to the encounter. Her presence there was proof that the Gospel message was still announced to the poor. The *cachot* authenticates the event of the Grotto.

CASTÉROT, LOUISE

The name of Castérot is still common in the Bigorre* today. It was the family name of Louise, Bernadette's mother, born in 1825, who was the daughter of Augustin and Claire Castérot. Around 1840, Augustin and Claire, lived in a mill, whose name would become famous, the mill of Boly in Lourdes. This mill stood against the large rock on which the castle had been built and it used the water of a small stream called the Lapaca. At that time the couple had four teenage daughters and two other small children.

On 1 July, the miller of Boly died in a cart accident. His widow, looking for someone to take over, turned to a certain Francois Soubirous and offered him the mill together with the hand of her eldest daughter,

Louise Castérot.

Bernarde. Francois was 34 and was still single. He was a likeable man and well known to the family. But Francois was in no hurry. It was not Bernarde he wanted, but her seventeen year-old sister, the one with the blue eyes.

The marriage of Francois and Louise took place on 9 January 1843 and Bernadette was born on 7 February 1844. Four women, the grandmother included, were there to admire the baby and so was little Aunt Lucile, aged 4. Bernarde, the 'heiress', was head of the household. This same status of 'heiress' would be devolved, later, to Bernadette, after the death of her parents.

The 'Castérot clan' as they were called, was to fall apart in 1848. Bernarde had a child outside matrimony with Jean-Marie Tarbes, whom she subsequently married. She was excluded from the Society of the *Enfants de Marie* (Children of Mary). The Castérots then left the mill of Boly. On the one hand, it meant more room and more freedom for the young Soubirous couple, but, on the other, they found themselves without a manager and, unfortunately, business would rapidly go downhill.

Bernarde played a significant role in the famous apparition of 25 February when, rather dramatically, the spring was revealed. Lucile, gentler and almost contemporary with Bernadette, accompanied her with Bernarde to the parish priest. Lucile was also to be a witness of the last apparition on 16 July. The mention of her death is the first line in the private diary which Bernadette kept from 1873 to 1875.

* The region of Bigorre takes its name from the ancient county of Bigorre, the capital of which was Tarbes.

C CASTLE

Bernadette was born at the foot of the impressive castle which towers over the town. This medieval building, of no real beauty, has always had an important military significance. Its strategic situation had been noted from very ancient times and the Saracens used it as a stronghold in the ninth century.

The Albingensians occupied the castle in 1213 and, on 8 May 1360, following the Treaty of Brétigny, it passed into English hands. The Count of Clermont razed it to the ground soon after, but it was rebuilt. During the religious wars, the year after the St Bartholomew's massacre, the castle was sacked by the Huguenots in 1573.

From 1607, when Bigorre was annexed by the Royal Estate, the situation became calmer; the castle became a state prison, a provincial bastille where the kings sent suspects including Fr Lacombe, friend of Mme Guyon during the 'Quietism'* affair, the Duke of Mazarin, Prince of Valentinois in the last

years of Louis XIV's reign, and members of Parliament opposed to the minister, under Louis XVI.

In 1894, the municipality of Lourdes bought it for 50,000 francs from the state, which had listed it as a 'stronghold of the third order' under Napoleon III. Nowadays it is a very interesting museum.

* a form of religious mysticism

CENTENARY

1958, the year of the centenary of the apparitions, was a particularly memorable time in Lourdes. A sign from 'heaven' seemed to confirm Bishop Théas's views. On 11 February, the day of the beginning of the centenary celebrations, the weather was awful - rainy and windy. The bishop stood by his idea of having a mass in the square of the Rosary Basilica. Suddenly a rainbow appeared in the sky and everything proceeded perfectly. Pius XII, in his address to the 60,000 pilgrims present, said: 'For so many favours received during the last century on this sanctified land, let your voices soar with ours towards the throne of the divine mercy in a hymn of thanksgiving. Answer the call of Mary!'

On 18 February, Archbishop Audrain of Auch spoke in praise of Bernadette and, for a fortnight, there were teaching sessions at the Grotto every day.

At last the day of 25 March arrived, the long-awaited day of the consecration of the underground basilica, the construction of which had required so much effort, so much money and had been the source of almost unbearable worries for the persons responsible. Cardinal Roncalli, previously nuncio in Paris and now Patriarch of Venice and, as emphasized by Bishop Théas, an assiduous pilgrim to Our Lady of Lourdes, had been asked to lead the ceremony. The crowds, the fervour and the enthusiasm were to exceed all expectations and, that same evening, a telegram overflowing with joy and praise, was sent to Rome by the papal legate. The financing for the construction was secured in less than three years.

The pilgrimages were more numerous and more fervent than ever; many would spend the night from Saturday to Sunday in prayer to ask for the conversion of Russia. This was first done in Walsingham, England, where in 1954 they had held an all-night vigil for this purpose during the centenary celebrations of the dogma of the Immaculate Conception. This had later also been introduced in Fatima.

In May, 1958, the first pilgrimage of the Order of Malta brought 250 sick people to Lourdes, and on 14 and 15 June, a splendid military pilgrimage brought 40,000 soldiers from all over the world. Bishop Ferreto greeted them on behalf of the Holy See: 'So much hope is being generated through Our Lady in this magnificent display of Christian brotherhood between soldiers of many nations. Is this not a sign that, despite so many accumulated obstacles, the cause of peace is progressing in the human heart?'

On 16 July, the feast of Our Lady of Carmel and the anniversary of the last apparition, mass was celebrated by a Carmelite bishop surrounded by many Carmelite priests and sisters. Pius XII had sent a message: 'Meditate anew the great lesson of the Lourdes apparitions.'

On 5 and 6 August, five thousand 'Children of Mary' gathered together from the five continents. (Bernadette had joined this movement two months after the apparitions). Ten days later, on the feast of the Assumption, 100,000 pilgrims gathered on the occasion of the international pilgrimage of the workers movement and the new basilica was unanimously admired. The mass was broadcast from Italy to Sweden. Cardinal Gerlier exclaimed in his enthusiasm: 'Your pilgrimage will remain a special date in the *Annales de Lourdes* and in the Church. If, only 25 years ago, anyone had spoken of organizing such a meeting, that person would have been called a dreamer or a visionary. And yet, here we are, having just lived through this magnificent spectacle.'

A few days later, a great national pilgrimage brought parliamentarians from France and from all over the world to the foot of the Grotto. The pilgrimage of the gypsies was to follow and, shortly after that, in September, a congress on Mariology was held, bringing together 400 theologians from universities, academies and various associations from all over the world. The sessions, in 29 languages, took place in various venues in the town.

It was at the time of the pilgrimage of the Rosary, on 9 October, that Pius XII died, who had loved and admired Our Lady of Lourdes so much. A funeral service was held the following day, led by Cardinal Feltin, and was attended by many civil, military and religious authorities. Another great friend of Lourdes, John XXIII, was called to replace him on 28 October.

On 8 December, the twenty-fifth anniversary of the canonisation of Bernadette, John XXIII authorized all cloistered contemplative sisters to go to the Grotto, where the former nuncio, Mgr Valerio Valeri, was to speak to them about religious life. On that day, at the instigation of the *Filles de l'Eglise* (Daughters of the Church), the daily and solemn adoration of the Blessed Sacrament started in the Shrine.

The Jubilee Year was closed, in Lourdes on 18 February 1959 and, on the same day, in Rome, by John XXIII, who went to meet the French ambassador to the Holy See at *Saint-Louis-des-Francais*. The Holy Father called this event: 'a Marian Pentecost'. The chapel master, Canon Alexandre Lesbordes, who had supported this special time so well musically, expressed the general impression poetically very well when he said: 'In the evening of this year, we feel the deep joy of hours anticipated for so long and lived so intensely; we also feel the melancholy which tinges the end of a beautiful day, over too quickly.'

CHAPLAINS

'Go and tell the priests to have a chapel built here and let processions be made to this spot,' said

The chaplains' house.

the Virgin Mary to Bernadette Soubirous on 2 March 1858, on the day of the 13th apparition.

After the Bishop of Tarbes had declared the eighteen apparitions of the Virgin to Bernadette to be authentic, on 18 January 1862, the construction of a first chapel, the Crypt, was immediately started, as a response to that request. The first 'chaplains' arrived in Lourdes on 12 May 1866, exactly eight days before the celebration of the first mass at the Crypt. Ever since that day, chaplains have continued to serve in the chapel asked for by the Immaculate Virgin, so that on the very spot where she encountered Bernadette, the celebration of the death and resurrection of her Son, our Lord Jesus Christ, could take place.

Nowadays, twenty-five priests and a few brothers constitute the community of chaplains of Our Lady of Lourdes. Under the authority of the rector of the Shrines, they have the role of welcoming the pilgrims, in six different languages: French, Italian, Spanish, English, German and Dutch. This explains the international nature of this community of priests, coming from different countries and from the five continents.

Their ministry is defined by the message of Lourdes. They transmit the accounts of Bernadette's experience. They enlighten the pilgrims on the meaning of the signs and practices in the pilgrimages. They celebrate the two sacraments which had a particular importance for Bernadette at the time of the apparitions: the sacrament of forgiveness and reconciliation (Bernadette made her first confession a few days after the first apparition) and the eucharist (Bernadette made her first communion a few weeks before the last apparition).

Certain chaplains receive from the Bishop of Tarbes and Lourdes a specific mission with particular attention to the service of the volunteer and of young people.

Some priests in the group of chaplains who have served Our Lady of Lourdes for many years by accompanying pilgrims in her Shrine may receive the '*Chapelain d'Honneur*' cross.

CHOQUET, GEORGES (bishop)

Georges Choquet (1878-1946), was Bishop of Lourdes from 1938 to 1946, which covers also the period of the Second World War. He played an important and discreet role in having the grounds of the Grotto returned to the diocesan association, thus putting to right a long dispute concerning the interpretation of the separation laws dating from the beginning of the century.

Born in Paris, he was ordained priest in 1903. He became known for his zeal, his all-conquering goodness and the wisdom of his spiritual direction. Named military chaplain during the First World War he was awarded the military medal and the *Legion d'Honneur* for his courage. After the war, he took his place among the diocesan missionaries, became their superior, and then vicar general for Cardinal Verdier. After being named Bishop of Langres in 1935, he was chosen by Pius XI to succeed Bishop Gerlier, who had become Archbishop of Lyons, in 1938.

Hardly had the new bishop celebrated with great joy the 80th anniversary of the apparition on 25 March 1938, than war broke out. Pope Pius XII was giving shelter, in Rome, to the Primate of Poland, Cardinal Hlond, who, according to the constitution, given the fracture of succession in Poland, had become head of state. Not wanting to have anything to do with the Nazis, he was hiding in Rome. Pius XII asked Bishop Choquet to hide the primate in the chalet where he had stayed at the time of the triduum for peace. And so, the Polish prelate left Rome, on 9 June 1940, to go to Lourdes where he remained hidden for more than two years. He never ventured beyond the garden surrounding the villa.

The following month, on 18 July 1940, Bishop Choquet wrote to the French head of state, Marshal Pétain, to negotiate the return of the estate of the Grotto to the Massabielle Association, of which the bishop was president. The estate had been confiscated by the State and then handed over to the municipality of Lourdes on 9 April 1910, which, in turn, let it to the Church. Everything was settled quickly and, on 15 October, the bishop was able to thank the Mayor of Lourdes officially.

Prevented by the war from realising his hopes, Bishop Choquet continued to acquire important pieces of land and work for the upkeep of the Shrine. On his death, Cardinal Gerlier summed the man up by saying that he was: 'a missionary soul with a resolute spirit, an apostolic worker of the greatest quality'.

CHURCH

The beautiful 'Lady' asked Bernadette to have a church built at the place of the apparitions. She was most certainly speaking of a construction which would be a place of prayer. But perhaps the immaculate mother had in mind that Lourdes should contribute to the revival of God's new people, the body and the spouse of Christ, the temple of the Spirit. These are precisely the images which the New Testament used to describe the Church.

The Church is the *new people of God* 'assembled in the unity of the Father, the Son and the Holy Spirit' (*Lumen Gentium 4)* which started to gather round Jesus. Unity is generated by his word and by his call to follow him, a call which has as foundation his commandment of reciprocal love.

Maintaining the continuity with the community of Israel, the Church reveals itself as a movement of people becoming new, in baptism, through the message of the Gospel; a movement of people called to establish and spread a new spirit, based on reciprocal giving. The Church is the *body of Christ* engendered by the eucharist: 'You are all one in Christ Jesus (Gal. 3: 28), his presence and his manifestation in the world. The Church is the *spouse of Christ* since it is not only identified in him but, as it is united to him at the same time, it is distinguishable from him and he regenerates it constantly; it receives life from him and maintains with him a relationship of love.

The Church is the *temple of the Holy Spirit,* identifying itself with him, it lives in the same way as him the Trinitarian love that it reflects and radiates. In this way it inspires a new social dimension, becoming leaven and giving a foretaste of the kingdom of God, which begins on this earth and will find its fulfilment in the heavenly Jerusalem.

In order to understand better the profound reality of the Church, that is, its vocation, we might ask first when it was born. Prefigured already in the community of Israel, the Fathers of the Church see its birth at the very moment of the incarnation, when the eternal Word became flesh in Mary and established the covenant with the whole of humanity which Mary expresses and incarnates.

We must then examine the public life of Jesus, with his preaching and the formation of a community of disciples; with the calling of the Twelve, so that 'they were with him as well as sent by him'; with Peter, the rock on which Jesus built his Church. But we must also consider the paschal mystery: Jesus on the cross with blood and water pouring out of his side pointing to the mystery of baptism and of the eucharist; Mary, at the foot of the cross, as the new Eve who is born from the side of the new Adam. Jesus on the cross is the seed which falls to the earth and dies to give fruit: his Church, which becomes visible on the day of Pentecost, when the gift of the Spirit - in many tongues, numerous peoples and cultures - gives life to a people with one heart and one soul.

Apart from the biblical images, and from those of the Early Christians, there are another three words which help us to understand more profoundly the nature of the Church.

The Church is *mystery* because its root is the life of three divine persons: Jesus reveals the Trinitarian mystery and makes the Church participate in it. Through Christ, the Church, in the Spirit, can thus reach the Father and in the Church the Trinity can live among men.

The Church is *communion* because its life is entirely fashioned on the model of the communion of the three divine Persons. Just like each one of the three Persons in the bosom of the Trinity lives with, for and in the other two, so the members of the community of the Church, the various vocations that it brings together, the charisms, and the institutions are all called to live with, for and in the others.

The Church is *mission* since, from its origins, it cannot close in on itself: it has the duty to make the whole of humanity participate in this communion and thus to bring it to its fulfilment. The Second Vatican Council called the Church 'sacrament', or rather, 'sign and instrument of intimate union with God and of the unity of the whole of humanity' (*Lumen Gentium 1)*.

Finally, the nature of the Church is revealed by four 'marks' which characterize it with more precision. It is *one* because it takes part in the Trinitarian life of unity, in conformity with the prayer of Jesus, addressed to his Father: 'May they all be one, as you and I are one'. The Church is *holy,* because it shares in the holiness of God thrice holy, because Jesus, the Holy One of God, lives in it, because it is the Holy Spirit which sanctifies it. It is *catholic,* because it reflects the Trinitarian dimension, it contains a great diversity of people, cultures and traditions and it presents a wide variety of gifts and charisms which make it beautiful and fertile. The Church is *apostolic* because it is founded on the apostles who continue to guide it through their successors, the pope and the bishops, through their teaching and through the sacraments.

Jesus wanted his Church to be like this. And we who are its members, although often fragile like clay vases, are on our way to the place where Jesus preceded us, towards the heavenly kingdom.

CHURCH OF ST BERNADETTE

The Church of St Bernadette stands near the place where Our Lady appeared to her for the last time on 16 July 1858. It is a multi-functional structure, intended mainly for liturgical celebrations, but it can also be used for conferences and forums requiring audio-visual equipment. The building is remarkable for the fact that it has none of the usual external features of a church.

The church comprises two buildings centred around a reception area. The first building is the church dedicated to St Bernadette, with a capacity of 5,000 including 300 wheelchairs; each wing of the nave can be partitioned off, depending on the number of people using it, or to allow several groups to use it simultaneously for conferences and

meetings. The sloping nave also allows space for some smaller meeting rooms.

The second building is the semi-circle (*hemi-cycle*), which takes it name from the shape of the large hall, and whose moveable equipment makes it suitable for a variety of different purposes: study sessions, conferences, even liturgical celebrations, with a capacity of between 350 – 500. The French bishops' conference meets here twice a year. There is a spacious sacristy from which processions can start on solemn occasions.

The church took 20 months to build. It was inaugurated on 25 March 1988, the day on which Mgr Sahuquet succeeded Mgr Douze as Bishop of Tarbes and Lourdes.

In 1995 a Blessed Sacrament chapel was added, specially reserved for adoration. It faces towards the Grotto and is dedicated as a place of permanent silent adoration for up to 150 people. Designed by Jean-Paul Félix, it was inaugurated on 18 June 1995, the feast of *Corpus Christi*.

The Chapel of Adoration was inspired by three biblical symbols: the tent of God's covenant with his people, symbolised by the ceiling tapestry; the luminous cloud by which God led his people to the Promised Land, symbolised by the gilded wooden column containing the eucharist; the new Jerusalem, symbolised by the twelve pillars representing the twelve apostles.

CINEMA

From its very beginning, cinema was characterised by a strong religious input. It found great dramatic inspiration in the Gospels and in the life of Christ, particularly in the scenes of the stations of the cross and of the passion.

Cinema inherited the vast patrimony handed down to it by the other art forms, a legacy of themes and representations and pictures of a religious character. These were drawn from paintings and the the-

Catre, with its vivid 'tableaux', its sacred scenes and its 'mystery, miracle and passion plays' - all extraordinary scenarios, ready to be used by this new invention. From the time of its pioneers, Louis and Auguste Lumière and George Melies, cinema was ready to leave behind the emphasis on newsreels and street scenes, moving locomotives and comic pranks or conjuring tricks, and from 1897 produced filmed scenes of the Passion (Images representing the life and the passion of Jesus Christ) and, in 1899, tableaux illustrating the life of Jesus (Christ walking on water).

In taking an interest in the sacred and in the religious, cinema, and later television, could not ignore such an important and popular phenomenon as the apparitions of the Virgin at Lourdes, a small town in the heart of the country which had seen cinema come to birth. Indeed, Louis Lumière was himself the first to take it as a topic only three years after the first public cinematographic show of 28 December 1895, with a documentary entitled simply *Lourdes.* Other documentaries were to follow: *Visions de Lourdes* by the Belgian Charles Dekeukeleire (1932); *il paese dell'anima*, produced by the two Italians, Victor De Santis and Remigio del Grosso for FIAT (1957); *Lourdes 93:Prvo hrvastko* under the direction of the Croatian Mislav Hudoletnjak (1993); the 8mm documentary by Enrico Zavalloni G*li angeli di Lourdes* (1999); the American documentary *In search of history: Lourdes – Shrine of miracles* (2000), where John Paul II can be seen. In terms of short and medium length films, one can recall: *Lourdes* by the English director Ken Russell (1958); *Milagre di Lourdes,* by the Brazilian Carlos Alberto Perrereia (1965); the French film *Lourdes, l'hiver,* by Marie-Claire Treilhou (1981); and *Madonna a Lourdes*, by the French producers Arnaud and Jean-Marie Larrieu (2001).

Naturally, fiction cinema also became interested in the story of the little shepherdess Marie-Bernarde Soubirous, with various full length films. In chronological order: *Credo ou la tragédie de Lourdes (*Credo or the tragedy of Lourdes), by French producer Julien Duvivier (1924); *Le Miracle de Lourdes*, by B. Simon (France 1926); *La vie merveilleuse de Bernadette,* by Georges Pallu (France 1929); *La merveilleuse tragédie de Lourdes,* by Henri Fabert (France 1933). In 1943, *The Song of Bernadette,* produced by the American Henry King (1943), certainly the most famous and the most accomplished version, won an Oscar for the actress Jennifer Jones for her powerful and sensitive interpretation. Afterwards, there came *Il suffit d'aimer,* by the French director Robert Darene (1960); the Spanish film *Aquella joven de blanco*, by Leon Klimovsky (1965); *Bernadette* (1987) and *La Passion de Bernadette* (1989), produced by French film maker Jean Delannoy with Sidney Penny as Bernadette. Among the various television films made are: *L'Affaire Lourdes,* by the French producer Marcel Bluwal (1967*);* *Lisdoonvarna – Lourdes of love,* by the Dutch Hans Heijnen (1999) and the Italian production *Lourdes*, by Ludovico Gasparini, with Stefania Rocca (2000). The little French town where the miracle of the apparitions of the Virgin Mary occurred is, incidentally, also mentioned in films dealing with other themes such as *Le Juge et l'assassin,* by Bertrand Tavernier (1976) and *Hommes, Femmes, mode d'emploi*, by Claude Lelouch (1996).

CITÉ SAINT-PIERRE

'To allow poorer people to come on pilgrimage to Lourdes and to welcome them respecting their dignity...' This wish of Bernadette was fulfilled in 1955 by the Cité Saint-Pierre foundation. On the request of Bishop Théas of Tarbes-Lourdes, Jean Rodhain, founder of *Secours Catholique*, created a *Cité-Secours* on the heights of the Pyrenean massif which overhangs Lourdes.

Since 1955, nearly a million poorer people have been welcomed in the *Cité*, as participants in diocesan pilgrimages or belonging to the *voyages d'espérance* (voyages of hope) operated by *Secours Catholique* and Caritas International.

Spread over 32 hectares of green land, the *Cité Saint-Pierre* can accommodate up to 500 pilgrims and provide 1,500 meals per day from 15 January to 15 December. Groups of pilgrims celebrate the liturgy in its ten venues, including the *Padre Pio* Hall, each with a capacity of 1,000 places. Forty permanent workers and more than a thousand volunteers, every year, put themselves at the service of the pilgrims. Various programmes are available during the pilgrims' stay: walks retracing the steps of Bernadette, exploring the symbols of the Grotto, workshops, festive vigils, the road of peace, etc. A shuttle service allows the pilgrims

to go down to the Shrines every day.

As a church facility, the *Cité Saint-Pierre* also welcomes movements, parishes, dioceses and chaplaincies, for retreats or gatherings. The mission of the *Cité Saint-Pierre* consists of revealing to the poor the hope which is within them, through the discovery of the message of Lourdes, the awareness of their talents and the acknowledgement of their dignity. This mission includes the raising of awareness within society and the Catholic Church of the importance of charity: the poor are our brothers and sisters; they build the world with us, they reveal to us the good news of the Gospel.

COHEN, HERMANN (Fr Augustin—Marie du Saint-Sacrement)

Hermann Cohen, known under the Carmelite habit as Fr Augustin-Marie (1821-1871), had a memorable encounter with Bernadette at the end of September 1858, and afterwards they remained spiritually very united. The cause for his beatification, a worthy recognition of an unforgettable life, has been submitted.

Hermann Cohen was born in Hamburg in 1821, into a non-practising Jewish family. From an early age he displayed a remarkable talent for music and became a child prodigy on the piano. In 1833, he was taken to Paris to be tutored by the great pianist Franz Liszt. Despite his tender years, he was made welcome in the home of the master who was living with the Countess of Agoult: there he met George Sand and Felicité de la Mennais.

Very handsome, and very gifted, he was to know success to a dangerous degree, accompanying Liszt to Germany, Italy and England. The Countess of Agoult became jealous and forced him to leave. He then fell into a dissolute life, slave to a passion for gambling and to the terrible temptations of that world. This existence lasted until 1847, but the Lord was waiting for him.

In May 1847 he was led to conduct an amateur choir, at the request of his friend the Prince of the Moskova, in the church of *Sainte-Valère*, in Paris (*Sainte-Clotilde*). During the adoration of the Blessed Sacrament, he found himself bowing his head, as if in worship. He was not a believer and was extremely surprised at this spontaneous reaction. In a flash the thought came to him to become a Catholic! The same experience occurred the following Friday.

As a result, he confided in a friend, a truly Christian lady, the Duchess of Rauzan. She put him in touch with a well-respected priest of the archdiocese, Fr Legrand, who gave him a book on Christian doctrine.

Some time later, he went to Ems, in Germany, for a concert. Fr Legrand recommended a Catholic priest to him whom he might wish to consult: on 8 August, during mass, just like St Augustine, he was flooded by grace, joy and light. He was baptized on 28 August, the feast of St Augustine, in the presence of the Ratisbonne brothers, eminent Jewish converts.

His spiritual progress led him to the Carmelite order. Ordained priest in 1851, he became a remarkable Carmelite whose preaching and example left a deep impression. While establishing a Carmelite monastery in Bagnères, in 1858, he took a trip to Lourdes on 20 September. He was completely overwhelmed by the Grotto and by Bernadette. At that time Bernadette was considering becoming a Carmelite – only her poor health would dissuade her. A great intimacy developed between them. Sent to England in 1864 to found the English Carmel, he wrote to Bernadette to congratulate her on entering Nevers, leaving behind such a dangerous world.

As a German Jew, he was sent back to Germany because of the 1870 war. He died there as a true saint, looking after French prisoners suffering from typhus, on 19 January 1871, at the age of forty-nine.

COURTIN, JEAN-BAPTISTE (historian of Lourdes)

Canon Jean-Baptiste Courtin must be counted among the privileged friends of the Shrines of Lourdes. Indeed, researchers have frequently referred and certainly always will have to refer to his important book: *Lourdes, le domaine de Notre-Dame de 1858 a 1947*.

Born in 1875 in the Diocese of Rennes, Fr Courtin took a close interest, from the early stages of his career, in the story of Lourdes and in the development of the place of the Grotto. But it was only at the beginning of the 1920s that he started to gather together precise documents on all its aspects of developments, without entering into the often fierce polemics that were raging at the time.

Thus, for twenty-five years, he was to work assiduously on this project, joining the Lourdes community in 1934 in order to be closer to his sources. He became chaplain to the sisters of Nevers who ran what was then called the *Asile de Lourdes*, a place which received the sick pilgrims and which is now called the *Accueil de Notre-Dame*. From 1933, he contributed to the *Annales de Notre-Dame*, a magazine of the Shrines, which merged with the *Journal de la Grotte*, in 1939.

He became honorary chaplain of *Notre-Dame* in 1934 and was made an honorary canon of the diocese of Tarbes and Lourdes in 1945, at which time he left Lourdes. Two years later, in 1947, his 400-page book was published. In it all sorts of details were given on the work achieved during the period under review, on all the monuments described in detail and on all the difficulties met on the way, the costs, the inaugurations, the personalities.

Canon Courtin died in the house of *Saint-Joseph de Châteaubourg*, in his own diocese, on 17 January 1955, on the feast of Our Lady of Pontmain. On 10 June that year, Cardinal Roques, Archbishop of Rennes, wrote a very positive preface to Canon Courtin's book: 'A wonderful project, within everyone's reach, fruit of conscientious work, of patient, meticulous and lengthy research and with a taste for precision. All this makes this work so valuable and gives it its charm.'

The book was not reprinted, but a sequel was written thanks to the efforts of Mgr Henry Branthomme and Mme Chantal Touvet: *Histoire des Sanctuaires de Lourdes,* NDL.

CROS, LÉONARD-MARIE (historian of Lourdes)

On 17 January 1913, Fr Léonard Cros, a Jesuit from Toulouse, died in exile in Vittoria, in Spain. He was the first of many great researchers of the story of the apparitions.

Born in 1831, his life had been illuminated by Pope Pius IX's proclamation of the dogma of the Immaculate Conception. He was 23 at the time. When the events of Lourdes occurred, he saw in them a striking confirmation of the Holy Father's proclamation and also of the eucharistic movement of which he was an ardent promoter. He became a passionate researcher, asking questions tirelessly, accumulating as many documents as possible, even the most humble, and wrote many pages of observations. These archives were later enriched by notes from Procurator Dutour and other sources.

Bishop Jourdan, 3rd successor to Bishop Laurence, gave him the responsibility, in 1877, of exploring the phenomenon of the apparitions from a scientific point of view. For three years he devoted himself unremittingly to this work. If hagiography is the art of embellishing holy things to render them more edifying, Fr Cros was at the opposite end of that spectrum. 'With unrelenting zeal,' said Fr Laurentin, 'and a sharp critical sense which reached the point of being a kind of phobia of any hagiographic conventions and of received ideas, Fr Cros gathered everything and anything that could have been written or said in newspapers, plaques, archives, correspondences or private diaries. Distance being no object, he pursued all who might have had even the slightest memory of the events, to the point of questioning people on their death bed, regardless of their suffering. The result is an impressive accumulated body of work, a unique collection of information on the events of Massabielle.' Moreover, the author wrote without any literary pretension: for him all that counted was the truth.

It is easy to understand why those three volumes, completed in 1879, could not readily be presented to the public: they revealed aspects which may have been considered indiscreet. It also contained errors, such as the account of an apparition on 26 February which did not take place. All the same, even the most exacting censors admired his work and were asking for its publication. However, due to the accusations made in the book against preceding historians, the author met with such opposition that his work did not appear until 1925: *Histoire de Notre-Dame de Lourdes* (Beauchesne). It became the principal source for Mgr Trochu's beautiful book on Bernadette.

One of the last answers Fr Cros received from Bernadette, on her death bed, on 17 April 1879, became the linchpin of all his writings on Lourdes: 'Whatever is written in the simplest way will be the best. When the Passion is being read, I am more touched than when it is being explained to me'.

CROWNED VIRGIN

The day after the consecration of the Basilica of the Immaculate Conception and of the coronation of Our Lady of Lourdes, on 2 and 3 July 1876 respectively, an anonymous benefactor made the gift of a statue in bronze, made in the workshops of the firm of Raffl, in Paris. It represented the Immaculate Conception as Bernadette had described her, but wearing a crown in the memory of the homage which had been given to her on the preceding 3 July. After some hesitation, it was decided to put the statue in the centre of the Savy field, at the foot of the Basilica of the Immaculate Conception, on the way to the Grotto. In this way, she watches over and blesses the chapel she had wanted and requested through Bernadette. One month after its blessing, which took place on 8 September, the feast of the Virgin's birthday, a pilgrimage from Anjou took the initiative of ending the candle procession at the foot of the statue to give her a last homage, singing the Salve Regina. This would become a ritual with other pilgrimages. This statue, very soon named the Crowned Virgin, was to become the rallying point for pilgrims before their ceremony of arrival at the Grotto and would mark the actual start of the pilgrimage.

CRYPT

When Bishop Laurence entrusted the architect Hyppolyte Durand with the project of building the chapel asked for by the Virgin, there was no question of building a crypt. However, to compensate for the different levels of the ground between the north and the south and to extend the surface on which the chapel was to stand, the architect suggested placing a crypt to the west, where, normally, the entrance to the chapel would be. In the end, he reversed his plan, placing the apse altar of the crypt above the cave of the apparition. The foundations of the Shrine are encircled by a thick wall, punctuated by elegant buttresses and its

C vaults are supported by double colonnades which reduce the view but contribute to the prayerful atmosphere. On the south side, two chapels dedicated to St Peter and the Sacred Heart open on to the nave, and on the north side are chapels to St Joseph and St John.

The first liturgical service was held in 1866, after the arrival of the missionaries of the Garaison who were in charge of pilgrimages to Lourdes. The first mass was celebrated on 19 May, on the eve of the feast of Pentecost, by Bishop Laurence, at the altar of the Immaculate Conception, for the intentions of M du Sordet, donor of the marble statue which adorns it. Created by the sculptor Fabish from Lyons, it represents the Madonna and Child. According to testimonies gathered twenty years later, Bernadette was present at the inauguration of the Crypt, among the *Enfants de Marie* (Movement of the Children of Mary).

In 1862, the architect had mined the more salient parts of the rock to obtain a wider level surface but he judged it prudent not to interfere with a compact mass of rock ten metres high which he bypassed, creating two corridors, one to the north, the other to the south. They would be occupied for a long period by thirteen, then twenty-six confessionals which were replaced in 1972, by altars. Only in 1903 was the digging done for the central corridor. The mosaic decoration by Facchina, applied in the lateral chapels in 1894, was covered over in the axial chapel in 1955 by green 'cipolin' (green-streaked, white marble) and the stone altar was replaced by an altar made of onyx, topped by an enamel tabernacle. The Virgin, by Fabish, stands out on a gilded background of large rays. Fabish (1812-1886) also sculpted two other well-known representations of the Virgin: the bronze statue of the Immaculate Conception in the Basilica of Fourvière, inaugurated on 8 December 1852, and the representations of Our Lady of la Salette.

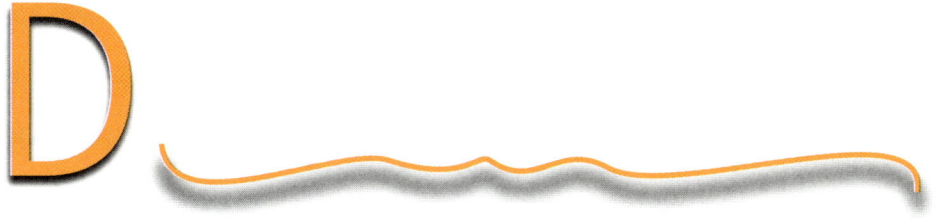

DANCE THEATRE

Unlike cinema, it seems that theatre is not an art form often inspired by the events of Lourdes. For this reason, we will limit ourselves to recalling only one piece of dance theatre, chosen because of its originality. It is called *Aquero*, the word from the local dialect used by Bernadette to name the apparition.

The show, which was created at the request of the Shrine's management, came to fruition in Florence (Italy), thanks to dozens of young people (singers, dancers, technicians) who gave their time voluntarily, with the assistance of a few professionals: Mite Balduzzi, composer of the music and lyrics, Walter Savelli, responsible for the arrangements, PierLuigi Grison, for the choreography and Enzo Gagliardi, for the sets.

Performed for the first time in the Church of *Sainte-Bernadette* on 16 August 1997, in front of thousands of young people who were on their way to the World Youth meeting in Paris, and then again in September of the same year, on the occasion of the official inauguration of the new *Accueil Notre-Dame*, the show presents a modern interpretation of the adventure lived by Bernadette. Without seeking to draw parallels with today's world and without getting lost in symbolism, the event itself is accepted as the starting point, as an established fact. This work manages to emphasize the beauty and the poetry contained in the real facts.

Aquero, which was performed in theatres all over Italy, is also, now, available as a CD.

DE SAINT-MACLOU, DUNOT (doctor)

Baron Dunot de Saint-Maclou (1828-1891), originally from Calvados, had studied philosophy and theology in depth before studying medicine at Caen, and later in Louvain, the famous Belgian university. His wife's health brought him to Lourdes in 1877. Unfortunately she died on 26 August of that year, having been given the last rites by Bishop Peyramale, assisted by Fr Sempé. Bishop Peyramale was to die just twelve days later.

Dr de Saint-Maclou then took refuge in a convent near Nice, while still retaining his link with the Lourdes Shrine, as a hospital assistant. He would become the third president of the *Hospitalité de Notre-Dame de Lourdes*.

In 1883, Fr Sempé asked him to remain in Lourdes permanently and to verify the healings. He accepted this invitation with all his faith and medical knowledge. He started receiving the pilgrims in a place near the pools, in a wooden shed which had been used during the construction of the Rosary Basilica. Later, he was provided with a more dignified office, and thus started what was called *la clinique du surnaturel* (the clinic of the supernatural) which Dr de Saint-Maclou would manage until his death in 1891. His successor, Dr Boissarie, was to give importance to what was to become the *Bureau des Constatations* (the office for reports and findings), by attracting numerous doctors from France and abroad

DÉSIRAT ANTOINE (priest)

Antoine Désirat is the only member of the clergy who was ever present during an apparition. His account of it is fascinating. Just ordained, but not yet in any post, he happened to be in Omex, a small neighbouring village, on 1 March 1858. There was nothing to stop him visiting the Grotto since he was not under the jurisdiction of the Lourdes parish priest who had forbidden his own priests to go there. He was present at the 12th apparition. Being a priest he had a good position, very close to the young visionary.

'Bernadette, while saying her Rosary, hardly moved her lips but, from her attitude, from the expression on her face, one could see that she was transported. The smile goes beyond any description. The most skilful artist, the most consummate actor, could never reproduce its charm! Impossible to imagine!

'What struck me was the joy and then the sadness that her face reflected. One phenomenon followed the other with lightning speed, and yet there was no brusque movement. It was a wonderful transition. I had observed the child as she was making her way to the Grotto with scrupulous attention. What a difference between the way she was then and how I saw her at the moment of the apparition - the same difference as between matter and spirit!

'Only Bernadette could see the apparition but everybody felt her presence. Respect, silence, recollection reigned all around. What a wonderful feeling it was. I felt as if I was at the entrance to paradise.'

Fr Désirat did not dare stay any longer and discreetly withdrew. There was great laughter at the college of Saint-Pé when he told of his experience on that day, so much so, that he did not speak about it for the next ten years. One of those who had laughed was Fr Remi Sempé, superior of the college, who was to become the first superior of the Shrine: a divine sense of humour!

DIARY OF BERNADETTE

Between 1873 and 1875, Bernadette kept a small private diary which is undoubtedly the most precious document we have from her. It is a very small, bound notebook, in which Sr Marie-Bernard wrote down, with meticulous care, extracts from her spiritual readings, notes of talks given at retreats, advice given by her confessor. On one of the last pages, despite her exhausted state, she had scribbled with a pencil a deeply moving text:

'Infallible ways towards holiness and consummated holiness:

1. Means which God puts at our disposal - the light - that is: our rules;

2. On our part, good will that is strong, courageous, constant, persevering.'

What a wonderful description of her soul!

This little diary has been published in various forms, including a facsimile version, and its reading invites a fresh discovery of this deeply evangelical soul. Let us content ourselves, in this brief presentation, with quoting the very first lines which describe so well the secret of the life of Bernadette, which is no other than the secret of Mary: 'What concerns me is no longer my concern, I must be, from this moment, entirely for God, and for God alone, not for myself.'

DIOCESE

If a poll were to be taken regarding such details about Lourdes as the diocese it is located in, or even

Bishop Jacques Perrier of Tarbes and Lourdes.

which department it belongs to, very few would be able to answer correctly. Lourdes is known the world over. Tarbes, the seat of the bishop and the administrative centre of the department, is a modest town: 15,000 inhabitants at the time of the apparitions. In those days the diocese had 251,000 inhabitants; today the number is 220,000.

The origins of the Tarbes diocese are unknown. Aper is the first bishop whose name is known. In 506 he sent a priest to represent him at the Council of Agde as he considered himself too old to participate.

The French wars of religion (1562-1598) have marked the region greatly. Many paintings and statues were destroyed at the time and churches pulled down. The cathedral also suffered, but the Bigorre remained Catholic despite the proximity of Protestant Bearn.

Marian devotion dates from ancient times and is particularly strong in that region. Marian Shrines abound, scattered over the whole territory. At the time of the apparitions, the most important one was that of Garaison, situated quite a distance from Lourdes. The Virgin had appeared at some point within the period 1510-1515, to Anglese de Sagazan, a young girl around ten years of age. Like all country children at that time, Anglese looked after sheep. Because of that example, and other similar ones, Bernadette was, wrongly, believed to be a shepherdess.

Under the *Ancien Regime*, the Diocese of Tarbes was linked to the province of Bigorre. The Revolution created the department of the Hautes Pyrénées, on a slightly modified territory. The 1801 Concordat abolished the diocese and attached it, as well as Bayonne, to Aire-sur-Adour. After about twenty years the diocese of Tarbes was re-established.

At the time of the apparitions, the diocese had, as bishop, a rather remarkable man, Bertrand-Severe Laurence, a native of the area. The Revolution and the Empire had left France in a deplorable spiritual state. Bishop Laurence drew strength and inspiration from the Marian Shrines to re-energize his diocese. For this, he brought priests together in Garaison and sent them out to organise missions and preach in the countryside.

The fathers of *Garaison*, who would become the *Missionnaires de l'Immaculée Conception,* were to be called upon by Bishop Laurence, from 1866, to serve the pilgrims. In 1903, the fathers were expelled from France. The priests of the diocese rallied to keep the service going at the Shrines. The fathers returned after the liberation, the rector of the Shrine remaining a priest of the diocese.

In 1912, Pope Pius X added the name of Lourdes to that of Tarbes, giving the diocese its current designation. Bishop Schoepfer, a 'guardian of the Grotto', was the first bishop to bear that title. Every year, the pilgrimage to Lourdes of the Diocese of Tarbes and Lourdes counts over six thousand participants and includes people of all ages. This goes to show how dear Lourdes is to the heart of the 'Bigordians'.

DONZE, HENRI (bishop)

Born in Canada, at Notre-Dame de Lourdes, on 11 October 1912, into a family originating from the north of France, Henri Donze was a student at the minor seminary of Saint-Jean de Maurienne, at the major seminary of Annecy, at the French seminary in Rome and, finally, at the Catholic Faculties of Lyon. He was ordained priest on 19 September 1936 and served in the Diocese of Maurienne. He was nominated Bishop of Tulle and his episcopal ordination took place on 26 January 1963. In 1970, he became Bishop of Tarbes and Lourdes and his duties there ceased in 1988.

He arrived in Lourdes in the

troubled years which followed May 1968 and the Second Vatican Council. Also, the people of the diocese wished to have more access to their bishop: his time was increasingly taken up with Lourdes. In addition, there were difficulties within the French episcopate regarding the construction of the St Pius X Basilica.

It was then that the *Conseil permanent de l'Episcopat* made public its S*tatut sur les Sanctuaires de Lourdes* (statute of the Lourdes Shrines), published in the diocesan bulletin on 25 June 1970. It noted the influence of Lourdes on the dioceses of France and on many other countries. The aim of the statute was to: 'bring into action an open and co-ordinated pastoral programme for the pilgrimages which specified the respective roles of the bishop and the rector: The Bishop of Tarbes and Lourdes remains the bishop of the Lourdes Shrines; but, so that he may be able to focus on his main duties in his diocese, the rector of the Shrines will be endowed with a specific role of management with the title of "episcopal vicar".' The statute also foresaw the creation of two councils around the bishop: a 'Conseil pour la Pastorale des Sanctuaires' (council for the pastoral management of the Shrines), and another for the finances, each with a bishop delegated from the French episcopate.

It was at that time that a general pastoral programme was put in place in order to ensure that Lourdes, at the time of Vatican II, would remain faithful to the founding event. With this perspective, Bishop Donze put in place the councils and named a new rector. It was a period of intense creativity in the light of the message. Bishop Donze welcomed the arrival of the *Action Catholique* to help pilgrims to unite faith and life. In a spirit of partnership with the directors of the pilgrimages he developed the *Journées de Fevrier* (the February days) and started new constructions: 'l'Accueil Bernadette' (no longer there), the Sainte-Bernadette church and the semi-circular room for the meeting of the French bishops. He also inaugurated the press office and promoted Christian art, etc.

Two main events marked his episcopate: the Eucharistic Congress *Lourdes ou l'appel des pauvres* (Lourdes or the call of the poor) in July 1981, and the welcoming of Pope John Paul II on 14-15 August 1983.

He died in Annecy on 25 June 2002.

DOZOUS, PIERRE-ROMAIN (doctor)

Dr Pierre-Romain Dozous (1799-1883) was to be the first doctor who would take an interest in the Lourdes healings and he was the only doctor to be present at the apparitions. He provided his reports to the Episcopal commission without, however, sitting on that commission.

This complex, colourful character was a doctor at the Lourdes hospital at the time of the apparitions. He was appreciated for his superior knowledge at a time when medicine was considered more as an art than as a science. He was attached to the courts in Lourdes and in Pau and enjoyed a certain celebrity status while deploring not being given the place in society he believed he merited. His passionate and spirited temperament sometimes made him too outspoken and his successor at the court of Pau, Dr Balencie, one of the three doc-

tors who examined Bernadette, said of him: 'He is intelligent but he lacks judgement.'

Aged about 60 at the time of the apparitions, he was no longer a believer. He was present at the apparitions, without believing in them, from the 21 February, which was the sixth one. It was on 7 April that grace would overwhelm him, just as it had done to the priest of Lourdes on 25 March. At Ade Bernadette had received a beautiful Easter candle and its flame, during the ecstasy, licked her fingers. People started shouting: 'She will be burnt!' As a man of science, Dr Dozous, there by chance on that particular day, silenced everybody and timed the duration of the phenomenon. After that, he put a little flame under the hand of Bernadette, who reacted sharply. After that, the doctor's heart changed radically.

The zeal which he had shown fighting against the 'facts of Lourdes' was now deployed to defend them. He would discuss them with Bishop Laurence whom he thought lukewarm. The latter, who was very astute, maintained his distance.

In 1874, Dr Dozous wrote a book *La grotte de Lourdes, ses fontaines et ses guerisons..* (The Grotto of Lourdes, its fountains and its cures). The book was very successful and remains an interesting testimony. His detractors went as far as accusing him of having 'fabricated Lourdes' – a comment which he would have rather enjoyed!

DUFO, BRICE (lawyer)

On 5 April 1858, Easter Monday, two days before the famous 17th apparition when doctor Dozous was converted after having seen the flames of a candle lick the fingers of the visionary, Bernadette was invited to dinner at the house of Maître Dufo (1799-1972), a former Mayor of Lourdes. The Dufos were one of the most prominent families of Lourdes, as we know from the notebooks of Inspector Jacomet, who, on that occasion, commented on the shrewdness of Bernadette who 'knew' how to get herself invited to good houses. There she met the eldest daughter, Marie, the pretty young girl with whom the same Jacomet wanted to compare the 'apparition', and Rachel, a personal friend of Bernadette's with whom she would correspond until her death. She also met Valery, a young boarder at the college of Saint-Pé. Maître Dufo had met, in March, the director of studies of that college, Fr Sempé, who did not believe in the apparitions. 'If you had seen her crossing herself, you would not speak in this manner!' he said. These words had struck the

priest. A few days later, Marie Dufo told Valery in a letter about the apparition of the 25 March and of Mary's words which she misquoted: 'Je suis Marie Immaculée...' (I am Mary Immaculate...). From that time Fr Sempé also began to believe in the apparitions. Eight years later, he was called to Lourdes to become the great builder of the Shrine.

DUTOUR, VITAL

The representative for law and order during the fortnight of the apparitions was the public prosecutor, M. Dutour, who had the power to imprison Bernadette should she cause a disturbance.

Vital Dutour was born in the Gers region in 1816 and began his career as a lawyer, before going on to become a magistrate. Having failed to be appointed as public prosecutor at Tarbes, he was appointed to Lourdes, a small town of little significance. He was an educated, conscientious professional, though somewhat timid. On 25 February, the day on which Our Lady was to show Bernadette the spring, M. Dutour summoned the visionary Bernadette to appear before him at six o'clock in the morning! Bernadette went with her mother and the session lasted for over two hours. They were kept standing the whole time. Louise Soubirous, dropping with fatigue, finally collapsed into a chair which M Dutour pushed towards her but Bernadette declined the offer of a chair, 'I would make it dirty,' she said, and sat on the floor instead. Bernadette so disconcerted the Magistrate who was also growing nervous at the noise of protests outside, that he could not even steady his hand to find the inkwell to dip his pen in. He later destroyed any drafts of this famous encounter. There would be plenty of opportunity for him to intervene at a later date.

Henri Laserre, writer and journalist, unjustly portrayed him as a 'bloodthirsty persecutor', intent on carrying out 'his detestable work'. Bishop Laurence was not at all happy with this description of the prosecutor, which marked him for the rest of his life. Right up until his death in Pau in 1887, he refused to hand over his papers to the Jesuit priest and researcher Fr Cros. Thankfully they were released later in 1891.

D

ECUMENISM

At Lourdes we find many elements that belong in a very specific way to the tradition of the Roman Catholic Church, such as the Virgin Mary, the mass and the pope. For some people these aspects may pose difficulties. Other smaller practices of piety and devotion can sometimes be off-putting too: for example, a group of nurses from the Protestant tradition entered into the heart of the Lourdes experience by coming on a pilgrimage for the sick, but felt that special moments, such as the bathing of the sick and the prayers which accompanied that moment, were very rushed, which took away some of their meaning, as did the commercialism in the town. We must seek to understand, as Newman did, the difference between 'faith and devotion'.

In spite of these difficulties Christians of other traditions love coming to Lourdes. It was during the 1970s that a hall was first reserved for their use and worship, making it possible to go beyond certain outward expressions of piety, to the real meaning of Lourdes. On coming to Lourdes, Lutheran theologians find the opportunity to consider the role of Mary in the Evangelical Church. Christians from the Anglican and Orthodox traditions hold pilgrimages, and beyond the Christian world, Jews, Muslims and Buddhists also come to pray at the Shrine. They understand that real unity comes from getting to know and love one another, without compromise or force. It is a gift of God. It is enough to open our hearts.

A Marian Church is one which welcomes; it does not wish to possess or dominate, but rather to continue the 'dialogue of redemption' which began in the womb of Our Lady, when God and man, separated by sin, were united once again. At Lourdes, Mary appears more mother than queen; her pilgrims welcome one another as brothers and sisters, children of the one Father and they experience the reality, not so much of a hierarchical Church but of the Church as a family gathered around the apostles. All the family are living servants of the Word of God, the least of whom, like Bernadette, are signs of the mercy and forgiveness of God, sources of hope for humanity.

ENFANTS DE MARIE
(Children of Mary)

Enfants de Marie was the name given to one of the numerous Marian congregations which the Jesuits founded from the 16th century to support the piety of the faithful. In Lourdes the group was made up of young girls who had been specially selected. On the occasion of parish events, processions for example, they wore a distinctive uniform. It was normal that Bernadette should belong to them since, on 28 July, Bishop Laurence had set up a canonical commission acknowledging the significance of the apparitions.

On 8 September 1858, at the end of a retreat preached by Fr Sempé to this Marian group, Bernadette was named *Enfant de Marie*. It represented, from many points of view a form of approval. Bernadette's aunt Bernarde, who had had a child outside marriage, had been excluded.

On 2 May 1866, at the time when the crypt, which was the first chapel asked for by the Virgin, was being inaugurated, Bernadette was there, hidden among the *Enfants de Marie*. There was a considerable crowd and Bishop Laurence celebrated the first mass at the Grotto. Fr Duboe, of the Garaison Fathers, gave a magnificent talk which was interrupted by a violent thunder storm. He had not made any mention of the visionary. The Virgin was protecting the precious humility of the one who was to leave Lourdes, a month later, to follow the admirable road on which the Lord was calling her.

ESPÈLUGUES

Coming down from the place called Calvary, at the end of the beautiful Stations of the Cross constructed for the Shrine, you pass by three caves situated on the left and called the Grottos of the Espèlugues. In fact, this is the name of the whole area and comes from the Latin 'spelunga' which means Grotto, or cave. The first one is around fifty metres long, five to ten metres wide and eight to ten metres high. This first Grotto opens on to another one, which is a bit bigger.

Geologists have explained that these caves were formed by the erosion of the crumbly limestone over the course of thousands of years. Specialists of prehistory are in no doubt that they were inhabited. Recently, some observant ramblers even have found sharpened flints nearby! The main part of the objects and artefacts unearthed after the apparitions can be seen in the *Musée de Saint-Germain-en-Laye* or in the *Musée Pyreneen de Lourdes*.

A famous Capuchin friar, Fr Marie-Antoine, a great preacher at Lourdes at the end of the 19th century, had asked Bishop Billère of Tarbes, to transform the caves into Christian Shrines with the help of an architect, M Rocher. It was thus that the first Grotto was dedicated to St Mary Magdalene, with an altar

and a statue. The second one was dedicated to Our Lady of Sorrows.

ESTRADE, JEAN-BAPTISTE

Jean-Baptiste Estrade (1821-1909), tax collector in Lourdes, is a first-class witness as regards the events of the Grotto, because of his objectivity and his abundance of good will. He lived in Lourdes, where he had been posted, with his sister Emmanuelite. A profoundly Christian man, he never married. After Lourdes, he was posted to Bordeaux, where he was to spend a great part of his working life. His whole life was permeated by the facts of Lourdes. At the end of his life, in 1909, having reached a great age, he would still be asked questions about his memories.

It was on 23 February 1858, five days after the beginning of the famous fortnight of the apparitions, that he visited the Grotto for the first time. It took a great deal of courage for a well-known figure to go openly to that place, to enter into such a bizarre adventure! Fr Peyramale, happy to get hold of a witness worthy of trust, had encouraged him to go. He set off, with his sister, in the dark of the night, at half past five in the morning. The apparition plunged him into boundless admiration. 'I had left home incredulous, I came back a believer!'

The account he gave of the event was taken up by the great journalist Veuillot in the *Univers*, a Catholic paper, and also by Henri Lasserre, in his book.

From that moment on, Jean-Baptiste Estrade was to follow the events closely. It was at his house that Bernadette was to learn the meaning of Mary's words, which she had heard that morning: 'I am the Immaculate Conception.' Bernadette trusted Emmanuelite and used to visit her from time to time. It is not hard to imagine the joy of those encounters: all three now knew that *aquero*, as Bernadette used to call the apparition, was in truth, the Holy Virgin!

Jean-Baptiste Estrade published a very engaging book in 1899, *Les Apparitions de Lourdes, Souvenirs Intimes d'un Temoin* (the Lourdes apparitions, private memories of a witness). In it he highlighted the extraordinary impression created on him and others by the apparitions, an impression which he would never forget: one could not see the Virgin, but her presence had a powerful influence and life was changed forever.

EUCHARIST

When Bernadette left Bartrès and went back to live in the *cachot* again, she was motivated, above all, by the desire to make her first communion. It can be said that Mary was her catechist throughout the meetings of the fortnight. After the apparition of 25 March, when she revealed her name, two other apparitions took place, on 7 April and on 16 July. It was on 7 April that what was to be called the 'miracle of the candle' occurred. Its news, worthy of credibility thanks to the witness of Dr Douzous, spread through the town like wild fire, all the while commented on, deformed, embellished and, alas, often distorted. An epidemic of apparitions, one stranger than the other, was reported in Lourdes. The civil and religious authorities decided to intervene to put an end to what was becoming comedy and superstition and had all the traits of collective hysteria. On 7 June, the mayor of the town, M Lacadé, forbade anyone to drink at the spring. On 15 June he had the Grotto closed, but some inhabitants of Lourdes pulled down the barriers during the night. They were reconstructed on the 26th only to be pulled down again on 5 July. The barriers were erected once more on the 10th and, on 12 July the bishop rigorously denounced the abuses which immediately ceased.

Bernadette kept away from all this confusion. She had gone back to school to try and learn some grammar rules and some paragraphs of the catechism. True to herself, as if detached from all that was happening to her, her only concern seemed to be to hide from the misplaced curiosity of the crowds. Besides, she had more important things to care about. She had finally been authorized to make her first communion for which she had prepared with the utmost care and which she received at the *Hospice des Soeurs de Nevers* (home of the sisters of Nevers) on 3 June, feast of *Corpus Christi*. The following day,

Emmanuelite Estrade put this question to her: 'Which of the two made you the happiest - your first communion or the apparitions?' The young girl's answer was, as always, disarming: 'The two things go together, but they cannot be compared! Both made me very happy!'

Holy Communion was very important to her. Her desire to receive communion went back to her early childhood. It continued to grow over the years that she spent at the 'hospice'* where she was a day pupil from January 1858 to 1860 and then a student at the secondary school until her departure for Nevers in 1866. Everyone confirms her desire for the eucharist. Her confessor, Fr Pomian, allowed her to receive communion every Sunday and also, on certain days of the week, which was unusual at the time. Sister Victorine would recall later that she 'prepared well' and that 'even when she suffered a lot, after sleepless nights, she would get up and go to receive communion.' The communion with the body of Christ already, for Bernadette, was her way of participating in the redemption of the world for 'sinners'.

The redemptive quality of the eucharistic sacrifice is thus linked specifically to the Lourdes message of penance. Benedict XVI says, in his apostolic exhortation *Sacramentum Cantatis*: 'In instituting the sacrament of the eucharist, Jesus anticipates and makes present the sacrifice of the cross and the victory of the resurrection. At the same time, he reveals that he himself is the *true* sacrificial lamb, destined in the Father's plan from the foundation of the world, as we read in the first letter of Peter (cf. 1:18-20). By placing his gift in this context, Jesus shows the salvific meaning of his death and resurrection, a mystery which renews history and the whole cosmos. The institution of the eucharist demonstrates how Jesus' death, for all its violence and absurdity, became in him a supreme act of love and mankind's definitive deliverance from evil'(No.10).

The eucharist is further associated with Lourdes by Mary's words, during her 13th apparition, on 2 March 1858: 'Let processions be made to this spot and have a chapel built here.' Indeed, it is the eucharist which builds the Church, since it is Christ who gives himself to all, by edifying us continuously: 'This is why Christian antiquity used the same words, *Corpus Christi*, to designate Christ's body born of the Virgin Mary, his eucharistic body and his ecclesial body ... It is significant that the second eucharistic prayer, invoking the Paraclete, formulates its prayer for the unity of the Church as follows: "*May all of us who share in the body and blood of Christ be brought together in unity by the Holy Spirit.*" These words help us to see clearly how the *res* of the sacrament of the eucharist is the unity of the faithful within ecclesial communion. The eucharist is thus found at the root of the Church as a mystery of communion' (No.15).

In Lourdes this mystery of communion is particularly significant during the season of pilgrimages, during the solemn celebration of the international mass, which takes place twice weekly, and also during the daily eucharistic processions. The eucharist is at the centre of every pilgrimage.

But there is also a third aspect which associates the eucharist with the message of Lourdes: the promise of happiness in the next world, made by Mary during the third apparition on 18 February. Benedict XVI also says: 'Man is created for that true and eternal happiness which only God's love can give. But our wounded freedom would go astray were it not already able to experience something of that future fulfilment. Moreover, to move forward in the right direction, we all need to be guided towards our final goal. That goal is Christ himself, the Lord who conquered sin and death, and who makes himself present to us in a special way in the eucharistic celebration. Even though we remain "aliens and exiles" in this world (*1, Pet* 2:11), through faith we already share in the fullness of risen life' (No. 30).

To conclude, let us remember the meaning of the word eucharist: thanksgiving. In the eucharist, Jesus himself becomes our 'Thank You' to the Father. Lourdes is a place where gifts are received. The celebration of the eucharist is the most elevated means given to us to express our gratitude.

* *T.N. 'L'ecole des indigents' (the school for the poor) of Lourdes was run by the Sisters of Charity of Nevers (Hospice des Soeurs de Nevers).*

EUCHARISTIC PROCESSION

It was in 1874 that the eucharistic procession came into being, in the context of the liturgical arrangements of the time. Pilgrims were invited to vespers, at the Basilica of the Immaculate Conception and then the procession would be formed and everyone joined the sick, who having gathered at the Grotto, were waiting for the blessing of the Blessed Sacrament, while

saying the Rosary. It is important to note that, from the beginning, procession, eucharistic adoration and the blessing of the sick formed an inseparable whole.

As the number of sick pilgrims continued to increase, those responsible for the Shrines would soon be forced to modify this procedure and to develop the ritual. From 1887, the sick gathered on the Rosary Esplanade for the recitation of the Rosary, while the other pilgrims sang vespers at the Grotto. Thus the procession would be formed and would reach the Saint-Michel door before returning to the esplanade, singing hymns. At that point, the blessing of the sick would take place. The Blessed Sacrament, accompanied by the bishops, the doctors and the senior manager of the *hospitalités* would pass through the rows of the sick, while all repeated the invocations, always the same and already translated into several languages. They were written by Fr Lagardère on the occasion of the French national pilgrimage in 1888. It is interesting to note the combined participation of volunteer workers, bishops and doctors, all in a position to notice any potential healing at the passing of the Blessed Sacrament.

The procession was to continue in this form until after Vatican II. A new perception of disabled persons and of the sick in society would soon be extended to the liturgy. In 1969, the sick were integrated into the procession itself. New hymns and new invocations were introduced: besides Latin, national languages took their due place.

In the context of the preparations for the great jubilee of the year 2000, other symbols were to enrich the procession in terms of the year's pastoral theme. A greater emphasis was placed on the Word of God, elevating it to the same status as the eucharist, and the pilgrim's prayer would be inspired by a gospel reading. Finally, since 2000, the procession leaves from the tent of adoration, where the faithful can pray in front of the Blessed Sacrament from the time of the first morning mass, and ends inside the Basilica of St Pius X with a moment for adoration, followed by the blessing of the sick. The depth of meaning in this sequence of celebrations, coming as a coherent whole, becomes more transparent: procession, adoration and the blessing of the sick can be seen, as the extension of the eucharistic celebration itself: 'source and apex' of our faith and of all Christian life.

EUROPEAN MARIAN NETWORK

Men and women today are nomadic, not only in their ideas, but also physically. They travel. But the nomad needs reference points, landmarks. In the desert, one must know where the water holes can be found.

This is true of Christians and of all other people. That is why pilgrimages and Shrines have become so important nowadays: they are pauses and oases in a world which is congested and spiritually barren.

Each Shrine has its particular grace. From one Shrine to another, pilgrims receive spiritual enrichment. The European Marian Network links twenty Shrines to one another: as many as the 'mysteries' of the Rosary. Many of those Shrines are situated in the former 'iron curtain' countries.

Almost all these countries belong to the European Marian Network. The Shrine which has been recognized as the most important by the people has been chosen for each country, albeit after some hesitation in some cases. Under different names, Mary is venerated in all countries to varying degrees, and in all Christian confessions.

The European Marian Network was established in 2003. From the beginning, it received encouragement from Rome. The directors for the Shrines of the Network meet once a year to get to know one another better, but above all, to learn more about the expectations of the millions of people who come to the Shrines nowadays, as pilgrims or visitors.

Here is the list of the Network Shrines:

Altotting (Germany), Banneux (Belgium), Brezje (Slovenia), Csiksomlyo (Rumania), Czestochowa (Poland), Einsiedeln (Switzerland), Fatima (Portugal), Our Lady of Europe (Gibraltar), Knock (Ireland), Levoca (Slovakia), Loreto (Italy), Lourdes (France), Mariapocs (Hungary), Mariazell (Austria), Maria Bistrica (Croatia), Mellieha (Malta), Vilnius (Lithuania), Walsingham (England), Zaragoza (Spain), Zarvanyzia (Ukraine).

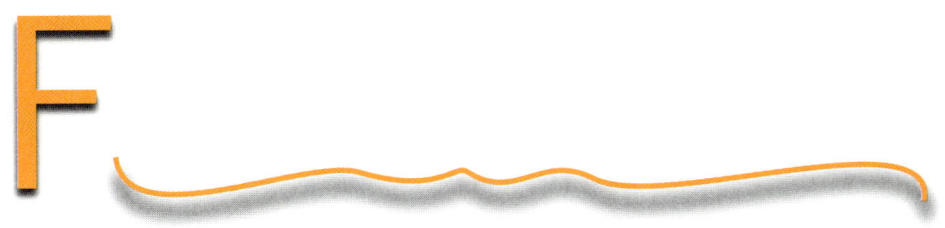

FESTIVAL OF SACRED MUSIC

In 1968, following the message of the Second Vatican Council to artists on the preceding 8 December, the first 'Easter Festival' took place in Lourdes. It was interrupted in 1987 and, in 1988, it continued under the name of International Festival of Sacred Music.

There are several features which characterize this festival:

1. It is organized by a small team consisting exclusively of Lourdes volunteers, under the artistic direction of Jean-Paul Lecot;

2. It lasts from Easter Sunday to Low Sunday;

3. The programme consists exclusively of sacred music from any era, while the music is chosen according to the liturgical period and the interpretation corresponds closely to the style of the chosen pieces. In general the music is being interpreted by the greatest national and international ensembles (over twenty years, 66 choirs, 41 orchestras and 73 renowned conductors and soloists have appeared at the Festival).

The concerts take place normally in the Basilica of Our Lady of the Rosary or in the parish church of Lourdes, but also in other places like the cathedral of Tarbes or the ancient Norman abbey of Saint-Savi.

Among the major works which are performed regularly at the Festival of Lourdes, let us mention: the *Vespers of the Virgin* by Monteverdi, the *Te Deum,* by Charpentier, *St Matthew's Passion, St John's Passion,* the *Mass in B minor* and the *Cantatas*, by Bach, the *Messiah,* by Handel, the *Creation* by Haydn, the *Resurrection Symphony*, by Mahler, the *Mass of Saint Cecilia,* by Gounod... Among the memorable events of the Festival there is one that stands out in particular: the presence, in 1989, of Oliver Messiaen (the greatest composer of the second part of the 20th century) for the interpretation of his work: *The three little liturgies of the divine presence.*

The audience at the festival is composed mainly of music lovers from the local region, from France and from the pilgrims of all the different countries represented in Lourdes at that time of the year.

GARAISON

Garaison, about 70 km from Lourdes, is now part of the Diocese of Tarbes and Lourdes. Before the Revolution, it belonged to the Diocese of Auch.

In that place, round about the year 1515, a graceful young lady dressed in a long white robe appeared to a shepherdess, Anglese de Sagazan. Anglese was tending her sheep not far from her family home and was eating her piece of black bread near a spring. 'Do not be afraid,' the apparition said to her, 'I am the Virgin Mary, mother of Jesus our redeemer. Go and tell the Rector of Monleon that he must have a chapel built here, as I have chosen this place so that my gifts become known.' The next day, there was again a request for the chapel: 'If the building is started, providence will help bring it to completion'. During the third apparition, the Virgin, to prove her identity, changed Anglese's poor black bread into white bread and filled her parents' bread store with white bread as well. Her last recommendation was: 'Do not forget to thank God for all his gifts.'

Then processions started. A cross was erected and a modest oratory built. The faithful came in great numbers attracted by the cures and the graces obtained through Mary. The shepherdess, whose personality was not unlike Bernadette's, entered the Cistercian convent of Fabas, 40 kilometres away.

It was only in 1540 that a chapel worthy of the name was built, but with no regular liturgical services being held there, it looked abandoned. However, this was the very place where the Missionaries of the Immaculate Conception came into being. They would become known as the Garaison Fathers, the first priests to be responsible for the running of the new Shrine of Lourdes.

GARICOÏTS, MICHEL (saint)

Canonised by Pius XII in 1947, Michel Garicoïts was involved directly, through Bishop Laurence, in the recognition of the apparitions.

Born in Ibarre, on a poor Basque farm on 15 April 1797, he became a priest after many sacrifices. He was a model parish priest and came to the attention of the Bishop of Bayonne for his intelligence and virtue. He was sent to the major seminary of Betharram where he became a lecturer, then rector. At that point he undertook the restoration of the ancient Shrine of the Virgin in Bearn and restarted the pilgrimages there.

In 1835 he founded a congregation of missionaries and of teachers which was to grow rapidly in importance. Committed apostle of the Sacred Heart and of the Virgin Mary, he was in great demand as a spiritual director, and Betharram's reputation as a wellspring of spirituality grew. Napoleon III would be told in the 1850s that in Betharram he had one of the most inspiring figures of his Empire. Never sparing himself, he died on 14 May 1863, the feast of the Ascension, at 3 o'clock in the morning, 'the hour at which he was used to starting his day.'

After the last apparition, on 16 July 1858, Bishop Laurence, being urged on by many, wanted to set up a commission for a canonical investigation. This came into being on 28 July, but before doing that he sought advice from that deeply spiritual man: Michel Garicoïts. Bernadette was invited to meet him. No one knows what passed between those two, but witnesses have spoken of their radiant appearances.

It has been recorded that, some time after the apparitions, Bernadette had gone to Betharram with her mother and had made her confession to Fr Garicoïts. It seems that her vocation developed from that moment, eventhough it was officially made public only on 4 April 1864, the day when the statue was installed in the Grotto. What is certain is that Jean Soubirous, the son of her brother Jean Marie, became a priest at Betharram and that he died in Buenos Aires, aged 32, on 4 April 1910.

GAVE

The beautiful river which runs by the Grotto is the Gave of Pau. The name 'gave', a generic term for all the rivers in the west of the Pyrenees, comes from the Bearnese word gabe, which means river. One can surely say that the Gave, together with the beautiful trees planted by Bishop Laurence make an important contribution to the well-being of the Lourdes pilgrims: they represent beauty and create an ambience which is profoundly biblical.

The Gave of Pau has its source in the *cirque* (corrie)* of Gavarnie, a splendid place, on the border with Spain, and receives water from the

tributaries of seven valleys. At the time of Bernadette, the power stations and the dams which nowadays alter its course, had not yet been built.

Having acquired the lands adjoining the Grotto, Bishop Laurence started to landscape the banks of the Gave to make access easier. The first great works started in 1864. After his death, they were resumed under Fr Sempé and Bishop Langénieux, in 1874/75. It was then that the Esplanade in front of the Grotto was created, allowing ceremonies to take place there.

At that time too, plans were made to put a cover over all the canals which led to the mills and, most importantly, to create a crossing over the Gave at the point which was to become the Saint-Michel bridge in 1877. This bridge was to prove very expensive and required enormous excavation works. President Mac-Mahon contributed to its financing to the value of 50,000 francs in gold. The sturdy bridge withstood the terrible floods of October 1937 and October 1965. In 1965, Bishop Théas had two additional bridges built, one upstream and the other downstream of the Grotto.

In 1872, Bishop Pichenot obtained permission to raise the dam which is at the level of the Poor Clares' convent. Thanks to this dam and the construction of canals that went with it, it became possible to install turbines for the generation of electricity. However, this was only a temporary solution, and Bishop Gerlier planned to have all the electric current needed for the Grotto generated locally as it would have been too expensive to purchase it elsewhere. This idea gave birth to the power station below the Saint-Michel bridge which was finished in 1937 and inaugurated on 2 October by Bishop Gerlier who was, by then, Archbishop of Lyons.

* Mountain valley head which has been shaped into deep hollows by the erosion of small glaciers.

GERLIER, PIERRE PAUL-MARIE (bishop)

His eminence, Cardinal Gerlier, *Primat des Gaules***, was a great friend of Lourdes throughout his life and was to preside over many of the most important events there. He was Bishop of Tarbes and Lourdes

from 1929 to 1938 and left behind significant improvements.

Born in Versailles in 1880, Pierre Paul-Marie Gerlier was soon recognized for the brilliance of his intellect. He showed exceptional ability in his role as a lawyer at the court of appeal of Paris from 1901 to 1913, all the while practising a first class lay apostolate with young people from France and abroad. Called to the priesthood, he entered the seminary in 1913 and was ordained in 1921. In a short time he became canon at Notre-Dame de Paris and later Bishop of Tarbes and Lourdes on 14 May 1929.

He was passionate about this role: 'I did all I could for Lourdes and I did it with all my heart,' he would say. He opened the *Bureau Medical* to doctors from across the world. He bought the large piece of land which was to become the young people's village and installed scouts there to protect the Stations of the Cross from excessive commercialism. He also bought part of the field of the Ribère, which was within sight of the Grotto, to keep property developers away. The *Musée Notre-Dame* (now *Musée Bernadette*) and the Notre-Dame Hall date from his episcopate.

His most important material contribution has been the power station which he had the courage to have built in 1935, to avoid the considerable costs of purchasing electricity for the Shrine. Pilgrims, if interested, can go and see the works which were carried out at that time, upstream of the Saint-Michel bridge. Large concrete structures had to be created to accommodate the portcullis, the drains and the locks for the canals and the discharge conduits. What is called now the *Quai Saint-Jean* was built over the canal. The power station was built on the right of the boulevard and below the Saint-Michel bridge.

The first international pilgrimage of veteran soldiers, 60,000 in total from 19 different nations, took place from 22 to 24 September 1934.

With Cardinal Pacelli, the future Pius XII, Bishop Gerlier presided over the glorious celebrations of the Jubilee of the Redemption, the 19th centenary of the death and resurrection of Jesus, which attracted a considerable crowd and was one of the greatest events held in Lourdes. He could not remain in Lourdes too long: this remarkable orator was destined to assume higher responsibilities in the Church and it was with regret that he wrenched himself away from Lourdes, a place to which he would often return.

**The title of *Primat des Gaules* is an honorary title given to the Archbishop of Lyons. It goes back to Roman times when the bishops of Lugdunum (Lyon) were given this title in recognition of the role of the town in the introduction of Christianity in Gaule. The *Primat des Gaules* automatically becomes cardinal, but the title does not carry particular powers any more.

GROTTO

The Grotto of Massabielle, the most famous and the most visited one in the world, was of no significance before the apparitions. A prehistoric cave, as any other of the great number of these in the Pyrenees, it was nothing like as beautiful as the Espélugues caves which are situated a little higher in the estate. When Bernadette went there it was covered with stones washed ashore when the Gave was in spate. It was dirty because the pigs of the town sheltered there on rainy days; occasionally, clandestine couples would meet there. If Bernadette and her sister took the decision to go there on 11 February, it was because, 'there, at least, we won't be called thieves,' as Bernadette had said. Their poor father had been imprisoned for a theft which he had not committed and they were on their guard. Such was the symbolic place which the Mother of God chose in order to come to the help of sinful humanity and invite everyone to conversion.

During the 9th apparition, on 25 February, a spring was uncovered under the hands of Bernadette. The first works would be carried out three days later, on 28 February, to channel the water. The main works started on 5 October, when the emperor himself ordered the removal of the barriers which the *préfet* of police had had erected in June, to prevent access, (on 16 July, for the last apparition, Bernadette was on the other side of the river). Stones and sand were removed and a little statue was put in place along with other pious images.

On 15 January 1861, Bishop Laurence approached the town and offered to buy the rock and the banks of Massabielle. This became a rather long and drawn-out process, as the approval of the emperor was required. Napoleon III gave his approval on 22 August and, on 5 September, the bishop became the owner. Bishop Laurence had the river rerouted and had a kind of esplanade built on the ground in front of the Grotto which had been previously very difficult to access. He had the surrounding area cleared and had various tree species planted. To avoid damage to the site, Bishop Laurence had railings erected close to the Grotto. These were removed by Bishop Théas in 1958, the centenary year. He took this opportunity to clear away all sorts of crutches, corsets and other 'souvenirs' which had been attached to the walls, and which impaired their natural appearance.

The work of transforming the surrounding area was pursued further by Bishop Langénieux in 1874, when the Gave was rerouted even further.

As to the liturgical celebrations in the Grotto, the first official religious event took place on the occasion of the installation of the statue by Fabish, a professor of sculpture in Lyon, representing Our Lady of Lourdes. This statue, commissioned at considerable expense, had been paid for by the Sisters of Lacour. Bernadette did not care for it. In fact, she was absent on that day, as was the parish priest of Lourdes, who was ill on 4 April 1864. There are illustrations depicting those magnificent ceremonies. On 21 May, in front of an immense crowd, Bishop Laurence celebrated the first mass, on the occasion of the inauguration of the Crypt, the first church built on the rock.

The Grotto possesses a mysterious attraction. Many people stay there a long time in prayer, others spend the whole night there and all want to touch it. Here are some evocative words pronounced by Cardinal Pacelli, the future Pius XII, during his first visit to Lourdes as papal legate: 'In you are gathered the enchantment of Nazareth, the sacred character of Bethlehem, the healing power of Bethsaida. How many miracles of the Redeemer have you not seen renewed here? What marvels of graces have been accomplished within your walls?' (25 April 1935).

GROTTO ESTATE

The Shrine of Lourdes is composed of vast spaces crossed by the river Gave, with a profusion of churches, basilicas, chapels, welcome centres, a dispensary, a museum, a bookshop, conference halls, projection rooms, meeting rooms and various other buildings, all of them dedicated to the service of the pilgrims. The founding bishops demonstrated great faith and prophetic vision when, in the final years of the 19th century, they created the Grotto estate.

The founders were Bishop Laurence and Bishop Langénieux who, between 1861 and 1875, bought the land situated on the left bank, as well as the Piedebat Mountains (where the Stations of the Cross were sited). The fields on the right bank were acquired over a long period, from 1874 to 1942. The total area is 51 hectares.

The Grotto estate, property of the 'Association diocesaine', is the responsibility of the Bishop of Tarbes and Lourdes. The bishop appoints a rector who represents him in all matters, spiritual and temporal.

On the temporal side, the Shrine is organised as a modern enterprise which uses the most up-to-date methods for the management of more than six million pilgrims per year. It has more than 400 salaried employees, of whom 120 are seasonal, spread over 60 different kinds of services: pastoral, reception, administration, security, technology.

The complex functioning of the Shrine could not do without the contribution of the 110,000 volunteers of the *Hospitalité Notre-Dame de Lourdes*, of all the other pilgrim *hospitalités* and services.

HOSPICE

On 16 July 1858, Bernadette was drawn to the Grotto once more. Despite the barricades barring the entrance to the Grotto, Our Lady appeared to her for the last time, closer and more beautiful than ever. The apparitions were over, but many people still needed Bernadette. The poor and the sick drew comfort from her and sought her prayers. The rich and famous too wished to meet her. Whoever it was, Bernadette was always herself, the girl she had been before 11 February 1858. Still poor, and still at school, she worked as a maid to help support the family.

After a few months, Fr Peyramale decided to protect her from being such an object of curiosity and publicity. So Mother Ursula Fardès took her in as a pupil at the hospice run by the Sisters of Charity and Christian Instruction which

provided schooling and shelter for young girls from poor families, as well as nursing for the elderly who were poor. Although Mother Ursula had her doubts about the apparitions, she was increasingly impressed by this young girl, who had been attending the class since January 1858. It was a great sacrifice for her parents when, at Fr Peyramale's request, Bernadette finally went to live full time with the other young girls at the hospice.

The building is still visible today on the hillside where the roads to Pau and Tarbes meet. A 19th century stone building, it has a rather austere façade, with its long double row of windows and imposing pillars (see photo). It still looks today as it did when it was built in 1834 for the Sisters of Charity and Christian Instruction who cared for the sick and needy. When Bernadette was a pupil, there were between seven and ten sisters working there in the school and the infirmary. Fr Pomian was the chaplain of their community. Today the hospice is part of the local hospital in the town. The original chapel where Bernadette made her First Holy Communion on 3 June 1858, as well as the long ground floor corridor, give us a good idea of what this period in Bernadette's life was like.

Bernadette stayed on at boarding school, even after she had completed her schooling, in September 1863. Her job, which she loved, was to help the sister in charge of the infirmary to take care of the sick. She was always very attentive towards the young pupils who came from very poor families.

One question, however, occupied her thoughts. It was put to her by Bishop Fourcade: 'And now, my child, what would you like to do?' At 19 years old, she could read and write, sew and embroider and speak French. She was a normal, well-balanced young woman, but perfectly aware of her limitations. She knew that her health was weak and that she was poor, and, indeed, chose to be so.

The apparitions had not indicated in any special way which path she was to follow. She found light and strength from two sources: her love for Jesus in the eucharist and her deep love for the poor. The idea of being able to live this double love as one of the Sisters of Charity of Nevers began to take root. Initially, she had not felt drawn to their community, and she had to admit that the sisters had never tried to persuade her to join their order, as they wished to leave her free to make her own choice. Six years went by before she finally made up her mind. Without giving in to pressure from other congregations, she weighed up the pros and the cons and in April 1866, made her final choice. Her departure for Nevers was postponed for a few weeks as she had been requested to attend the inauguration of the Crypt of the new chapel. She finally left Lourdes for good on 4th July 1866.

HOSPITALITÉ

Bernadette Soubirous never went to the Grotto alone. She always had someone with her, and there was always someone there to welcome

her. It is this same twofold dimension, to welcome and to accompany, that has become a tradition at Lourdes.

On 11 February 1858, Bernadette was led to the Grotto by her two companions. During the apparitions that followed, others helped in a practical or spiritual way to make her meeting with 'the Lady', possible. First Fr Pomian, who by reassuring her ('who can stop you, Bernadette?'), accompanied her in a spiritual sense to the Grotto, where he was unable to go himself. Had he had not done so, it is unlikely that Bernadette would have been able to keep her promise to Our Lady to return to the Grotto for the next fifteen days.

At the Grotto, it was Our Lady herself who welcomed Bernadette, smiling and beckoning to her to come closer. Very soon, others started to reach the Grotto ahead of Bernadette, so it was a community in prayer, the Church, that welcomed her as she arrived and were with her throughout the visions. Some welcomed Bernadette in a very practical sense by helping her through the crowds to her place in front of the niche (Bernadette's special place).

The first *hospitalité* (association of welcome) in the history of Lourdes, *l'Hospitalité Notre-Dame de Salut*, is a *hospitalité* of assistance. It started because of the need for people to accompany and look after the sick. The original charter for the first *hospitaliers* or helpers was simple but strong:
- Accompany the sick to Lourdes on their national pilgrimage led by the Assumption Fathers;
- help to meet the expenses of those who accompany them; - be at the disposition of other pilgrimages helping to care for their sick;
- in time of war, to serve the country by nursing the wounded.

This first *hospitalité* was soon found to be too restrictive, and became the international *Hospitalité de Notre-Dame de Lourdes* founded in 1886, which has overall responsibility for the welcome of all pilgrims and visitors to Lourdes. In that period other *hospitalités* were set up and still today new ones are being born.

There are now around 230 *hospitalités de Lourdes* worldwide. They are all at the service of accompanying groups. They are run by a great variety of groups and associations linked to dioceses, religious orders, and other specific pilgrimage organizations, both national and international. They are known as the smaller individual *hospitalités* but they are all affiliated in a pious association with the permanent international *Hospitalité Notre-Dame de Lourdes*, which has overall responsibility.

Such is the family of the helpers of Lourdes which welcomes us today; approximately 100,000 volunteers from every part of the world, through 230 distinct and independent associations, put themselves at some point during the year freely at the service of the sick and of people with disabilities, and come to Lourdes to relive the experience of Bernadette in their encounter with Our Lady, and through her, with her son, Jesus.

IMAGES

In the 19th century, the Pyrenees fascinated artists, such as William Oliver from England, for example, who left behind admirable lithographs, including a view of Lourdes dating from Bernadette's childhood years. The apparitions were to be a prime subject. Photography, which had been invented a little before Bernadette's birth, would play an important role in the spreading of the news of the Lourdes events. In 1978, Fr Laurentin published an invaluable study, in two volumes, the fruit of twenty-five years work, on the photographic portraits of Bernadette. He had discovered seventy-five of them, dating from 1861. In that year, Bernadette was past 16, the age which Fr Peyramale had said she should reach before she could be photographed. He allowed one of his brother priests, Fr Bernadou, to do so. Unquestionably, those snapshots bring out the overwhelming mystery of her soul. Several specialists (who were not believers) confirmed this fact. Bernadette was photographed until her death; we even have the snapshot of her exhumation, on 18 April 1925. In relation to painted portraits, one has to admit that they have never been satisfactory, even though artists such as Maurice Denis tried to portray her. A touching example, by a local artist, painted in 1858, has been reproduced as a postcard, the original having been retained in the

Lourdes in 1858

Soubirous household. It shows Bernadette, wearing a blue bonnet.

The Grotto itself was first photographed in 1858, by Lemmonier de Bagnères. From it one can appreciate the considerable works which were carried out and which culminated in the construction of a retaining structure for the Basilica of the Immaculate Conception. Between 1883 and 1889, an enormous excavation was created to shelter the Basilica of the Rosary. The hill of Calvary, now covered by trees, used to be a barren rock when Bishop Laurence acquired it at the end of November 1869.

There are also many paintings and engravings. The most interesting engravings tell us about significant events such as the great ceremony of the installation of the statue of Our Lady in the Grotto, on 4 April 1864. An impressive procession, with the bishops at the end, meanders its way up the hairpin bends, with a great many priests and a huge crowd. No tree is to be seen yet; the Grotto is closed by a barrier and the retaining wall has been built.

Certain engravings, representing great gatherings, such as the pilgrimage of the banners, in October 1872, have become stereotypes. They are always being reproduced, with an ever changing décor as the Shrine is developing all the time. These precious witnesses speak a universal language to the glory of the extraordinary reality.

IMMACULATE CONCEPTION

After three weeks of apparitions (from 11 February to 4 March) and three weeks of silence (from the 4 to the 25 March) Bernadette again felt the impulse to run to the Grotto. She went there at the crack of dawn and found the Lady at the rendez-vous. She still did not know the name of the apparition and could not therefore obtain a favourable response from the parish priest to the request she had made to him on her behalf: 'Go and tell the priests to have a chapel built here and let processions be made to this spot.' But, on that day, the little Lady was waiting for Bernadette, standing in the posture which is depicted on the miraculous medal, the arms stretched in a wel-

Imaculate Conception's statue at the Tresor Museum

ception). It is important to integrate this answer in the sequence of the apparitions: there was the joyful period of the first meetings, then the instructions for penance and, finally, the request to build a church. This church would certainly not be just made of stone of course, but would mainly be built through the patient unfolding of a new humanity in the image of the apparitions: emerging from the soil, a transparent, limpid spring, a new creation.

On the Easter journey, there emerges the face of a new humanity converted by the Holy Spirit like the anticipated grace of the salvation offered on the cross. The Son of Man crossed the waters of sin and death to be reborn victorious on the morning of the Resurrection, into a life which was no longer ephemeral but which was renewed every instant from the heart of God. This life is not only his, he shares it with all those who open themselves to him in faith. The first to have allowed her heart to surrender itself to the work of a new life was Mary of Nazareth, who thus became the mother of God, a small piece of earth entirely at the disposal of the Spirit of God. Eternally, the Father gives life to his Son in a kiss of love. This creation of new life, he can also operate in the secret of Mary's heart; she allows herself to be completely open to the divine life with which she is entrusted.

coming sign; then she lifted her joined hands to heaven and said: 'Que soy era Immaculada Councepciou' (I am the Immaculate Con-

On her part, there is no prior merit but, simply, the welcome, the perfection of her 'yes', an echo of the eternal 'yes' of the Father and the Son: that 'yes' is the Spirit of Love, and Mary corresponds to the

Spirit. Fr Kolbe, founder of the Militia of the Immaculata, who died as a martyr in the hell of Auschwitz, underlined the fact that Mary, in Lourdes, says: 'Je suis' (I am). She gives the secret of her being; and her being is to let God through, to be 'conception of God'. As, in the Trinity, the Father conceives, the Son is conceived, and the Spirit is the pure conception of the Son of the Father, so on earth Mary 'is' this Immaculate Conception of the same Son of God: there is her identity; she does not exist in any individual zone where she would endeavour to find her own fulfilment in an autonomous manner: her being is completely relative to the divine work of God. The Gospel says this, when it points to her, at the foot of the cross as 'the mother of Jesus' and then, in all simplicity as 'the mother'. She exists, like God, only in the gift of her life.

It has been emphasized that this designation was given four years after the definition, by Pope Pius IX, of the dogma of the Immaculate Conception. But, in Lourdes, Mary's answer was not given on 8 December, the day when this unique privilege is celebrated: she gave her name on 25 March, on the day when the Son of God was conceived in her. The Immaculate Conception is not to be confused with the virginal conception of Jesus. Mary was conceived by the completely ordinary union between her mother and father. But, in her, the grace, the free gift of God, was able to grow without obstacle. Retrospectively, we realise that, if God could be incarnated from her, if the Spirit could accomplish in her what he has done in God from all eternity, it is because there was in her not a trace of withdrawal or refusal – she has always been nothing but 'yes'. Otherwise, the One who is love and who forces no one to love would never have allowed himself to force the door. We are here, at the source, at the heart and at the summit of the work of salvation. We know humanity's vocation, already realised in Mary, is to welcome and to give God.

INFORMATION FORUM

The Information Forum has existed in its present form since 1991. Its role is to welcome, give directions and inform everyone passing through the Shrines. The present team can answer pilgrims' questions in eight languages. Also available is a leaflet showing a detailed map of the Shrines and a timetable of the masses and other features of the liturgy.

The forum is responsible for the reception of all groups, both those that have announced their visit, and those that arrive unannounced, but

who like to book venues for services, meeting places, visits to the Stations of the Cross, etc. On average, 2,000 groups inform the secretariat of their arrival and 2,000 arrive unannounced every year.

The forum has at its disposal 3 projection rooms where pilgrims can watch a twenty-five minute film on the message of Lourdes, translated into thirty languages and another one, on the theme of the year, in six languages. It also offers the free loan of wheelchairs to persons of reduced mobility who have come on their own.

On the 1st floor, there are five meeting places of varying capacity, from 30 to 160 places. On the 2nd floor there is a large room with 500 places. These rooms are at the disposal of pilgrimages and groups, by reservation.

INTERNATIONALITY

In the 19th century, Lourdes was just a small town of less than 3,000 inhabitants in the Pyrenees. Yet, the police inspector declared, on 4 March 1858, that between 10,000 and 20,000 people had gathered around Bernadette at the Grotto. Supposing that all the Lourdes inhabitants had been present at the Grotto on that day, they would still have been in a minority as four out of five persons were well and truly 'strangers' to Lourdes.

Indeed, the news of the apparitions spread extremely quickly beyond Lourdes through the local and then the national newspapers. As those were read in the great world capitals, pilgrims came to Lourdes from other countries and other continents. Those same pilgrims became in turn witnesses, as active as they were enthusiastic and, very soon, pilgrimages were organized. In fact, in a few decades, an enormous network would become established which allowed pilgrims from the whole of Europe and from other continents to converge towards Lourdes.

However, this rapidly-acquired reputation could not be viewed as ephemeral. Be they from near or far, the millions of pilgrims discovered that, through the internationality of Lourdes, the 'catholicity' of the Church shone through. The message of Lourdes does have a universal dimension, it is, like the Church, 'catholic'.* Nowadays, the Shrines welcome, yearly, more than six million pilgrims, coming from around a hundred-and-fifty different countries. The rise in the number of pilgrims is linked to the diversity of their place of origin.

The great celebrations of Lourdes are 'international'. Be it the 'international mass', celebrated on Sundays and Wednesdays, or, every afternoon, the eucharistic procession, the adoration, the blessing of the Blessed Sacrament and then, in the evening, the Marian candle procession. Prayers are never said in less than six languages: French, Italian, Spanish, English, German and Dutch. It is in those six languages that the Shrines welcome pilgrims. However, every group is invited to pray in its own language. Prayers are said in Lourdes in hundreds of different languages.

* From the Greek *katholikos*: 'general' 'universal'

INTERNET

http//www.lourdes-france.org is the official website of the Shrines of Our Lady of Lourdes. Every day, thousands of internet users from all over the world invite themselves to Lourdes via the website and discover or rediscover the message from heaven entrusted to Bernadette. Apart from the news and other forms of information which are constantly brought up to date, they can follow, almost live, the events in the Grotto or on the esplanade of the Rosary, thanks to ultra modern webcams. This visual access to the Shrines, by day and by night, 24 hourly, is the key to its intercontinental success.

Adding to the transmission of the Rosary of Lourdes, which is broadcast with a slight time lapse on the radio every day at 15.30, the integration of reporting media, since March 2007, has contributed to the fuller participation of the Shrines' website in the multi-media era. As the internet is becoming more accessible, people from practically every country in the world have the possibility of going to Lourdes with a simple click. In 2006, for example, the website registered connections from Barbados (at the frontier of the Caribbean and the Atlantic Ocean), Cape Verde (off Senegal), Kiribati (Pacific Ocean), Lesotho (South of Africa), the Solomon Islands and Samoa (Pacific Ocean) and Tajikistan (Central Asia). The countries most present on the website are France, Italy and the United States of America.

On the occasion of the 150th anniversary of the apparitions, a website was created to allow the whole world to follow the event: *www.lourdes2008.co*

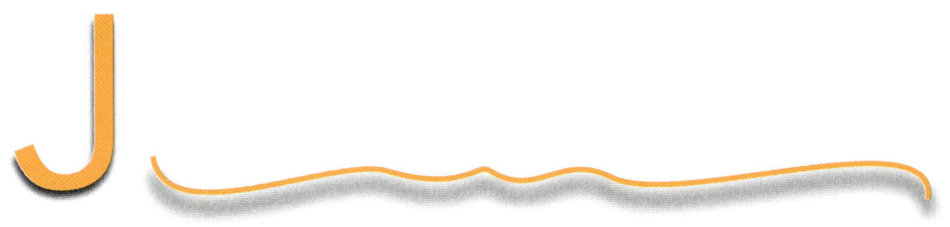

JACOMET, DOMINIQUE
(police inspector)

For Lourdes historians, Inspector Jacomet is a valuable ally, for he felt it very much his duty to keep M Dutour, the public prosecutor (and thereby the magistrate) closely informed about events at the Grotto.

Born in Argèles, South West France, in 1821, Dominique Jacomet had been the police inspector of the town of Lourdes for five years when the apparitions began. Only the year before, in 1857, he had dealt with Bernadette's father, François Soubirous, who was wrongly accused of stealing flour. Jacomet had him put in prison for seven days, much to the distress of his family. Inspector Jacomet, kept a notebook in which he meticulously recorded the number of people who went to the Grotto, the number of candles and any gifts of money that were left there. Even after the final apparition was over, he continued to follow and note down certain details concerning Bernadette's behaviour.

Jacomet first interviewed Bernadette on the evening of 21 February, having 'arrested' her after Vespers,

with the deliberate intention of confusing her. He did not succeed, for Bernadette met his questioning with such disarming honesty that she outwitted him – 'Monsieur, you have changed everything I have told you.' She was interviewed by him several times in all.

An educated man, Jacomet carried out his duties diligently. Whilst previously stationed at Barèges, Bishop Laurence had highly commended him for a housing project for the poor, which proved extremely useful to the Church.

When it came to the apparitions, however, Jacomet was out of his depth, struggling with facts and events he just could not comprehend. His wife, who had been present at two of the apparitions, did not believe in them, whereas his mother-in-law had not missed a single one. A famous page of Jacomet's notebook is on display at the Museum of Saint Bernadette (*Musée Bernadette*), situated behind the underground Basilica. It has been of great interest to researchers, notably Canon Laurentin.

Jacomet ended his career in Paris in the service of the Governor. He died on 5 August 1873 at the age of 52.

JOHN XXIII (1958-63)

Cardinal Roncalli, Patriarch of Venice, became Pope John XXIII in that wonderful year 1958, the centenary of the apparitions. An unforgettable experience was the moment in which he came to consecrate the new underground Basilica of Saint Pius X at Lourdes. A year later, on 15 February 1959, in the church of St Mary Major in Rome, he recalled that moment as follows: 'In between Venice and Rome, another providential arrangement presented itself, like a divine inspiration: the task entrusted to us was to go to Lourdes for the inauguration of a church as vast as it is original, dedicated to the Mother of God, under the auspices of the most venerated and in-

Cardinal Roncalli in Lourdes .....

voked sovereign pontiff of modern times, St Pius X. The moment of consecration of this underground basilica in Lourdes on 24 and 25 March, has left a deep impression upon us, the memory of which will always be a sweet delight for our soul.'

Bishop Théas of Lourdes welcomed the cardinal with this greeting: 'Besides being apostolic nuncio in Paris, these last eight years, you have also been a devoted pilgrim of Lourdes.' As nuncio he had indeed come to Lourdes as often as possible, ever since his first pilgrimage in 1905 as the newly ordained Fr Angelo Roncalli.

Bound by a deep mutual understanding, which stemmed from their similarly modest backgrounds, Bishop Théas, as apostolic administrator of Tarbes and Lourdes since July 1946, had been able to be of support to the papal nuncio when he took up his post in difficult circumstances (the previous nuncio was judged to have compromised with the Vichy regime and the nunciature's reputation had been damaged). Cardinal Roncalli willingly broke his journey to stay with Bishop Théas in Lourdes on his way to Spain. After the death of Pope Pius XII, the new pope gave his support to Bishop Théas in the form of financial assistance for the new basilica, which had become a bone of contention in Rome.

Let us end with an interesting quote from the Patriarch of Venice: 'My fondest memories of my brief time in office as papal nuncio include my visit to Lourdes on 26 August 1947, as part of the national pilgrimage. The most venerable and amiable Pierre Théas, Bishop of Tarbes and Lourdes, confided to me his deep desire to build a chapel in memory of Pius X, next to the two other churches. Together we searched painstakingly amidst the twists and turns of the three churches already in existence, the Basilica, the Crypt and the Rosary, for a small space that just didn't exist.' The rest of the story is history!

JOHN PAUL II (1978-2005)

Lourdes had been eagerly awaiting the visit of the Holy Father to celebrate the International Eucharistic Congress in July 1981, but the attempted assassination on 13 May made that impossible. Cardinal Gantin came in his place. It was an unforgettable gathering with the Holy Father uppermost in everyone's hearts and minds.

Two years later, the town of Lourdes and the president of the republic finally had the honour of welcoming their exceptional guest. 'I am overcome to be able, at last, to add Lourdes to my pilgrimage of Marian Shrines throughout the world, in order that I might pray with my Christian family. This devotion of mine is fundamental to my life and I wish to draw the whole Church with me in prayer. Prayer is the first task and the first message of the pope. It is good that I too kneel at the Grotto of Massabielle.'

The Holy Father was filled with awe in this place of grace. 'Here one prays, one wants to pray, and reconcile oneself with God; here one wants to venerate the eucharist and give place of honour to the sick. Lourdes is a place of exceptional graces.

Praise be to God.' On 15 August, he addressed the vast crowd of young people: 'I believe that France is lucky to possess a place of such grace! Or rather, not to "possess" it, for it was a gift of pure grace; not a gift that is out of date, but rather a mystical source of life for pilgrims from all over the world.' As he was leaving, he added: 'Yes, I will remember this feast of the Assumption as one of the most beautiful in my life.'

In 2004, he was old and weary and had great difficulty speaking, but the crowd, greatly moved, welcomed John Paul II once again. 'As I kneel close to the Grotto, I am filled with the sense that I have almost completed my pilgrimage.' With total humility, the elderly pontiff placed his life into the hands of the most Holy Virgin, repeating with Bernadette: 'Good mother, have pity on me; I give myself totally to you, so that you may give me to your dear son whom I love with all my heart. Sweet mother, give me a heart that burns for Jesus.'

Highlights of his visit were the recitation of the Rosary with comments from Jean Vanier, and the open air mass in the meadow: 'It is here that the Virgin invited Bernadette to recite the Rosary. This Grotto has become the seat of an incredible school of prayer where Mary teaches us to contemplate the face of Christ with ardent love.' He felt a great affinity with the sick: 'Above all I greet you dearest friends, who are ill, and who have come to this blessed place to find solace and hope. May the Holy Virgin fill you with her presence and comfort you!'

After a long period of intense and silent prayer, the Holy Father returned to Rome to be reunited with his heavenly Father.

JOURDAN, CÉSAR-VICTOR

Mgr Jourdan (1813-1882), vicar general of Paris, became Bishop of Tarbes in 1874, as successor to

Bishop Langénieux. Born in Marseilles in 1813, César-Victor Jourdan was ordained in Beauvais, and held the post of professor of philosophy for the next 5 years, before being called to Paris by Bishop Darboy. There he became Archdeacon of Notre-Dame, and accompanied his bishop to the First Vatican Council.

In the infamous uprising of the Paris Commune in 1871, both were held hostage. Mgr Jourdan miraculously escaped but Bishop Darboy was shot.

On becoming Bishop of Tarbes, Jourdan entrusted his ministry to Our Lady of Lourdes, and many great things ensued: the episcopal residence was completed in 1875, followed by the impressive chaplaincy in 1878. Most significantly, Bishop Jourdan gave full support, as had his predecessor, to Fr Sempé's plans to alter the course of the River Gave for a considerable distance and construct the Saint-Michel Bridge, thus creating the Avenue of the Grotto (*Boulevard de la Grotte*). The bishop managed to keep a delicate balance between co-operating with the townspeople, whose barrage of protests clearly demonstrated their feeling that changing the River Gave's course would be the ruin of their town, and safeguarding the long-term needs of the Shrine (the future volume of visitors).

In 1875 the bishop laid the first stone of the new parish church of Lourdes (the original church where Bernadette was baptized no longer exists). Its spire rose to a dizzy height, before lack of funds prevented it from climbing any higher.

Trials were certainly not lacking

for Bishop Jourdan, whom people regarded as wise, good and pious. During his episcopacy the Basilica of the Immaculate Conception was consecrated in July 1876 by the apostolic nuncio, and the statue of the Immaculate Conception was crowned. ('The Crowned Virgin' - *La Vierge Couronnée*). Bishop Jourdan died on 16 July, 1882, the 22nd anniversary of the final apparition.

LACADÉ, ANSELME
(solicitor and Mayor of Lourdes)

Anselme Abadie-Lacadé (1804-1866) had been mayor of Lourdes for more than ten years when the events started: this man appeared to have been chosen by divine Providence, just like the bishop and so many others. He was to have a subtle role in preventing anything which could have harmed either the Soubirous family or the unfolding of the phenomenon of the apparitions.

Honest, open and very likeable, this portly young man put on a naïve front to deal with all the delicate matters he was confronted with and he coped remarkably with everything. He followed the apparitions attentively, from the end of February to the beginning of March, when the crowds continued to grow. From successive letters which had been sent to Massy (the *préfet*), we can gather precious details, especially the one written on 4 March 1858, which he composed at one o'clock in the morning. It was the end of the fortnight and the crowd was considerable. In it he foresees that this Grotto could attract people to his city: 'It is a most picturesque place and I presume that "strangers" will visit it during the season.' He could not have imagined how prophetic his words were to be. And, writing about the crowd during the apparition, he said: 'Perfect order reigned at all times: there were no accidents' (despite the great number of people).

In May, he had the water analysed by two pharmacists and the result was excellent, so good in fact that this spring, which now flows generously, could perhaps have competed with the most famous thermal stations of the region? Here again, he showed himself to be skilful and discreet.

On 10 June, given the considerable bustle which was growing around the Grotto, he forestalled *Préfet* Massy, having secretly been informed of the latter's intentions, and suggested the closing of the Grotto. This again was a skilful manoeuvre designed to temper the zeal of the authorities and to avoid tiresome and useless prohibitions. He did of course supervise the maintenance of the barriers, which would be taken down several times, but was enthusiastic at the removal of these same barriers, ordered by the emperor, Napoleon III, on 5 October 1858.

It was with the mayor that Bishop Laurence, one year before the recognition of the apparitions, on 15 January 1861, wished to negotiate the purchase from the town of the Grotto and its surrounding area. The town council gave its agreement; the experts gave a price for the property which was of little commercial value. The Emperor was to give his approval in August and all was settled on 5 September 1861. Three years had passed, the bishop and the mayor, long before the recognition by the Church, had prepared everything, silently, in anticipation of a formidable adventure! That is what St John of the Cross called 'God's style'!

It is striking to see, on reflection, how Lacadé - just as Bishop Laurence - would have seemed to be, in the eyes of his contemporaries, such as Dr Dozous, as a man given to procrastination, incapable of appreciating the extent of the event. However, both gave remarkable service to the cause of Lourdes, each in their own way and place, and neither of them liked Dr Dozous very much.

In February 1859, *Préfet* Massy was posted to Isère and left Lourdes. As for the mayor, he would live to see the growing celebrity of his humble little town.

LAGUËS, MARIE (née Avant)

Eleven months after Bernadette's birth, in November 1844, her mother Louise fell asleep near the fire; a resin candle fell on her blouse and burnt her. She had to stop breastfeeding her baby daughter who was left to the care of a customer of the mill, Marie Laguës from Bartrès, who had just lost her

only child aged 18 days. For five francs per month, Bernadette became a resident in the 'Maison Burg' in Bartrès. She would remain there until 1 March 1846.

In September 1857, Marie Laguës asked if Bernadette could come to help with the children, the ewes and general house chores. Bernadette was 13 and her parents were in great poverty. It was with regret that Bernadette left Lourdes, as she had been hoping finally to make her first communion. Marie Laguës did try to teach her the rudiments of the catechism used by the diocese, but Bernadette did not understand the abstract points and it reduced her to tears. On the other hand, she found peace in silent prayer, with the ewes and Pigou, the dog. Marie Laguës emphasized that she was very good with her hands.

LANGÉNIEUX, BENOÎT (bishop)

Bishop Langénieux (1824-1905) was Bishop of Tarbes for just a year, from the end of 1873 to the beginning of 1875, which makes his achievements in Lourdes all the more extraordinary. Having begun his priesthood in Paris, he went on to become vicar-general; later, Archbishop of Reims and finally cardinal.

Since 1866, the care and running of the Shrine had been entrusted to the Missionary Fathers of Garaison. Their superior, Fr Sempé, found in his new bishop, a person who deeply shared his own vision for developments to the Shrine. In

fact, no sooner had he been appointed, than Bishop Langénieux proceeded to acquire key areas of land and property around the cave of the apparitions, destined to become the so-called domain area of the Shrine. He also acquired the surrounding farmland of Espélugues on which he commissioned the future building of the bishops' residence (chalet des Évéques) as well as a permanent home for the Missionary Fathers. He approved plans to alter the course of the River Gave, making access to the Grotto possible, as well as plans to develop Rosary Square (Place du Rosaire) and the Esplanade. Together with Fr Sempé, they envisaged the construction of St Michael's Bridge (*Pont St Michel*) which would extend the existing Esplanade and pave the way for the Avenue of the Grotto (*Boulevard de la Grotte*). Naturally the local people objected strongly to this new layout, as they felt that their own livelihood, their shops and businesses, would be ruined by the flow of pilgrims from the station to the Shrine who would simply forget that the town of Lourdes ever existed.

However, there was something so logical and enlightened about the ideas of these two men that the plans went ahead and the president of the republic, Mac-Mahon gave his official approval, plus the sum of 50,000 francs towards the construction of the bridge.

On 7 April 1874, Bishop Langénieux laid the foundation stone of the Hospital of Our Lady of Sorrows. He welcomed the first large-scale pilgrimages from Belgium and the United States, whilst not forgetting the building plans for the parish church of Lourdes put forward by Fr Peyramale, which he approved. It was hard for the bishop to leave these new developments behind him when he was called to take up his appointment as Archbishop of Reims, but he was able to follow their progress from his new position.

Later, as cardinal and papal legate, he was delighted to return to Lourdes for the Eucharistic Congress in 1893 and again in 1901 to consecrate the Basilica of the Holy Rosary (the lower basilica).

LASSERRE, HENRI (journalist)

Henri de Monzie, known as Henri Lasserre, was to play an essential role in the broadcasting of the actual details of Lourdes. Born in Carlux (Dordogne) in 1826, he was a brilliant writer and essayist. A refined and cultured man, he was at ease in the high society of the Second Empire.

At the age of 36, as he was on the point of losing his sight, and following the advice of a very well known scientist, M de Freynet, a Protestant, he had recourse to the benefits of Lourdes water. Miraculously cured in 1862, he was approached by Fr Peyramale on the possibility of writing about the apparitions. He collected a great deal of documentation and eventually wrote, in 1869, *Notre-Dame de Lourdes*, a very large volume which would meet with immense success. Translated into many languages, it reveals the meeting between Mary and Bernadette to the whole world. Bishop Laurence had reservations about the book, which he considered to be too subjective.

Unfortunately, the author was to associate himself with the Lourdes parish priest against the chaplains who, themselves, had done their historical research. A sad polemic ensued which lasted until the death of the author in 1900.

LAURENCE, BERTRAND-SÉVÈRE (bishop)

In a preface to a book on Bishop Laurence, Bishop Théas remarked that, in appearing at Lourdes, Our Lady had not only chosen her messenger but, also, her 'bishop'. What a true statement that was. One cannot help but be filled with wonder at the rare qualities shown by the bishop of the apparitions in accepting divine and human realities.

Today's pilgrims can never guess how much they owe to him.

Bertrand-Sévère Laurence was born in 1790 in a humble peasant family at the boundaries of the Bigorre and the Bearn. Noticed early by two parish priests for his intelligence and piety, he started thinking of the priesthood. Despite the poverty of his family he was able to enter the seminary and received a very good formation in the Betharram and Aire seminaries, since the Tarbes diocese, abolished by the 1801 concordat, no longer had a seminary. He was ordained priest by Bishop d'Astros, Bishop of Bayonne, on 29 April 1820. When an ancient Benedictine abbey in Saint-Pé was restored and transformed into a small seminary, he became its superior, a task which he fulfilled admirably. At the request of the bishop of the new diocese of Tarbes, re-established by the 'Restauration', he worked to bring peace to the town of Lourdes, which had been left in turmoil by the Revolution. Having become vicar general in 1832, he was chosen by King Louis-Philippe as Bishop of Tarbes, at the end of 1844, the year of Bernadette's birth.

The new bishop strove to restore faith and Marian devotion in his diocese by founding, with Fr Peydessus, the Garaison Fathers, *Missionaires de l'Immaculée* and guardians of many Shrines dedicated to the Holy Virgin.

During the apparitions he kept his own council, while being kept informed regularly by Fr Peyramale and by the civil authorities. Urged to do so by his colleagues, in particular by the Bishop of Montpellier, he set up a canonical enquiry to study the facts on 28 July 1858, twelve days after the last apparition. On 7 December, he summoned Bernadette for a meeting with some selected judges: this rather cold man, master of the situation, was deeply moved by the humble visionary as she demonstrated Mary's gestures, and tears rolled down his face. His doubts evaporated and he started buying up land and in particular the Grotto, all before the official recognition in the apostolic letter of 16 January 1862. For him, in this document, it was the person of Bernadette that was the main topic, more than the miracles that had already occurred in the meantime: 'We judge that Mary Immaculate, Mother of God, has really appeared 18 times to Bernadette Soubirous, on 11 February 1858 and on following days in the Grotto of Massabielle.'

From then on, Bishop Laurence started to work for the construction of the future basilica. To accomplish this, it was necessary to construct a retaining wall. Looking attentively at this formidable work, one can only guess at the boldness of the architects, and of the bishop, whose responsibility it had been. After 140 years, it has not moved.

The bishop transformed the Grotto, built the temporary residence of the chaplains and bought all the appropriate pieces of land. On 24 November 1869, just before going to Rome for the First Vatican Council in 1870, he bought the rock of the Espélugues, which is now the hill of the Calvary.

One of his greatest joys was to bless the marble statue installed in the Grotto on 4 April 1864 and to preside, on 20 and 21 May 1866, in the presence of Bernadette, hidden among the *Enfants de Marie* (Children of Mary), over the blessing of the first Shrine, the Crypt, asked for by Our Lady.

He always showed remarkable tact and skill in the very difficult negotiations, which one can only imagine, with the civil authorities, the *Préfet* Massy and others, often very hostile to the apparitions. The great pilgrimage of 11 April 1868, which brought together thousands of pilgrims from his diocese, took the form of a consecration.

Despite his eighty years, Bishop Laurence set off for Rome 'carrying out his great duty as bishop', to take part in the Council. He died of acute kidney failure on 30 January 1870. His majestic funeral was celebrated at *Saint-Louis-des-Français*. He was brought back to Tarbes and mourned by a population who venerated him.

LAURENTIN, RENÈ (historian of Lourdes)

René Laurentin was born in Tours on 19 October1917. He was to make an exceptional contribution to the recorded history of the Lourdes events. He spent his childhood in Cholet then entered the Carmelite seminary at the *Institut Catholique* of Paris, where he achieved brilliant results. Mobilised during the war, he spent five years in captivity in Germany. He was ordained priest in 1946 and devoted himself to Marian theology, visiting many European countries in search of documentation.

In 1952, he obtained a doctorate in philosophy, with distinction, from the Sorbonne and in 1973, from the *Institut Catholique*, a doctorate in theology, again with distinction. He was named professor of theology at the Catholic University of Angers in October 1953 and, in October 1954 he participated in an international Marian congress, in the context of the centenary of the definition of the dogma of the Immaculate Conception. It was at that time that Bishop Théas met him and felt that here was the theologian he had been looking for: 'I have the feeling that you have been chosen by Our Lady to be the theologian of Lourdes'.

In the spring of 1955, René Laurentin's book, *Le Sens de Lourdes* was born. 'This book goes beyond my greatest hopes' wrote the bishop in his preface... 'nothing was

Bishop Théas with a young René Laurentin

ever written more beautifully or so luminously. You have revealed the mystery of Lourdes and its place in the life of the Church.'

With the assistance of a Benedictine from the neighbouring abbey of Tournay, Dom Bernard Billet, he was to complete a series of interesting in-depth studies on Lourdes: *Lourdes, dossiers des documents authentiques* (Lourdes, the authentic document files) 7 volumes (Lethielleux – 1957-1965); *Lourdes, histoire authentique des apparitions* (Lourdes, authentic story of the apparitions) 6 volumes (Lethielleux, 1961-1964) - a critical study of the apparitions of Lourdes.

Everything could be revealed, scrutinized, criticized... Many more works popularizing the life of Bernadette were to follow: *Les paroles de Bernadette, Le Message de Lourdes, Le sens du pelerinage* (Bernadette's words, the message of Lourdes, the meaning of pilgrimage). A set of three volumes, written in collaboration with Sister M.Th. Bourgeade, is of particular interest. They were published in February 1971, in subscription form: *Logia de Bernadette*. Every word spoken by Bernadette after her departure from Lourdes, as recalled by witnesses at the various formal processes with a view to beatification, was recorded and analysed. New editions of all those documents are now being prepared or have already been published.

Nothing makes for a better introduction to Bernadette and the incomparable world in which she had her being, a world full of grace, than these writings and words.

This is how the author of *Le Sens de Lourdes* expressed himself in 1955: 'We shall go from the historical and terrestrial dimension to its mystical and celestial dimension, passing through the witness of Bernadette who is like the focal point. It is this witness which permits the discovery, through the material fabric of the events, of the spiritual intentions which manifest themselves in transparency.' Canon Laurentin kept his word.

Mosaic of Leo XIII, made in the Vatican, on the wall of the Rosary Basilica

LEO XIII (1878-1903)

Leo XIII demonstrated his devotion to Our Lady of Lourdes in a remarkable way. Shortly after his election as pope in 1878, he made a request to Bishop Jourdan of Lourdes, to offer a special mass for his intentions. Chaplains, helpers and pilgrims alike were enriched by his many spiritual gifts.

In 1883, the 25th anniversary of the apparitions, he donated a chalice in vermillion red and delegated Cardinal Desprez, Archbishop of Toulouse, to bless the foundation stone of the Basilica of the Holy Rosary, first envisaged by Bishop Langénieux in 1874. In 1901, the former Bishop, but then Cardinal, Langénieux, returned to perform the consecration. He had also been the main celebrant at the International Eucharistic Congress, two years earlier.

Pope Leo XIII had his own Grotto made in the Vatican gardens, similar to that of Lourdes, where he often went to pray, fondly referring to it as 'my little corner of France'. Following the example of Pius IX, he commissioned a mosaic of himself for one of the Lourdes churches.

LIGHT

Whoever passes through Lourdes cannot help but be struck by the number of candles of all sizes which burn night and day in front of the Grotto all year round: visible even from the train!

Certainly this is a common sight in Shrines and churches, but nevertheless it started with Bernadette herself when she came to the Grotto on 19 February 1858 (4th Apparition) with a lighted candle which she left there at the express wish of the Lady. Since then, the flame of the

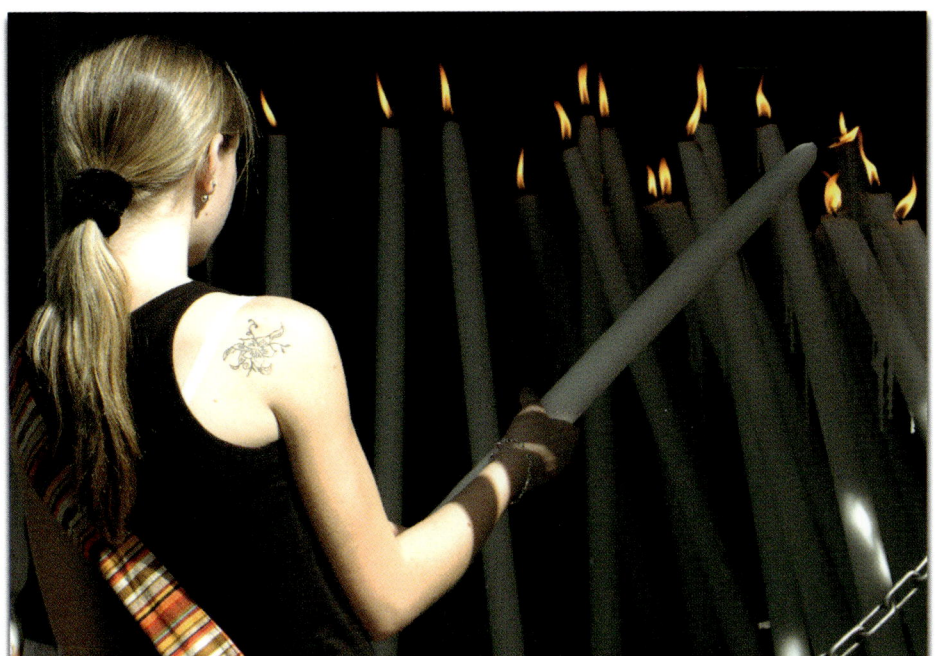

candle has always accompanied the recitation of the Rosary and silent contemplation. During the 17th apparition, whilst in ecstasy, Bernadette held a candle which burnt right down to her fingers though she felt nothing, and upon examination afterwards by the amazed Dr Dozous, who had witnessed the miracle, her hands were found to be without any trace of burns. Ever since the apparitions, pilgrims continue to burn candles at the Grotto, illuminating its darkness, like a great burning bush.

The symbol of the candle is light which illuminates the darkness, and flame which burns and purifies. In the great poem of creation, the first of God's works is to separate light from darkness. To see a light in the night chases away fear and restores courage. This was the experience of the people of God who were guided by a pillar of fire during the night as they came out of exile from Egypt. 'The Lord is my light and my help' (Ps 27).

Then there is the light of the Transfiguration on Mount Tabor and the light of the Resurrection: 'I am the light of the world,' and also 'You are the light of the world.' The pilgrim who lights a candle often utters a silent prayer, conscious that he has come to be illuminated by the one who is without sin, and that he must live as a child of the light, faithful to his baptism. To light a candle is to ask that our hearts too might burn with love for others and that we might shine as a light for others by freely giving of ourselves. If these candles could only speak as they burn through the night even in winter, how many supplications and deeds of grace we would hear!

For some, the prayer may be a simple 'Sweet Virgin Mary, it is time for me to go, but with this candle my prayer will continue.' The message of Lourdes is Mary herself, the immaculate one, virgin of light, woman clothed with the sun, all holy. Bernadette was overwhelmed by the Lady's beauty: 'I could only gaze at her as much my eyes would allow me.' Whenever she recounted the apparitions to others, it was as if that beauty imprinted itself upon her own face, in her expression, especially when she made the same gesture that the Lady had made when she gave her name. Bernadette herself imitated this gesture for the sculptor Fabisch who recounted his memory of it afterwards: 'She stood up with such simplicity and joined her hands together and raised her eyes towards heaven. I have never seen anything so beautiful.' The more we contemplate, the more we resemble what we contemplate. Just like Bernadette, the pilgrim who contemplates Mary at the Grotto, can be radiant too, like light shining through a stained glass window.

The pilgrim's day ends with the Marian torchlight procession: in the night of our world, the night of our doubts, our suffering and our weaknesses, this procession of light gathers everyone into the church, to acclaim Mary Immaculate resplendent with the clear light of God.

LITERATURE

There is an undeniable fascination about Lourdes, with its splendid scenery, the captivating beauty of the story of Bernadette, the mysterious presence of all those pilgrims from all over the world and the fervour which emanates from certain ceremonies. One can understand why writers have been attracted by those features.

We shall limit ourselves to the works which have had the most impact and which are still being discussed. Many Catholic writers have spoken of Lourdes, but four or five of them have left their mark: the great Francis Jammes (1868-1938), who still has many admirers in the world; the famous novelist Emile Zola (1840-1902); another very original novelist, Joris-Karl Huysmans (1848-1907); a biologist and surgeon, famous for his research on human tissue, author of a bestseller *L'Homme, cet inconnu* (Man, the unknown) (1935) and, unfortunately, also known for his eugenic theories: Alexis Carrel (1873-1944); and Francois Mauriac (1885-1970) great novelist, and member of the Academie Francaise.

Francis Jammes was brought to Lourdes by his mother in 1872, on the occasion of the very first pilgrimage. He was not yet four. In 1889, he returned there with his mother and beseeched God, in a beautiful poem, *J'allai a Lourdes* (I went to Lourdes), to heal a young girl, aged 18, whom he had seen on a stretcher:

> Dieu, ne la tue pas!
> - Ne serait-ce que
> pour son père nu-tête
> qui priait Dieu.
> (God, do not let her die !
> Be it for no other reason than
> for her bare-headed father
> who was praying to God.)

Lourdes was to play an important

role in his conversion which would take place in 1905, in a little Basque village, where he received communion with Claudel. Moreover, he went to Lourdes with him to confirm his new resolutions. From then on, the praying of the Rosary became very important in his life and also became the theme of many poems, poems in which Lourdes would continuously be alluded to.

In 1936, not long before his death, he published *Le Pèlerin de Lourdes* (the Lourdes pilgrim) in which he expressed all that this magical place meant to him: 'Virgin of the holy Rosary (...) it was you who gave me these wooden beads in the year one-thousand-nine-hundred-and-five, when I was converted.' The poet is like this other Lourdes poet, Jean Escuyot, who 'held his Rosary in the hollow of his hand and pressed it firmly on the sacred rock as though to make it absorb the spirit of the place. (*Le Pèlerin de Lourdes*, p.41).

Emile Zola, the novelist and leader of the naturalistic school of writers, had a passion for meticulous social studies. A non-believer, he was fascinated by the extraordinary atmosphere he found in Lourdes. He decided to go there in 1892, for a short stay, during which he would try and see everything: the pilgrim trains, the reception of the sick, the processions, taking part in one of them, behind the Blessed Sacrament. From this experience he produced a large book *Lourdes*, which would become famous, to the scandal of the believers, who felt insulted. They would, with the support of Bishop Billère, take steps to ensure atonement which included, in particular, gifts of important works of art to the Shrines.

Zola told of the journey of a priest, Fr Pierre, with a sick young girl, Marie, and wove all sorts of adventures, meetings and intrigues which allowed the description of everything with a striking number of details. This priest is full of doubts and expresses, in a way, the state of mind of the author. He sees miracles and does not deny them but attributes them to the electric atmosphere which reigns all around, or to auto-suggestion. Moreover, by his account, people who had been miraculously cured had had a relapse on the return train journey and the final impression is of an artificial faith, fuelled by fanatical preachers, an all-consuming commerce, one vast and terrifying fraud.

Dr Boissarie, who succeeded Dr de Saint-Maclou, at the *Bureau des Constatations Medicales* (office for medical reports and findings) in 1891, decided to re-establish the truth. He sent for people who had been cured, during one famous confrontation, to show the difference between the treatment those poor people had received at the hand of Zola compared to that of the Virgin. Zola, who had always promised to give a truthful, objective account of the facts, shrugged the whole thing off and declared that a novelist: 'could do what he liked with his characters.' Before his death, he was to publish *Les quatre évangiles* (the four Gospels) and to demonstrate a 'messianic' side, in the literary sense, signalling an evolution in his thinking.

The path which Joris-Karl Huysmans's life followed was very chaotic as he frequented esoteric, rather doubtful circles, far from the Christian faith. This man from the north, a decadent novelist, experienced a curious discovery of faith, through his association with the Trappists. He found his Catholic faith again, in those final years of the 19th century, in contradiction with a cultural climate in which writers, apart from Leon Bloy, were vehemently anti-Christian. Claudel, who had become a convert in 1886, had not yet published anything by that time.

When *Lourdes*, by Zola, was published in 1894, Huysmans was struck by it, as was everybody else, and decided to conduct his own research. He went to Lourdes in 1904. He lived, with great intensity, this meeting with pilgrims from all over the world, with sick people, with all the daily realities of Lourdes around this 'blazing Grotto'. In fact, everything appalled him in Lourdes. Nevertheless, he would publish a captivating description *Les Foules de Lourdes* (the crowds of Lourdes) in 1906, which met with great success. He was ill at the time and died the following year.

A lover of the arts, he had been a great admirer of medieval Gothic art and was literally stunned by the ugliness of those constructions of the 19th century, those statues, the pious bric-a-brac sold everywhere, the Basilica of the Rosary, of such composite styles: he compared it, with its lateral chapels, to a locomotive shed, expressing astonishment at the walls not being blackened every time a whistling locomotive launched ahead towards the esplanade. He found Lourdes the capital of ugliness which he saw as the devil's revenge for all the graces obtained by Mary.

His book contains selective passages on the processions, the symbolism of candles, Marian piety and of the numerous activities one can witness in Lourdes. It has been reprinted regularly for the last hundred years.

At the same time exactly, a young agnostic surgeon, Alexis Carrel, a native of Lyon, was also becoming curious about all that was happening in Lourdes. A researcher with a brilliant mind, he was awarded the Nobel Prize in 1912. He accompanied a young patient who seemed to be at death's door, to the point that there was doubt about her continuing her journey. To Dr Carrel's great astonishment, she recovered rapidly in front of him, in a way which could only be considered miraculous. This would mark Dr Carrel for life and he felt it his duty to bear witness to what he had seen in a short essay entitled *Le voyage à Lourdes.* This book, which is still being sold, has deservedly remained famous.

Francois Mauriac, who knew Lourdes from childhood, made it the theme of a book in 1931: he created two characters, two young men from good families. One, Augustin, represents the author himself and the other, Serge, is a Calvinist from Geneva. Their discussions form the basis of the short book *Pèlerin de Lourdes*, (Pilgrim of Lourdes), published in 1932. One *can guess the profound interest that place would arouse in the author and the questions which would present themselves to such a deep mind.*

LITURGICAL MUSIC

Liturgical music occupies an essential place in Lourdes, in the course of the daily celebrations of the 'season' for pilgrimages (April to October), i.e. eucharistic processions, Marian processions, masses, including international masses on Wednesdays and Sundays, and, during winter, Sunday vespers.

The service of liturgical music is the responsibility of a chapel master and is run by paid singers and organists (as well as volunteers). They take charge of the service of scheduled celebrations in the French language and of the international celebrations.

There is no official choir of the Shrines of Lourdes. There are three reasons for this: the small size of the town of Lourdes, the 'season' of the pilgrimages being restricted to a certain time of the year (April to October) and the wish to involve pilgrims in the singing at all celebrations. This does not prevent the presence, very much appreciated, of visiting choirs, coming from all countries.

Since 1969, thanks to the multilingual setting of Lourdes, the repertoire has become more international, consisting of a collection of songs usually sung all over Europe along with Lourdes songs translated in the six languages used officially in Lourdes: French, Italian, Spanish, English, German and Dutch. Other languages can be added according to circumstances. It has been noted that sometimes, during the Marian torch procession, both for the reciting of the Rosary as for the *Ave Maria* song, more than twenty five languages were being used. The official hymn of the great jubilee of 2000, 'Christ hier, Christ aujourd'hui' (Christ yesterday, Christ today), chosen by the Vatican in a competition, comes from Lourdes; it has been translated into twenty-seven languages.

Every year, the pastoral theme chosen by the bishop inspires the production of a song for the theme of the year – often emphasizing the 'signs' of Lourdes, like, over the past few years: water, rock, light... This song is a particular feature of the Wednesday international mass.

The organ occupies an important place in the sequence of the day's events, either for the accompaniment of songs or as a solo instrument (meditative or festive). Other instruments may sometimes be played alongside (trumpet, brass ensembles, etc.).

On the occasion of the 2008 jubilee in Lourdes, a double CD (NDL Editions), entitled '150 years of songs in Lourdes' was made available, consisting of several works by various chapel masters of Lourdes since 1858: Dargein, Antzenberger, Darros, Lesbordes, Décha and Lécot. It has to be noted that, in this album, there are works recorded for the first time, among them, the Missa Festiva, by Lesbordes, with orchestra.

LITURGY

Those responsible for the Shrines have always ensured that the riches of the liturgy are made available to as many people as possible. Also, before and after the Second Vatican Council, Lourdes has always endeavoured to anticipate and innovate, thus contributing to the renewal of 'pastoral liturgy', while taking account of its own uniqueness: diversity of cultures, presence of sick people, management of great crowds. But, unlike the practice in other Shrines, the celebration of the sacraments in Lourdes has focused mainly on the sacrament of reconciliation, the eucharist and, more recently, the anointing of the sick.

As far as the sacrament of reconciliation is concerned, from the beginning, the chaplains have been aware that Lourdes was a place for the discovery or the rediscovery of the sacrament for pilgrims who were more or less distant from the Church or, more recently, for young people. In this context, the Shrines wished to prepare pilgrims for the sacrament. For example, up until the 1950s, chaplains celebrated, several times a week, 'votive' masses 'for the forgiveness of sins' or 'for the grace of a good death'. The chaplains also developed, from the 1930s, a simplified document for the preparation for the sacrament. Lastly, as shown by specialised press reports, in the 60s and 70s, there were initiatives by pilgrimage organisers, in relation to the collective celebration of penance. As regards these initiatives, the Shrines made a significant contribution to the elaboration of successive rituals.

The collective celebration of the sacrament of the anointing of the sick is, in itself, a unique characteristic of the Shrines, even though some attention had to be given to cultural and pastoral differences. As it is, such a liturgical celebration is foreign to Italian and Spanish tradi-

An international mass in the St Pius X Basilica

tions. It is conducted in a different way in the Anglo-Saxon world, where it is limited to a laying on of hands. By contrast, French pilgrimages, from the end of the 1960s, well before the advent of the official ritual, had already integrated the celebration of this sacrament into their programmes. In this respect, Lourdes has truly been a source of innovation in this new form of the sacrament.

In terms of the celebration of the eucharist, the Shrines have always ensured that the sacrament is offered to the greatest number and, with this objective in mind, from the 1890s, successive bishops have fully exploited the resources of church law to facilitate the celebration of mass, for priests and for the faithful, to liberalise the rules of eucharistic fasting and to favour Marian masses. The liturgical regulations of the Shrines contain multiple 'indults'*, granted by popes or bishops. Two examples are revealing: Bishop Billère obtained from Pope Leo XIII in 1894 permission to celebrate the feast of the Immaculate Conception on 8 December, even though the date falls on a Sunday of Advent. Even better, in 1933, Bishop Gerlier obtained permission from Pope Pius XI to celebrate the feast of St Bernadette in February (and not on 16 April) so that Holy Week, or the Octave of Easter, could not supercede it.

The great pilgrimages have long raised the question of private masses by priests. From the 1950s, due to restricted facilities, the Shrines introduced 'synchronised' masses, with several priests celebrating their own mass on the same

podium, while the main celebrant presided on the main altar. It was to open the way to what was going to become, fifteen years later, the concelebrated mass in the Shrines: the international mass. The latter became an official rite in 1954. At that time, it was celebrated on the altar of the esplanade, in Latin. But, already, the liturgy of the word was read in several languages and the celebrants were invited to omit homilies.

Nowadays, the fundamentals of the international mass have not changed: liturgy of the word in several languages, Latin kept as the language for the ordinary of the mass and for the eucharistic prayer. Over the last few years the concelebrated character of the mass has been reinforced: the concelebrants all wear a chasuble, venerate the altar and surround it during the eucharistic liturgy. The Shrines are linking back to what was being practised in the 1960s, when Lourdes was considered as a state-of-the-art Shrine for concelebration. Also, one cannot forget the contribution of successive chapel masters towards the compositions of a repertoire adapted to the needs of an international assembly. It is

Lourdes' privilege to have at its disposal a multilingual repertoire. Finally, the Shrines make a particular effort to present the pastoral theme of the year in liturgical terms in order that it can be received by pilgrims of different cultures.

* from the Latin 'indulum, indulgere' – to be indulgent – any favour granted by the Holy See, for the benefit of either communities or individuals, which is a dispensation from the norms of the Church.

LOURDES MAGAZINE

The magazine of the Shrines of Lourdes is presently published eight times a year, in five languages, and has subscribers from more than 140 countries. The extra numbers and the special issues are particularly appreciated by the passing pilgrims who can obtain them in the kiosks of the estate or at the Librairie des Sanctuaires (the Shrines Bookshop). The French edition of the Lourdes Magazine has been distributed since the jubilee of the year 2000 all over France, thus reaching a very diverse readership. Founded in 1991, the Shrines Review is printed in Italy, a country extraordinarily appreciative of Lourdes. The themes published in the Lourdes Magazine explore, for example, the story of the Marian apparitions (number 150 of May 2007) and news about pilgrimages, and they also give an important place to the teaching of the faith and to the life of the universal Church. Many of the people who subscribe to this magazine find in it spiritual resources which, for some, may be their only link with the Church. The number of subscribers, around 20,000, only partly reflects the impact of the Lourdes Magazine which can be measured by the reproduction of its articles in thousands of pages of bulletins and newspapers in the four corners of the earth. In Cuba, for example, the magazine is photocopied and used for the catechism of young people, as shown in readers' letters. The website of the Lourdes Magazine is now being developed. It was linked to the websites of the bookshop and of the publishing house of the Shrines of Lourdes (NDL Editions) on the occasion of the jubilee of 2008. The celebration of the fifteenth anniversary of the Lourdes Magazine, on 17 May 2006, was presided over by the Indian Cardinal Ivan Dias, Prefect of the Roman Congregation for the Evangelization of Peoples, underlining the missionary zeal of the team who manage this unique magazine.

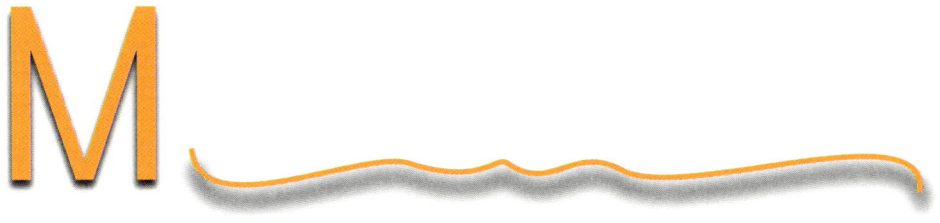

MARIAN PROCESSION

The Marian procession constitutes without doubt the best known image of Lourdes. It is also its most popular celebration. Bernadette often used to repeat, at the time of the apparitions, that all she knew was her Rosary. The Rosary still constitutes, today, the central element of the Marian procession, together with the Ave Maria song. The torchlight procession, it seems, goes back to the origins of the pilgrimages, when the *Enfants de Marie* (Children of Mary) came on Saturdays, after vespers, to recite the Rosary, holding a candle. But the first organised torchlight procession, on 28 August 1872, was the inspiration of Fr Marie-Antoine, a Capuchin and famous preacher from Toulouse. After the evening meal, pilgrims come to the Grotto holding a candle with the famous paper 'ruffle'. Everyone says the Rosary, meditating on the various sets of mysteries (joyful, sorrowful, glorious or luminous). Then the procession forms, always following the same itinerary: along the Gave, on the incline to the north up to the square of the Crypt, then along the south ramp on to the esplanade up

to the Calvaire des Bretons, returning finally to the square of the Basilica.

During the procession, pilgrims sing the sixty verses of the *Ave Maria*, which were sung for the first time on 27 May 1873. When the procession ends, a bishop gives the blessing, before the *Salve Regina*. This procession used to be reserved for able pilgrims only. Until 1970 the sick were not included in the procession: the late hour and the route were too demanding, at least according to the thinking of the time. From 1970, the participation of the sick has meant a modification of the route and a simplification of the ritual: the Rosary is said during the procession itself. Further, during the 1970s, new hymns accompanied the Ave Maria and the procession became multilingual. Since the beginning of the nineties, a *lucernaire** and sung litanies precede the blessing. Finally, in 2004, the luminous mysteries were introduced to the procession (on Mondays and Thursdays). Since 2008, their illustration – in mosaics by Fr Rupnik – can be seen on the façade of the Basilica of Our Lady of the Rosary, around a sculpture of the Virgin offering the Rosary to St Dominic.

* an evening liturgy

MARIE-ANTOINE, (priest)

On 8 February 1907, in Toulouse, Fr Marie-Antoine, a Capuchin Franciscan, who had become very famous and was called the 'saint of Toulouse', died at the age of 81. His fate was closely linked to the life of Lourdes at the end of the 19th century, as he was the most sought-after preacher, the one most people came to hear. Huysmans described him as having an eloquence 'toute en cris' (punctuated by outbursts), when commenting on the style of his famous invocations which would be taken up by the crowd.

Born in Lavaux, in 1825, of a good Christian family, he thought of the priesthood from a very early age and was ordained in 1850. As curate in Gaudens, he displayed remarkable zeal and was greatly appreciated. However, aged 28, during the Stations of the Cross, he heard an inner voice telling him: 'You will be a Capuchin!' Bishop Laurence asked him to think about it for a year. Amidst general consternation, he entered this very poor order, which was born in the 16th century, from a desire for radical reform from within the Franciscan community.

After a noviciate in Marseilles, he became a Capuchin in 1856 and started a career as a preacher which he was to pursue with rare energy, profundity and enthusiasm. He heard about the apparitions and, at the beginning of July 1858, before the 18th and last apparition of 16 July, he met Bernadette and was conquered: *Tout est vrai* (It is all true). He would give a description of this meeting in one of his first books, in 1873, *Le lis de l'Immaculée,* (the lily of the immaculate one) and Bishop Fourcade, who had known Bernadette very well in Lourdes and in Nevers, would recognize her in what Fr Marie-Antoine said, much more than in the romantic accounts of Lasserre.

Already famous for his preaching in the Marian Shrines such as Rocamadour and others, he would soon become the greatest preacher of Lourdes, very much in demand by all the pilgrimages, speaking everywhere, in the churches, at the Grotto, at the baths, tackling all sorts of subjects without ever repeating himself. As it was, he published a *Manuel du Pèlerin,* (a pilgrim's manual) in 1873, which is a real treatise on theology. One day, the great Parisian Dominican preacher of Notre-Dame, Fr Monsabré, pushed his way through the crowd in order to convey his satisfaction to him: 'This is how we should preach!'

It was because of him that the first important regional pilgrimages from 1868, six years after the official recognition of the apparitions by Bishop Laurence, took place. He too was responsible for the famous torchlight procession, started on 28 August 1872. One night, seeing all those shining torches, motionless against the Grotto, he exclaimed: 'These must walk, they must sing!' He invited people to circulate, singing and praying, holding a torch. We know how well this idea was to be received!

Fr Marie-Antoine finished his days, after innumerable missions, greatly honoured in the convent of the *Côte Pavée*, which he had been called to re-establish in 1857, rekindling a tradition which went back to the 13th century.

MARIOLOGY OF LOURDES

In the simplicity of the story of the apparitions we are able to detect a light which illuminates the mystery, the presence of Our Lady at the heart of our faith. Mary was manifested to us because, in her, the reality of our salvation was initiated by her 'yes'. If we forget about her, if we put her aside, we can no longer unite God and humanity, in one flesh, in a common history. God is sent back to his heaven, well beyond our contingencies. Men and women are left to their loneliness, their fear or their pride, at the mercy of their heart's fantasies. Mary is therefore witness and partaker of an alliance. She makes us see and understand Christian 'life' and the mystery of Christianity as an ineradicable alliance between God and his creatures. God is a living being and not an abstraction: 'An abstraction does not need a mother.' Humanity is, for eternity, in partnership with God. Human beings are not the 'dream of a shadow', they are of infinite value.

At the apex of the Lourdes message, there is the revelation of 25 March: the incarnation of the Son of God in a woman's womb. Mary makes herself one with the mission which is entrusted to her, to bring the world the gift of God. The mariology of Lourdes puts us at the source of the very being of Mary, who makes no claim in an individualistic way; she is total relationship with the One who gives himeself through her. She is the mother of Jesus, the mother of God. And that is why, at the time of the apparitions, and all along the history of the pilgrimages, we discover, with the Grotto as a departure point, the God who heals and who saves, the God

who forgives and who nourishes the faithful.

M   Mary, through her transparency, expresses God, his breath, his spirit. If she is able to communicate him, it is because, first, she receives him, she has, at all times, made herself attentive to his presence. The 'sound of a breeze' which preceded the first apparition reminds us of the tremor felt at Pentecost by the disciples of Jesus. And with the breeze, there was the light and then, the spring that wells up from the porous earth prepared by the work of creation. Mary does nothing but display the power of the Spirit in the midst of the chaos, the primitive confusion caused by humanity in God's creation.

Mary is a sign of starting again and of an ever-present hope, whether in the dirt in which our humanity flounders, or at the foot of the cross, where death seems to have taken this hope away. She is the mother who remains standing and who consoles broken, exhausted hearts at the end of their pilgrimage. In Lourdes she invited Bernadette to sink her face and hands into the dirt and to eat grass *comme les bêtes* (like the beasts); only then was it possible for the spring to gush forth; it had been running, but had been forgotten. After Bernadette, how many sick and disabled people were to occupy the first row in pilgrimage gatherings: Mary makes us contemporaries of the newness of the Gospel, which was born from the gift of God himself, nailed on that cross on which still the most vulnerable people are being put to death, denying their human dignity. Mary, here, is their mother.

Mary accompanied Bernadette through the whole of Lent 1858, right up until the light of Easter. She was the catechist who prepared her for her first communion. She was the mother who introduced the disciples to the new life in Christ: 'Do everything he tells you,' she said to the servants at the wedding of

Cana. She was in a position to say that, as she herself had answered to the angel on the day of the Annunciation: 'Be it done to me according to your word'. Mary allowed the Word to become flesh in her; because of this she can be close to everyone and, by her faith, by her prayer, she can open all hearts to trust. In her we shall be modelled by the breath of the Spirit.

Thus can she can call herself the 'Immaculate Conception', the one who, in the depth of our world, corresponds with the Holy Spirit; she assures us that nothing is ever lost, that grace is more original than sin. In Lourdes, Mary allows the pilgrims to live the grace of their baptism, of their birth as children of God.

MARY

The story of Lourdes starts with the meeting of two young girls under the grace of the prayer: 'In the name of the Father, and of the Son, and of the Holy Spirit'. The sign of the cross inaugurates the road of the apparitions which will go on towards an exchange of promises: 'Will you do me the favour of coming here during the next fortnight?' Bernadette said yes. She then received an assurance: 'I do not promise to make you happy in this world, but in the other.' We are involved in the narrative of an alliance between two female partners, which is grafted, in some way, to the eternal alliance of the three divine persons. The writing of a holy story was started in Lourdes, which makes us contemporaries with the covenant of God with humanity, a covenant which constitutes the very heart of God's love.

That is why Mary, in Lourdes, cannot be separated from Bernadette. Witnesses of the apparitions could not see anything in the hollow of the Grotto. But, every day, before their very eyes, they saw that the face of Bernadette was transformed; they followed her dialogue with the 'something' which she saw and which motivated her to proceed. Mary is thus revealed as a teacher of spiritual growth. Bernadette was drawn towards this hollow in the rock where she would be reborn to hope. Gradually, she was being released from the *cachot* in which she had been confined. From the very beginning of the apparitions, a noise like a sudden breeze had seemed to symbolize the beginning of a new phase. Mary allowed a little asthmatic to hear the breath of the Spirit. Her horizon, which had been limited to the tiny courtyard of the *cachot*, now revealed a light which took the form of a young girl, 'as young and as small as me'. Bernadette could see herself, transfigured in those eyes which invited her to have complete trust.

Mary is a creature and not an intermediary between God and humanity. She is a little Bernadette of Nazareth. But she is totally at the disposal of the work of the Holy Spirit and she radiates in its light. Mary is the creature who is perfectly saved and redeemed from sin, from mistrust, from the doubt which humanity has always opposed to the call of God.

Mary shows the way which God

has always kept open to our sinful humanity. She is also a testimony to the price God had to pay for this. Half way through the fortnight of the apparitions, Bernadette had to dig in the mud until a spring spurted out: she had embarked on a form of penance 'for sinners'. Mary chose to accompany her Son right up to the Cross, from which Life burst out, when, from the side of Jesus, 'there came out blood and water...'. God wants to be accompanied in his gift: then his creature is not only saved but also able to communicate the love received.

Mary participated in the mission of the Son of God: she is not the source of salvation but she participates in its reality by her faith and the confidence she has in the Word which is given to her, this Word which became flesh in her bosom. God does not save us from the outside but he gives rise to the 'yes' of our freedom and makes us participants in his work. Mary responded fully and perfectly to his expectations. And she would know how to recognize, in our humanity, those little ones and those poor, like her, whom God chooses as his instruments.

Mary is also the model of that Church which she wishes to see renewed at the Grotto of Lourdes by the construction of a chapel and the organisation of processions and pilgrimages. The priests were invited to start on their way by a little one, from the lowliest origin. God wanted to visit his people and needed them to be at the service of a Marian Church, open to the Holy Spirit, and attentive to the humblest messengers of the Gospel.

Mary is the model and the mother of the Church, the heart of the new humanity which, to the point of the greatest suffering, never ceases to beat to the rhythm of the Spirit of the risen one.

Bernadette was the first pilgrim; she relived the adventure of Mary of Nazareth, before a multitude of others who would discover that, here, poverty, illness, the monotony of an ordinary existence, can be the setting for a joy hitherto unknown. The experience of the intimacy with that presence in the Grotto does not bring passivity but, on the contrary, it opens a new way, in the footsteps of Jesus.

MASSY, OSCAR (préfet)

Oscar Massy was born on 25 November 1810. His father, a colonel in Napoleon's armies, had died in action. He had been made a noble by the emperor in 1813 and his son Oscar inherited the title of baron.

He made his career in the civil service and became *préfet* (head of regional administration) of the Hautes-Pyrénées in 1849. There he met the new Bishop Laurence. The latter was to be of great assistance to him when he was removed from office due to his attitude after the *coup d'état* of 2 December 1851. Bishop Laurence approached the minister and intervened for his reinstatement as *préfet* of Tarbes. These events were to prepare for the future.

Highly disconcerted by the apparitions in which, while being a practising Christian, he could not believe, he was in constant commu-

nication with minister Rouland, who recommended firmness and tact. He also tried to obtain information from Inspector Jacomet and from the mayor of Lourdes, Lacadé. As people had begun to organize a veritable cult at the Grotto, bringing flowers, candles and money, for which people had mass said in church, he wanted to close it at the beginning of May. The mayor implemented this bye-law at the beginning of June. How great would Massy's embarrassment be when, on 28 July, despite the ban, the lady admiral Bruat, governess of the imperial prince and the eminent journalist Veuillot, were interrogated by the local gendarme Callet! The emperor was to end these difficulties by re-opening the Grotto the following 5 October.

The minister of state, Fould, a native of the Hautes-Pyrénées, disliked Oscar Massy and wanted his departure. Massy was then named *préfet* of the Isère region in January 1859 and left, with little regret on the part of the clergy, taking with him several hundred personal documents from the archives which, later, would become a treasure trove for researchers. Unjustly criticised, he died 3 years later, on 10 August 1862, sustained by the sacraments, in his castle of Saint-Yriex.

MEDIA

From the time of the apparitions, Lourdes has not ceased to arouse the curiosity of the media. *L'intérêt Public*, the Tarbes newspaper, on 6 March, recounted the turmoil provoked by the story of Bernadette. From then on, the attraction of the media to Lourdes would continue to grow. For example, eighty journalists were present at the consecration of the Basilica of St Pius X in 1958.

At the journalists' request, Bishop Donze created the *Bureau de Presse* (press office) in 1971 and named Fr Ramond its director. Apart from exceptional events, such as the Holy Father's visit in 2004, on average, more than 800 journalists get in touch with the Shrines each year; they represent more than 500 media contacts. Displayed as a diagram the following division can be made: 1/3 work for the press, 1/2 for television, the rest being shared between radio, press agencies, pilgrimage organisations and internet. While the presence of the press and radio remains stable, there has been a notable increase in the presence of television channels and of press agencies, as well as the emergence of journalists who work specifically for the web.

The geographical origin of the press is varied. Alongside the bulk of European journalists (96%), we see, since the jubilee of the year 2000, journalists appearing from the American, African and Asian continents.

The challenge for the managers of the Shrines is to broadcast the message of Lourdes by means of the press. Even though the main interest is usually directed at the healings and miracles of Lourdes, the discovery of the phenomenon of pilgrimages remains a constant surprise. The Shrines' communication services elicit the visit of the media by means of *communiqués* and press conferences. Their objective is to present to the media the great events which give the life of the Shrines its rhythm and to inform them of the current validity of the message of Lourdes. Thus, the media participate in the broadcasting of that message and respond in their own way to the request made by the Virgin Mary to Bernadette: 'Go and tell…'.

MESSAGE

The message of Lourdes is what the Virgin said to Bernadette, but also everything she accomplished, in Lourdes, at that particular time - that is 19th century France. This message is sober and low key. In Lourdes, as in the Gospel, the Virgin speaks little: through the story of Bernadette, through a few words and a few gestures, which we had to receive for our life in today's world and in the Church of Vatican II.

The time of Bernadette.
The time was 19th century France, marked by unprecedented industrial development: the steam engine, the railway, flour mills. It enriched some and impoverished others; it deepened social inequalities. It was also the time of triumphant emphasis on rationality. There was a belief that progress would bring happiness to everyone: science rather than faith. In this context, the apparitions were a manifestation of the other world, with its demands and its beauty, where the poor and the sick came first.

A Fact
The message of Lourdes is, first and foremost, a fact. 'She really appeared to Bernadette Soubirous,' said Bishop Laurence. By appearing, Mary demonstrated that there was another world, one of beauty, in which humanity was called to live as children of God.

A Choice
The message is, also, a choice – the choice of Bernadette, from a 'lowly class', daughter of a miller who had faced ruin, living in the *cachot*. 'The Virgin chose me because I was the poorest'.

A Place
It is also the choice of a place for the apparitions, the Grotto of Massabielle, a disreputable area at the time, beside the Gave, dark, damp and dirty, a shelter for pigs. And it was in this place of darkness, an image reflecting our hearts, that Mary would manifest herself as the immaculate one. God wanted to

join us in the depth of our troubles and fill them with his light.

A Meeting in Real Life
A meeting between two women: 'Heaven has visited the earth'. Why did Bernadette come to Massabielle on that 11 February 1858? There were two reasons: the first, an immediate need: in the *cachot*, there was no wood left for the fire. But Bernadette had come back to live in the *cachot* for one reason only – she wanted to make her first communion and had left Bartrès, which was without a priest, to come back to the *cachot*, in the middle of winter!

Silence and Prayer
And suddenly, an overwhelming meeting: a light, a presence, a smile, the surprise soon turning to peace with prayer and the beautiful sign of the cross the Lady taught Bernadette. The words of the message are as if sealed in a casket of silence: the first two apparitions to prepare her heart to listen, the last two for the words to be engraved in her heart. Always in a climate of prayer, all the apparitions started with the rosary.

A Call
There had already been signs: a sound like a sudden breeze (Pentecost), a light, a presence, but on the third apparition, on 18 February, the Lady spoke to Bernadette and she was speaking in a language which was known to her, the *patois* (dialect) of Lourdes. 'In French, I only knew my Rosary'.

Would the Lady write her name on the sheet which Bernadette was holding out to her?

'It is not necessary... Would you do me the favour of coming here for a fortnight?' Never had anyone spoken to Bernadette, the girl of the *cachot*, with such respect. 'It was the first time I was addressed as "vous"'. (the polite and formal form of 'you').

'Do you want to?' It was a call, a suggestion, as in the Gospel: 'If you want'.

'To come here'. The pilgrimage is a journey, a response to a call.

'For a fortnight': it is a commitment and also a mark of trust. Our religion is an invitation to a more beautiful life and not an imperative without choice. For Bernadette, as for us, the call would cause difficulties: curiosity, mockery, trouble with the authorities, being the laughing stock of newspapers, accusations of acting as though in a cataleptic state. A call which would also be the cause of questioning: who is this Lady? Tongues were wagging in the *Café Français*, the town was divided.

A Promise
Bernadette would not be spared anything in her life and yet she was happy through her tribulations, with the joy of the other world, living the beatitudes.

A Request for Conversion
After the 8th apparition, during Lent, Bernadette's face changed; it reflected the sadness of the Lady when she spoke of sinners, of penance, of conversion. One had to turn to God, believe in his love and change one's life. The Lady asked for gestures of penance from Bernadette: to kiss the ground, to

eat grass, to drink from the spring and to wash herself in it. But the crowd could not hear anything during the apparitions. All that those present could see was Bernadette going to the Gave, then scratching the earth in the Grotto, emerging later with her face all dirty, looking slightly lost. She is mad, thought some, she is laughing at us. In reality she was only obeying the Lady while performing these actions 'for sinners'. But the spring, discovered beneath the Grotto under the Lady's guidance, was dirty and muddy. 'At the fourth attempt, I was able to drink from it. It cost me to drink that dirty water.'

With Bernadette, we have to purify our hearts, clarify our desires and find again the grace of our baptism in order to live as children of God.

A Mission
'Go and tell the priests': it was to someone from the laity, a woman, a young person that this message was given: the message of Lourdes is of the Church. 'Let processions be made to this spot': that is, together, within the mantle of the Church, and 'to have a chapel built here': Lourdes is a place where the Church is being built. The chapel is the place where people gather together, the place of the proclaimed Word of God, of the sacrifice offered in the eucharist.

A revelation: 'I am the Immaculate Conception'
It is the apex, the signature of the message, the answer to the question everyone had been asking regarding who the Lady was. On 25 March, Bernadette asked that question three times without result. The fourth time she had an answer at last: 'I am the Immaculate Conception.' Bernadette did not understand this expression but, when recounting the apparition, her face was transfigured, reflecting the supernatural beauty she had seen that day: Mary, the *panagia*, from the depth of her being, virgin of light, in the obscurity of the Grotto and the darkness of the world, perfect creature, as wanted by God from all eternity, face of the Church and sign of God's design: 'that we should be holy and faultless, before him in love' (Ephesians, 1.4). Beyond the words, Bernadette, dazzled by this beauty, enters into contemplation: 'I looked at her as much as I could'.

In conclusion
The message can be summarized thus: in Lourdes, the immaculate one calls sinning humanity to come together, in the Church, to return to God, to build the Church with a missionary spirit.

A universal message
By its simplicity, its limpidity, the message becomes universal. In Lourdes, everyone can feel at home since there is no political or any narrowly national dimension in the fact of the apparitions. There is no threat in the message, only an invitation, a call. There is no secret concerning the world's destiny, no prophecy on the future, no spectacular prodigy, nothing that could provoke curiosity or exalt the imagination.

There is nothing but the Gospel

in its simplicity and its radicality, given to us right up to the self-effacement of Nevers by Bernadette, yet lit up by the soothing, luminous, maternal presence of the immaculate one, like a clear spring for our poor humanity.

MILL OF BOLY

This is where Bernadette was born, on 7 January 1844, in one of the five mills spread along the stream of Lapacca, at the foot of the stronghold. It was there that her father François had set himself up as miller after his marriage to Louise Castérot who was half his age. Despite all the social conventions, he had refused the eldest daughter, Bernarde, and had chosen to marry the youngest. This marriage of love rather than social convention had been celebrated on 9 January 1843.

However, Bernarde, as the 'heiress', remained head of the household. Louise and François accepted this situation and Bernarde would be the godmother of their eldest daughter, who would bear her name.

Bernadette would always be influenced by the atmosphere of the mill, an atmosphere filled with love and shared labour. She died saying: 'I have been ground down like a grain of wheat.' It was not merely imagery. From the beginning her happy life was marred by suffering: her mother burnt her breast and the baby was left in the care of a wet nurse from Bartrès, who had just lost her child. It was the father who found it hardest to be separated from his little daughter and he would never miss an opportunity, or often create one, to go to Bartrès, until the time when he could bring her back. In Boly, alas,

death would also hit the family when the baby of two months, Jean, was taken away. Then difficulties accumulated: the mother-in-law and her children left the mill, a mill where the easy-going nature of François avoided trouble but did nothing to improve business.

Also, he lost an eye, hit by a bit of stone as he was drilling holes in his millstones. And, even though the atmosphere in the mill stayed joyful, the remaining customers came mostly to exploit the generosity of the Soubirous: kind-hearted, their welcome was always generous. But they themselves were forced to leave the place in 1854. François's arrival had followed the death of the Castérot father, after a cart accident in 1841. Bad luck seemed to repeat itself. Are the misfortunes of the poor to be part of their lot always?

MIRACLES

'While the Jews demand miracles and the Greeks look for wisdom, we are preaching a crucified Christ' (1 Cor, 22-23). Perhaps the apostle Paul might reply, still today, to all those who ask for miracles, that the 'miracle' is that we are loved by God to a point which we cannot imagine. He loves us to the point of giving us his son who, in his turn, loves us with the greatest of love, that of giving up his life.

By 'miracle', normally, we understand a phenomenon, or an extraordinary occurrence which causes us to marvel or leaves us astounded. We might also think of events such as the wonders performed by Moses in Egypt, or an upheaval of the order of things, an apparent suspension of the laws of creation. A miracle appears as an event the causes of which we do not know. We wonder, at the same time, whether what seems to go against the normal course of things, seems like that to us because we do not yet understand all the laws of nature. Could it be that the things that seem 'miraculous' to us now, may be revealed, tomorrow, in the light of new scientific discoveries, as completely natural.

Miracles must be seen, rather, as a particular intervention by God in our history, in our life, a manifestation of his power, a sign of his presence, of his compassion. When Jesus healed a sick person, he showed, by his action, that he had come to bring back that person to his/her integrity, to the natural beauty which had been corrupted by sin. When he ordered storms to cease, he wanted us to believe that all had been created by him and that nature lay in his hands. When he chased demons out he wished to show us that we are not at the mercy of malevolent and dark forces – he had delivered us from evil. When he changed water into wine, or multiplied bread, he was leading us to understand that, with him, a new world was born, overflowing with love. A miracle is like an invitation to look towards heaven to recognize the greatness of God and his benevolence towards us, to hope with unwavering faith that he is triumphant over all forms of evil, over sin and over death itself.

In his extreme generosity, God

also allows others to achieve great things in his name, first Mary who, already at Cana, 'urged' Jesus to perform his first miracle.

All the same, the miracles which are recognized in Lourdes are few. Why are so few people cured and not all those who present themselves at the Grotto? Because only one sign is needed to make us remember that the love of God and of his mother for us embraces us all. One person touched by a miracle makes us understand that the new world, the world of heaven, is here, on earth, already.

MIRACLES OF LOURDES

To speak of Lourdes is to speak of miracles. Contrary to popular belief, however, a miracle needs to be more than a sensational or incredible occurrence - it needs to have a spiritual dimension. Two criteria, in fact, must be fulfilled before a cure can be verified and formally recognised:

1. The cure itself must be 'abnormal', that is to say, completely unpredicted given the medical circumstances.

2. The nature of the cure must 'be a sign', that is, it must lead us to believe that a special intervention of God has taken place through the intercession of Our Lady of Lourdes (in the case of Lourdes).

When faced with cures of an extraordinary nature, it is essential that both criteria be treated as part of the same single reality. The investigation will be conducted on specifically medical grounds as well as on pastoral and ecclesial grounds. A cure cannot be recognised unless, firstly, it has exceeded all known outcomes normally associated with the progression of the illness in question and secondly, unless both beneficiary and witnesses

The first two miracles of Lourdes: Catherine Latapie and Louis Bouriette

have recognised its spiritual significance in their lives.

Discernment is required at two levels. At the scientific and medical level, at which a doctor must submit his professional opinion having carried out a medical examination with the utmost rigour, in line with guidelines from the medical authorities, and in accordance with his medical training and experience. At the spiritual level, where faith enters in and reaches beyond the boundaries of scientific examination.

A dialogue between medical science and the Church is therefore essential and such a dialogue has always existed at Lourdes, thanks to the permanent presence of doctors in the medical bureau at the Shrine, whose job it is to receive every notification of a cure and to put in motion the processes required by the Church to study the authenticity of a possible miracle. When presented with a cure, their primary task is to certify that a cure has indeed taken place, whilst also keeping in mind the personal life of their patient, who, in being cured, has received a unique, unforgettable grace. It is the Church's task to discern such an experience and to judge its spiritual fruits

In conclusion, in the space of 150 years, only 67 miracles have been formally recognised out of more than 7,200 cures registered and documented at the medical bureau.

MISSIONARIES OF THE IMMACULATE CONCEPTION OF LOURDES

The cradle of this religious congregation is Garaison. As indicated by its name, it has had a privileged connection with the Shrines of Lourdes to which, in 1866, it provided its first chaplains. The congregation in fact had three founders: Pierre Geoffroy, in the

The arrival of the new missionaries at Garaison

17th century, and Bishop Laurence and Fr Peydessus in the 19th century.

Pierre Geoffroy came to Garaison for the first time in 1600, accompanying, in his capacity as bursar, the Archbishop of Auch on a visit of his diocese. The chapel, built here at the request of the Virgin Mary, seemed abandoned. Geoffroy, captivated by Mary, asked his archbishop to put him in charge of this chapel. It was a real resurrection, with a service provided by a corps of chaplains, the number of which rose gradually to around twenty. They lived in community, welcoming pilgrims and preaching missions in the area. As a result, that place of pilgrimage became the most frequented in the region. The Revolution put an end to it all; the chaplains went into exile, the chapel was abandoned and Garaison became once again, a desert.

It was to rise again around fifty years later, thanks to Bishop Laurence who was then vicar general to the Bishop of Tarbes. He had conceived a plan of evangelization based on the ancient Marian Shrines of the diocese. Once restored, each would help spread Christian life to the neighbouring populations. This project required a solid team of priests to implement it. The vicar general knew the priests of the diocese very well: they had been his students in the seminaries. He chose four ardent, young men of great Marian piety. At their head, he placed Pierre Laurence, his nephew, who, at 30, was their senior. His right arm was Jean-Louis Peydessus. This project would start with the Shrine of Garaison, the most important and the most frequented one.

The new chaplains arrived at Garaison on 31 May 1836 and, having consecrated themselves to Our Lady, they started work immediately. From the very first days, pilgrims started to arrive and, a few months later, the parish missions began. The vicar general followed the work of his missionaries closely and shared it on the days when large numbers of people came. Even after having been named Bishop of Tarbes, he never changed his ways. This collaboration was soon to intensify. In the hands of their bishop, in December 1848, the missionaries made their three religious vows. They also 'committed themselves to going any time and for any occasion wherever the bishop needed them'. The latter, following his evangelization plan, sent them to restore the Shrines of Héas (1848), Poueylaün (1856), Piétat (1861). Meanwhile, there came the great surprise, the apparitions of Mary in Lourdes, in 1858, and the request for a new Shrine: 'Go and tell the priests to have a chapel built here and let processions be made to this spot'. At Bishop Laurence's request four Garaison missionaries arrived in Lourdes in May 1866. Their superior, Fr Sempé, worked ceaselessly until his death in September 1889, to give the Shrine a structure which would allow it to function up to the centenary of the apparitions. In 1868, Bishop Laurence, wishing to secure the future of the young congregation, asked for and obtained Rome's approval. He died two years later, in January 1870, while in

Rome for the Vatican Council.

From then on, responsibility for the congregation rested solely on the shoulders of Fr Peydessus. In 1850, Pierre Laurence had been called to serve beside his uncle, the vicar general and the Garaison community had elected Fr Peydessus superior. He would remain in this role until his death, being constantly re-elected. 'He was the tenderly loved "good father",' said one of his religious brothers, 'never giving orders, always obedient, forming his disciples by the example of his virtues.'

His great preoccupation was above all to unite the constitutions which specified the missionary and Marian character of the congregation. Those constitutions were brought up to date after Vatican II. This is how the charism of these religious is defined: 'They will see themselves, following Mary's example, as witnesses of God's loving eye over humanity. An optimistic view of themselves and of any person they meet should be their decisive mark.'

Fr Peydessus died on 13 February 1882. The cause for his beatification was raised in Rome and brought to the point of the declaration of recognition of heroic virtues (1994). The Missionaries of the Immaculate Conception of Lourdes are present in various communities of the Tarbes diocese: Garaison, Piétat, Tarbes, Lourdes, Héas (during the summer), Galan (retreat house) and also in Argentina, in the dioceses of Tucuman, Catarmarca and Buenos Aires.

MUSEUM OF BERNADETTE

The old *Musée Notre-Dame*, near the large statue of Bernadette praying on her knees, which can be reached by the exit of the Saint Pius X basilica, behind the great organ, is now the *Musée Bernadette*.

With its historical and pastoral perspectives, it helps the visitor have a deeper understanding of the message.

At the entrance, a great three-dimensional model represents Lourdes at the time of the apparitions. It is very interesting to spend some time studying it and particularly to compare the course of the Gave and its banks, then and now. In chronological order, there is a series of rooms on Bernadette's baptism, her childhood, 11 February 1858, the eighteen apparitions, the development of Lourdes and, finally, the signs of Lourdes.

Among the numerous objects and pictures which can be admired in this museum, the following merit particular attention: the Virgin of gilded wood which used to be in the choir of the old parish church, the original of Bernadette's baptismal certificate which had been rescued from a fire, the small portrait of Bernadette which is, also, the only authentic painting of her we possess; the portraits of Bernadette's parents; a picture of the Grotto as popular imagination represented it a few years after the apparitions; the photograph of Bernadette's two companions on the morning of 11 February: her friend Jeanne, nicknamed Baloume, and her little sister Marie, nicknamed Toinette; the first text written by Bernadette, three years later, where she recounts the first apparition; the holy water font from the parish church where, on Sunday 14 February, Bernadette went to fill her bottle to sprinkle at the apparition; some poor souvenirs such as two pieces of the wild rosebush of the Grotto above which the Virgin appeared, a few flowers glued together to make a picture, and the first engraving of the Grotto; the photographs of some of the protagonists of the story, such as Fr Peyramale and the Inspector Jacomet with, in a glass case, the

small notebook where he wrote down all that happened and the words of witnesses; a photograph of Bernadette between the ladies of the town, just before leaving Lourdes in 1866; a few souvenirs reminding us of her religious life.

MUSEUM (TREASURE)

From the very beginning of the pilgrimages, the thanksgiving of the pilgrims was often expressed in the form of gifts, from the humble to the sumptuous. Visitors find whole walls of the basilicas covered with votes of thanks engraved in marble and placed, anonymously or by celebrities, on the occasion of graces received through the intercession of Our Lady of Lourdes. Often they relate to healings, but also to prayers by mothers or wives for the protection granted by the Virgin to their children or their husbands who returned from the front in either of the 20th century's world wars.

They tell the story of the Shrines and of the pilgrimages. This is why the persons responsible for the Shrines, at the request of Bishop Perrier of Tarbes and Lourdes, decided to open collections hitherto reserved to researchers. The Treasure Museum was opened in 2001 and was developed considerably in 2004. It records 150 years of history, with photographs, liturgical ornaments, exceptional jewellery pieces, presents from popes and princes, but also humble objects of piety and devotion. With the richness and diversity of jewellery and altar cloths of the 19th century, representative of the neo-gothic trends, but particularly of symbolism and 'art deco', it is one of the most beautiful exhibitions in France today.

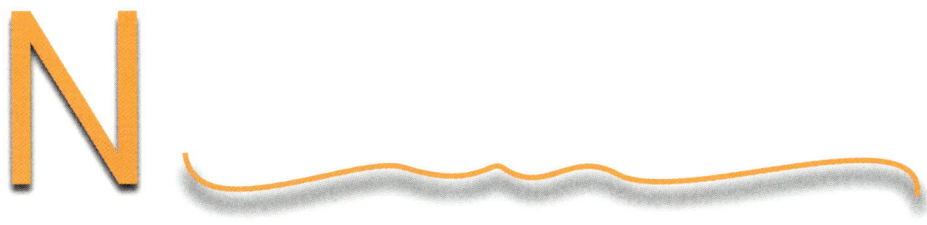

NAPOLEON III

Napoleon III (1808-1873), was the emperor of the French at the time of Bernadette. An admirer of modern British institutions and enterprises, his reign was marked by considerable industrial, economic and financial development.

The Lourdes facts were reported to him in a negative way by his administration, through the judicial apparatus and the *préfet* Massy. However, providence was watching. The Empress Eugenie, as a good Spanish Catholic, was a pious woman. Moreover, since 1856, she had enticed the emperor to Biarritz, a pretty fishing village on the Atlantic, very close to the Spanish border, and was in the process of having a residence built there. The imperial couple enjoyed going there every year.

Thus it was that, in July 1858, on Wednesday 28, twelve days after the last apparition, the lady admiral Bruat, governess of the imperial prince, accompanied by her three daughters and by a celebrity, Louis Veuillot, editor in chief of the Catholic newspaper *L'Univers*, had

the idea of going to the Grotto. It was closed by municipal decree and a wooden barrier had been erected all around it. Braving the ban, these illustrious visitors went there to pray and encountered the local gendarme, Callet, who asked for their names and declared them in breach of the law. What stupor at the town hall and at the prefecture when the news arrived: 'The governess of the children of France, questioned! And Louis Veuillot! Fr Peyramale rubbed his hands: thus the emperor would know at first hand of 'the rigorous measures taken against a religious and peaceful population'. On that blessed day, Bishop Laurence set up the commission for a canonical enquiry.

Many approaches from the bishops were received in Biarritz and things began to move. On Saturday 2 October, the Ministry of Religious Affairs advised the Bishop of Tarbes that His Majesty wished 'access to the Grotto to be free as well as the use of the water.' The measure would come into effect on 5 October.

The emperor would intervene again directly three years later, at the time of the acquisition of the Grotto and of the neighbouring field by the bishop to build a chapel, as the Virgin had asked. Those negotiations lasted several months, during 1861, and the apparitions had not yet been recognized. On 22 August, the emperor signed the decree of the *Conseil d'Etat**, authorizing the bishop to become the owner of what would become the Lourdes estate. As always, Bishop Laurence was continuing in his mission.

* the executive branch of the government.

NEVERS

Nevers is the capital of the department of the Nièvre, in the region of Burgundy. More than 500 km from Lourdes. It is situated in the Massif Central, at the confluence of the Nièvre and Loire rivers.

It was in the evening of 7 July

1866 that Bernadette stepped over the threshold of the convent of Saint-Gildard, mother house of the congregation of the Sisters of Charity of Nevers, where she had chosen to be a religious. The convent owes its name to a celebrated priest of the Nièvre, who lived in the 7th century and who was buried in an abbey built in that same place.

'God is charity' were the words which, on arrival, Bernadette could see engraved on the stone of the pediment of the house in which she was to spend the rest of her life. It was the essence of the experience she had lived through in Lourdes during the apparitions: that of the love of God for all humanity, and in particular for the humble and for sinners.

Bernadette made her first vows on 25 October 1866: simple vows for the length of her novitiate, which would end on 30 October 1867, and perpetual vows on 22 September 1877. During her thirteen years at Saint-Gildard, she was, successively, assistant nurse, in charge of the infirmary and the sacristy.

In her humble and hidden life, she would feel, deep inside her heart, a profound solidarity with the poorest. Attached to Jesus who had

loved to the point of giving his life, she would always seek to manifest, in each of her words and of her actions, her only desire: 'I shall not live a single moment without loving'.

Often ill towards the end of her life, Bernadette spent long periods in the infirmary of Sainte-Croix. Those close to her described how 'the suffering during her last illness was atrocious. Her exhausted lungs were on fire; the bones of one knee were eaten away by a raging infection', but they also added: 'One leaves her side feeling stronger and more confident than when arriving!' Those weeks lived in the sick room were for Bernadette a time of great trial, physical of course but also, spiritual: the dark night of the soul.

On Wednesday 16 April 1879, during Holy Week, in the middle of the afternoon, was the hour when the spiritual adventure of Bernadette was accomplished. Like Jesus, she put her life into the hands of God.

Her body, exhumed three times during the process of beatification and canonisation (1909, 1919, 1925), and always found intact, has, since 18 July 1925, been displayed in the chapel, in a glass case, a small sign of a great story which moved millions of people.

N

Bernadette's infirmary at Nevers

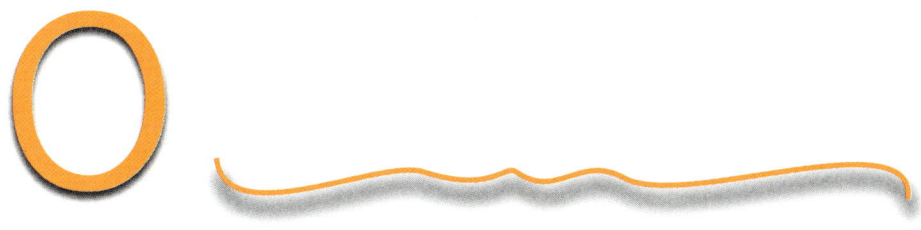

OBLATES OF MARY IMMACULATE

It was 3 March 1813, in Aix-en-Provence. In the church of St Mary Magdalene, early in the morning, a young priest of 31 was addressing the assembly in the Provencal language: 'Artisans, what are you according to the world? A class of people bound to a life of hard, obscure work which makes you dependent on, and having to submit to, the vagaries of all those you seek to work for. Domestics, what are you according to the world? A class of people, enslaved by those who pay you, exposed to scorn, to injustice and even to ill treatment from demanding and sometimes barbarous masters who believe they have the right to be unjust to you because of the paltry wages they pay you. And you, small farmers, peasants, what are you according to the world? However useful your work may be, you are valued only on the basis of the amount of work your arms can do and if the world may take account of the sweat of your brow, it is only inasmuch as this sweat can water the earth.'

Eugene de Mazenod, founder of the Oblates of Mary Immaculate

This young priest was called Eugene de Mazenod and his language was that of a revolutionary. And yet, son of a noble president of the court department of accounts, all the French Revolution had brought him, when he was only an eight year old child, was exile to Italy, which would take him from Turin to Venice, then from Naples to Palermo, until 1802, the date of his return to France.

On 27 March 1807, on Good Friday, in front of a crucifix, he experienced, in tears, the love of God. The way he would look at the realities around him from that moment would be Christ-like, in the light of the paschal mystery. 'Come now, and learn from us what you are, in the eyes of the faith. You, the poor of Jesus Christ, the afflicted, the suffering, the infirm, covered in ulcers, all of you who are oppressed by the direst poverty, my brothers, listen to me! You are the children of God, the brothers of Jesus Christ, the heirs to his eternal kingdom, the chosen portion of his heritage.'

Eugene was a strong character, a lively and impetuous man, animated by ardent desires, firm in his resolutions, whole in his will and in his feelings. He entered the seminary of Saint-Sulpice in Paris, in October 1808. After his ordination in Amiens, on Christmas Eve 1811, on his return to Aix, he never ceased to take initiatives to announce the Gospel. Along with the poor, a call which he could not resist, it was the young who retained his attention. He soon came to realize that he could not undertake this immense task on his own. On 25 January 1816, two priests, de Mazenod and Tempier, started their life in common in the ancient Carmel of Aix and, with three other companions, they sent a supplication to the vicars general of the chapter in which they asked for permission to form a regular community of missionaries. Ten years later, on 17 February 1826, Pope Leo XII approved the constitutions of this new congregation: the *Missionnaires de Provence*, by inspiration of their founder, had become 'Oblates of Mary Immaculate', a name which Fr de Mazenod defined as 'a passport to heaven and a sign of predestination'. Nowadays, more than 4,000 Oblates of Mary Immaculate, called to 'walk on the trail of the apostles' operate in sixty-five countries, spread over the five continents.

Although their name associates them closely to the dogma of the Immaculate Conception, and their founder was alive at the time of the apparitions in Lourdes, one must not deduce that the Oblates have always been present at the Shrine. The many writings of Eugene de Mazenod, who died on 21 May 1861, three years after the events, make no mention of the apparitions.

However, from the beginning, several Oblates became part of the story of Lourdes. Among the numerous events which took place, we shall cite here just three of the more significant ones:

1. At the time Bernadette was learning to read and write she met Fr Ferdinand Gondrand who had been invited by Bishop Laurence to preach at the priests' retreat in 1860. This Oblate, conquered by the visionary and convinced of the truth of her story, started to correspond with her and even asked her to give him a written account of the apparitions. In May 1861, he came to Lourdes for the second time,

again to preach a retreat, and lodged at Bétharram. Bernadette agreed to his request on 28 May 1861; this was the first written account of the apparitions. Unfortunately, having learnt of the death of Mgr de Mazenod, Fr Gondrand had to leave immediately for Marseilles. The letter was returned to Bernadette who kept it until her death.

2. In 1876, Pope Pius IX delegated Cardinal Guibert, Archbishop of Paris, Oblate of Mary Immaculate, to consecrate, in his name, the Basilica of the Immaculate Conception.

3. Foreigners started to come to Lourdes from the very beginning, but it was not until 1883, that a pilgrimage came from abroad which would equal the scale of the average French ones: 300 English pilgrims, brought by Fr Ring, O.M.I., among them, the Duke of Norfolk.

From September 1995, the Oblates of Mary Immaculate, have played an official role as chaplains, dedicating themselves to the young and to the international pastoral services.

ORGANS

The Shrines of Lourdes contain six organs. In chronological order, they are:

1. Basilica of the Immaculate Conception (often called: *Basilique Superieure*)
   a) Anonymous, small Italian organ (around 1760), restored by Barthelemy Formentelli. Wooden case painted green. Nine registers & *Tiratutti*. One manual keyboard

The organ in the St Pius X Basilica

only with short octave and small pedals. Mechanical transmission.
   b) Great organ – Aristide Cavaille-Coll (1872), of 'romantic' style. A gift to the basilica after fund-raising launched throughout all the dioceses of France: a 'manifestation of faith and hope towards Our Lady of Lourdes' and inaugurated by the most famous French organist of the time: Charles-Marie Widor. Twenty-five registers. Two manual keyboards & pedals. Mechanical transmission.

2. Basilica of Our Lady of the Rosary.
   a) Small organ for choir (1980), rebuilt by the *Pesce* firm from an old Cavaille-Coll instrument. 'Neoclassical' style. Eleven registers. Two manual keyboards & pedals.
   b) Great organ – Aristide Cavaille-Coll (1897), 'symphonic style'. Case: 'neo-Byzantine'. Also inaugurated by Widor. Forty-two registers. Three manual keyboards & pedals. Mechanical transmission.

3. Church of St Bernadette.
Great organ – Barthelemy Formentelli (1991), in the 'French baroque' style. Inaugurated by Jean-Paul Lécot. Thirty-six registers. Three manual keyboards & pedals. Mechanical transmission.

4. Basilica of St Pius X (underground)
Great organ – *Pesce* (1998), rebuilt from a Spanish organ dated 1968 and of 'neo-classical' style. Inaugurated by Jean-Paul Lécot. Fifty-four registers – 3,585 pipes. Four manual keyboards & pedals. Electrical transmission.

This organ has the greatest *chamade* – set of horizontal trumpet pipes – in France and a 32-foot *contrebombarde*.

OUTREACH OF LOURDES IN THE WORLD

In 1858, during the eighteen apparitions of the Virgin Mary to Bernadette Soubirous, one remarkable fact was the extraordinary multiplication of the number of people present at the Grotto. On the day of the first apparition, only two young girls were with Bernadette. The news of the Grotto event spread so rapidly that, twenty-one days later, more than ten thousand people had gathered round her. In addition, as soon as the national daily newspapers got hold of the news, the information reached the great cities of the five continents. France's standing in the world and that of the French language in the nineteenth century made that possible.

Very soon, pilgrims crossed the oceans to visit the Lourdes Grotto. Back in their own country these visitors would give witness by word and also by what they brought back as proof: Lourdes water. But how can one give an account of that which cannot be expressed, explained or told? They can only give their message by saying the rosary, singing the *Ave Maria* or making replicas of the Grotto. During the same period missionaries also contributed to the growing fame of Lourdes outside Europe. In the nineteenth century, three out of four missionaries were French. France had the greatest number of religious. For example, Italy had 30,000 women in religious orders, compared with 180,000 in France. Missionaries sustained their preaching by speaking about the Virgin, by building dispensaries and schools. The missionary priests, before going on the missions, would have been pilgrims in Lourdes. They knew Our Lady of Lourdes; they loved her and placed themselves spontaneously under her protection. In addition, the grace of Lourdes, that grace of love and witness, was in harmony with the foundations they were laying down. Indeed, it was in the midst of trials, illnesses, perils and anguish that they invoked Our Lady of Lourdes, promising, if they survived, to dedicate to her a church, a chapel, a Grotto. Their prayers were answered beyond their expectations, to the extent that one might say that, before the missionaries made Our Lady of Lourdes known, it was Our Lady of Lourdes who herself made the missionaries known and, through them, the Gospel. In the missions, priests and religious benefited from her presence, her help and her support. So we see a lesser known aspect of Lourdes, that of the place of the immaculate Virgin in evangelization.

While, in Europe, pilgrims and associations of welcome wove a veritable web around the Grotto, the rest of the world was also living more and more the reality of Lourdes. The publishing of the first book on Lourdes, translated into eighty languages, gave Lourdes universal fame. However, the local churches were also embracing the outreach of Lourdes. Indeed, many bishops wanted to have, in their diocese, parishes, churches and chapels, Grottos placed under the protection of Our Lady of Lourdes. Among the replicas of the Grotto of Lourdes, some constitute today the heart of the Shrines, sometimes as important as the Lourdes Shrine in France. However, nothing is set in stone. Indeed, some Grottos and churches bearing the name of Lourdes in the past, do not exist anymore, whereas, every day, somewhere in the world, other constructions, based on Lourdes, are created.

Through this incomparable outreach, Our Lady of Lourdes helps, on a worldwide basis, every one of her children to journey along the way, through a well-intentioned Marian devotion, to a life with her, Mary, mother of Jesus. This is the way how, like for Bernadette, Our Lady of Lourdes shows us Jesus Christ, leads us to him, and gives him to us, not only in Lourdes, but everywhere in the world.

PARISH CHURCH

In the church square, in the centre of the Ville Haute (upper town) stands the parish church of the Sacre-Coeur de Lourdes, visible from afar with its 65 metre spire of Pyrenean stone. On that same square is the Cénac house, where illustrious participants in the story

The present-day parish church

of the apparitions have lived: Inspector Jacomet, Fr Pene, curate of Lourdes, and Jean-Baptiste Estrade, civil servant at the Income Tax Department.

Bernadette was never in this church because its construction was planned after the apparitions. The first stone was laid in 1875 but, after Fr Peyramale's death, work was interrupted and did not start

The old parish church

again until 1896. It was inaugurated on 8 September 1903, the year that saw the demolition of the old church of St Peter, which had been Bernadette's parish church.

Two important features of the story of the apparitions are kept there: at the entrance, on the left, the baptismal fonts, made of granite from the Pyrenees, where Bernadette was baptized on 9 January 1844 and, in the crypt, the tomb of Fr Peyramale, who died on 8 September 1877. From the old church there are also two beautiful statues representing the Virgin and St John the Baptist. The sacred vessels and other objects from the church of St Peter are kept in the chapel of the castle.

The parish of Lourdes has some 17,000 inhabitants but it also serves numerous seasonal workers and the crowds of pilgrims who come to follow in the footsteps of Bernadette.

PASTORAL MINISTRY

If you do a search for 'pastoral' on the Internet, the first result would be: 'La Pastorale des Santons de Provence'. If you are a music lover, 'pastoral' may remind you of Beethoven's Pastoral Symphony. But the word 'pastoral' here in this entry doesn't have the same meaning. Where does the ambiguity come from?

The 'pastor' (shepherd) is the one who looks after his sheep in 'pastures'. The Old Testament did not hesitate to use this image for God himself: 'The Lord is my shepherd, in pastures green, he leadeth me' the psalmist sang (Ps 23). 'We are the people of his sheepfold, the flock of his hand' (Ps 95). God is the true 'pastor', as he is the true king.

If God entrusts a person with a mission, that person is not to use it in his own name but in the name of God. It was not by chance that the king, who remains the ideal king in the memory of Israel, David, was chosen as he was looking after the family flock. He never put himself in the place of the Lord God. In contrast with the surrounding peoples, Israel never divinized its kings. If the 'pastors' seek their own interest and 'feed' themselves, God will withdraw the mission entrusted to them. (Ezekiel 34)

In the New Testament, the parable of the lost sheep which the shepherd sets out to find, or that of the good shepherd who gives his life for his flock, have to be heard against the sonorous background of the Old Testament. In the same way, by the designation of Peter as the shepherd of the flock in chapter 21 of John's Gospel, Jesus entrusts this task to him because he had professed, first, his love for Christ. The scene by the lakeside ends with the obedience of Peter to Christ's order: 'Follow me', and by the announcement of his martyrdom. Let us make no mistake about it: when Jesus speaks of the Church, he says: 'my' Church, 'my' sheep. The 'pastoral ministry' is, first of all, Christ's task, acting through his Spirit.

David was the youngest of Jesse's sons. From a human point of view, it was not he who was the best placed to become king.

Bernadette, in the same way, was astonished that she had been chosen to be the Virgin's messenger. Like David, Bernadette also kept watch over sheep during her stay in Bartrès, from June 1857 to July 1858. She loved those long, quiet hours which allowed her to say her Rosary in peace.

This temporary activity must not make us imagine Bernadette as a shepherdess. Bernadette was not a country girl. Her normal life was in the context of the small town of Lourdes. Yet, the representation of Bernadette as a shepherdess has a true side to it. From 1858, an immense flock, millions of women and men have come to the Grotto to seek 'grace and happiness' as said in psalm 23, verse 6. This psalm, which we have already quoted, includes a verse which could just as well be applied to Bernadette: '… he leadeth me, the quiet waters* by'.

Bernadette had been entrusted with a message to give to Fr Peyramale: that processions, pilgrimages be made. The request from the Virgin has been fully carried out if the pilgrims, even the occasional ones, drink from the one who is the source, the spring. This objective synthesizes the pastoral role of Lourdes. In the measure in which it is accomplished, Bernadette has fulfilled perfectly her role of shepherdess according to the heart of God.

*In Lourdes, the 'quiet waters' are those of the spring which Mary indicated to Bernadette. A spring which recalls the water spurting forth from the rock to quench the thirst of the people of Israel in the desert. Spring of living water, flowing from the pierced heart of Jesus on the Cross. Spring of baptism, permeating the Church to give life to the people of the new alliance.

PAUL VI (1963-1978)

Paul VI's predecessor, Pope John XXIII, was very familiar with Lourdes. In fact, three days before he died he confided to Bishop Théas that 'Lourdes was in his heart and on his lips.' Paul VI was no less a keen Lourdes pilgrim. In 1957, as Cardinal Montini, Archbishop of Milan, he celebrated a solemn mass (Ambrosian rite) at the Shrine, and bequeathed to the Treasury Museum some priestly ornaments. In 1962 he came back with some Italian journalists.

In November 1962, at the Sec-

ond Vatican Council, on the basis of his experience as bishop of Lourdes, Bishop ThéasB asked for permission to concelebrate. On the feast of All Saints in 1963, the pope granted the Council Fathers access to the Grotto so that they could celebrate from dawn to nightfall. At this time Paul VI spoke of a new title for Mary: 'Mary, Mother of the Church' (which he later proclaimed officially on 21 November 1964). In February 1964 permission to celebrate mass in French was granted, and on 26 July 1964, *ad experimentum,* the first concelebration in France took place at Lourdes. The Holy See sent the great Italian lover of ceremony, Fr Braga, to this mass celebrated by Cardinal Ferreto, during the pilgrimage of the Diocese of Rome : twenty-four priests concelebrated and 25,000 faithful attended this unforgettable ceremony. Two days later, Bishop Théas presided at the first concelebrated mass at the Grotto, surrounded by sick priests from Italy.

The following November, accompanied by 23 bishops from other Marian Shrines, Bishop Théas concelebrated mass with the Holy Father. One week later pilgrims joyfully proclaimed the new title pronounced by the Holy Father, 'Mary, Mother of the Church'. Bishop Théas was very much aware of the role Lourdes had to play in the development of Marian devotion and the spreading of the Rosary. He prayed solidly for three days from 5-7 December 1965, as the Council drew to its close.

At Pope Paul VI's request, the year after the Council was designated a Jubilee Year to begin a time of spiritual renewal. In Lourdes, the Jubilee was memorably celebrated by the apostolic nuncio, Archbishop Bertoli, on 25 March 1966, which was a special anniversary year for many aspects of the Shrine, commemorating the consecration of the Crypt and first mass at the Grotto, the arrival of the Garraison Fathers (Missionaries of Mary Immaculate), first administrators of the Shrine, the departure of Bernadette from Lourdes to Nevers and the founding of the Sisters of Saint-Frais. The Holy Father sent his representative Cardinal Tisserand to give thanks for the exceptional work of these nuns in their care of the sick over the preceding hundred years.

Paul VI also called for the participation of artists in this spirit of renewal, and Lourdes held its first festival of sacred music in April 1968, which was a great success.

Sadly, a very different kind of movement was also making itself felt, unsettling for the Holy Father, Bishop Théas and for Christians everywhere. 'After the Council (which had wonderfully spoken of the Virgin Mary), there were those who tried to minimise its Marian theology, in order to reduce Our Lady's redemptive role, and undermine Marian devotion in the Catholic soul.' This suffocating movement, 'The breath of Satan' as the Holy Father called it, was to have far-reaching consequences, whilst bringing much sadness to Bishop Théas in his retirement. In 1970, his jubilee anniversary as a priest, Paul VI paid him a great honour saying 'It is thanks to you that great and courageous works have been undertaken at Lourdes, in order to promote and to better equip this Marian Shrine, admired by the whole world, where the marvellous spring of the Queen of Heaven and of Earth wells up and overflows, never tiring in its healing mercy.'

What Pope Paul VI appreciated very much in Lourdes, as he would later say to Bishop Donze and to the other French bishops, was popular devotion, something certain theologians tended to look down upon: 'The Grotto of Massabielle has become the meeting point for so many pilgrims, near and far, the world over. And more and more people from the diocese of Rome are benefiting from it... Popular piety can express itself in Lourdes with ease - something which is important for the vitality of the People of God' (1978). Paul VI certainly had a great love for Lourdes.

PAVILIONS

Since Vatican II, new services, based on reflection and sharing, have been offered to pilgrims in the 'pavilions' of the Shrine. The organization of those services is entrusted to the various movements concerned.

Pax Christi

To be a member of Pax Christi is to believe that peace is a gift from God and the fruit of people's labour. It is being informed about, and concerned with, the world's events to discover aspirations for peace. It is to act and to engage with all persons of good will.

Legion of Mary

'With Mary, we learn to open our heart to the grace of forgiveness and to walk on the road to conversion.'

Pastoral Service to the Family
Marriage and family counsellors offer personal consultations, family group meetings and information, to reflect with visitors on the difficulties which confront them.

Faith and Life
Through various initiatives such as readings, reflecting on the Lourdes message, talks and debates, dialogues in cafes and family orientated receptions, the objective of this pavilion is to integrate a deepening faith into one's life.

Mission
Missionaries from all five continents welcome pilgrims in this pavilion. They present to them a living Church spread all over the world. They explain to them how they live today's mission in the service of the poor and in dialogue with believers of other religions. They invite pilgrims to be witnesses of Christ: 'As the Father sent me, so I am sending you' (Jn: 20-21).

Vocations
This pavilion is part of the mission initiative for vocations by the bishops of France: 'to be, in communion with the diocese, witnesses of God who calls us to live of his love.' It invites pilgrims to follow the road leading to the source of life, Christ, and to respond to the call of the Lord to follow his way.

The CCFD (Catholic Committee against Hunger and for Development)
By looking at Bernadette as a 'person' Mary gave respect and dignity to the one who, in her own words, was 'among the weakest according to the world'.
To give to each man, each woman, each child, respect and dignity, thus allowing them to participate in humanity's transformation. Such is the hope of the CCFD in their witness.

Fr Kolbe's Mission of Mary Immaculate
This presents the life of St Maximilian Kolbe, apostle of Mary Immaculate, as an inspiration to deepen the love of Mary.

The Way of the Niglo*
Spiritual welcome for travelling people: to cater for their needs and allow them to advance in the light of the Gospel. To make the little known world of travelling people be better understood by others. To help people in general on their spiritual journey.

*Niglo means hedgehog in the language of the travelling people.

The Nest Movement
This movement is involved in the fight against prostitution and its trail of misery. God, the Father of mercy, invites all his children to conversion: clients, procurers, prostitutes having become victim of trafficking, and those who are actively fighting against this form of slavery.

PENANCE

On 24 February 1858, when Bernadette was preparing to pray in front of the Grotto, glancing briefly

The Chapel of Reconciliation

around her, she was astounded at the ever-increasing number of people present: 200, perhaps 300. Ignoring the crowd, she knelt down and, holding a candle, started saying the Rosary. As on the preceding days, her face grew pale: she was in ecstasy, transported into another world. That day, however, during that eighth apparition, something new happened: at a certain moment she stopped smiling, she seemed sad even and she got up, looking anxious, appearing to look around for something. The people nearest her saw her move her lips and saw tears rolling down her cheeks. Right to the end of this apparition, Bernadette remained agitated, moving continuously backwards and forwards.

On the way home, her teacher, Fanny Nicolan, found the courage to ask: 'Did the Lady speak to you?' Bernadette, surprised, answered: 'But how come - you were so close to me and you did not hear anything?' From the visionary's point of view, the conversation had taken place aloud. 'How did she speak to you, in French or in dialect?' 'Well, how could you think that she would speak French to me with me not knowing it!'

That evening, at the Cénac house, having been assured that Inspector Jacomet would not be present, Bernadette revealed that *aquero* had pronounced a new word: penance. And she had asked to pray to God for the conversion of sinners. She had even asked her to walk on her knees and to kiss the earth as signs of penance for sinners. The Lady seemed sad.

The following day, the people of

Lourdes rushed to the Grotto at two in the morning: all wanted the best places which, by five o'clock, were becoming difficult to find. It started raining. Comical scenes could be observed: a boy from Ade had settled himself inside the cavity where the apparitions had taken place, just at the entrance. Shouts from the crowd persuaded him to look for a better viewpoint and he found himself hanging from a rocky ridge.

Bernadette arrived, accompanied by three of her aunts and, having made her way through the crowd, started to say her Rosary. At about half past five, she took her hood off, handed her candle to one of her aunts and started advancing on her knees towards the back of the Grotto. She could be heard murmuring: 'Penance, penance, penance...' Then she went towards the Gave, but something seemed to stop her. Once again, she made towards the back of the Grotto, this time to the left, then again towards the exterior, only to turn back again. Then she started digging and raising to her face and lips, several times, the mud that she had found. And that was not all - she went as far as eating the grass. Somebody saw her Aunt Bernarde, who had remained near her all the time, wipe her face with a handkerchief and slap her face. Disappointment reigned among the people who were there: this young girl was insane!

Later, at the Cénac house, in the presence of Fr Pène and of M Estrade, the tax inspector, Bernadette explained the reasons for the strange gestures she had made on that day. '*Aquero* told me to drink and wash at the fountain. Not seeing any I went to drink from the Gave, but she signalled to me with her finger to go under the rock. I went there and found a little water, like mud, so little that it just about filled the hollow of my hand. Three times I threw it away as it was so dirty'. But why did you do all this? 'For sinners.'

In the course of those two crucial apparitions, Bernadette understood something which she repeated throughout her life: how sad it was to be far from God, and that it is necessary to intercede for the conversion of sinners. It was in those two apparitions that the message of penance, of conversion and reconciliation, so strong in Lourdes, drew its roots. They are not however to be separated from the whole of the message, which is, primarily, a promise of happiness and of a new world still to come, but already fulfilled in the Immaculate Conception.

The innumerable public testimonies of conversion which the Lourdes pilgrims have given and continue to give are an established fact. A demonstration of this is the chapel of reconciliation, transferred recently from the earlier site in the *Accueil de Notre-Dame*. A great number of priests, both Shrine chaplains and visiting priests, are available for the sacrament of reconciliation. It is therefore one of the missions of the Shrine of Lourdes to respond to the expectations of those who come, to understand that God forgives them, and wants to be reconciled with him and draw new strength from love, in the same way as one finds new energy when one washes at the spring.

PEYRAMALE, DOMINIQUE
(parish priest)

Bernadette used to say, when speaking about Fr Peyramale and Fr Sempé: 'They are the two people I love the most on earth: they accomplished the work I could not do.' Indeed, Fr Peyramale, parish priest of Lourdes from the end of 1854, was to play a major role in the events which turned his parish upside down.

Born in Momères, in the Hautes Pyrénées, he was 47 in 1858. Described by his friends as intelligent, full of imagination and sensitivity, He was rather severe-looking but with a heart of gold and a tremendous love for the poor. He was taken aback by the apparitions and did not know what to think or what to do. Undoubtedly, he should go and see… 'Go,' Bishop Laurence said. 'But people will think I am involved.' 'Then, don't go.' He knew the family and its extreme poverty and asked his curates to be prudent. M Estrade, a well-respected personality in the town, told him of his admiration for the events at the Grotto.

On 2 March, he received Bernadette who had come, trembling, to tell him about the request for a 'procession' by the unknown lady. The priest became angry and told her companion, her Aunt Basile, not to 'let her go anywhere'. The visitors left in fear. But Bernadette had to return: she had forgotten to speak about the chapel asked for by the Lady! Bernadette made her request in front of several priests and came out relieved to have given her 'message'. On 25 March, the priest was overwhelmed when hearing the name of the Lady: the 'Immaculate Conception', all the more since Bernadette did not understand its meaning. He soon became an ardent champion of Bernadette and noted the extraordinary fervour that reigned in his parish at Easter.

He prepared Bernadette for her first communion on 3 June and secretly marvelled at her piety and her progress. From then on, in his role as pastor, he did all in his power to protect the Soubirous family, particularly Bernadette, and to help in the difficult times they were about to face.

His central role would diminish progressively after the arrival of the missionaries in May 1866. The more the latter got organized to establish the facts and started to build, the more the priest was put in the shade. The historian, Lasserre, who made Lourdes famous with his book *Notre-Dame de*

Lourdes, would soon join him in an increasingly open resistance to the chaplains: the historian and the priest admired each other but did each other harm through 'a kind of exaltation which benefited no-one' (Canon Dantin).

In 1874, Bishop Langénieux made the priest of the apparitions a prelate. Immediately after, Mgr Peyramale submitted the plans for a new church which, he hoped, without saying it, would become the centre of the pilgrimages that had become such an important feature since 1872. Based on the misguided advice of his friends, he thought he would have all the money he needed. But, instead of the budget of 350,000 gold francs recommended by the bishop, Mgr Peyramale wanted to build something 'big and beautiful' and anticipated more than double that sum. The poor man had to stop all work due to lack of money and died completely ruined, on 8 September 1877. The church was only completed in 1903 with help from the Grotto estate. Bernadette had predicted that this church 'would be his tomb': he was buried in the Crypt.

His story illustrates the grave difficulties which often accompany the signs of God when they become linked to the affairs of men: Mgr Peyramale did not join in the wonderful celebrations of the coronation of the statue of the Virgin of the esplanade in July 1876, under the pretext that, being a monsignor, he should have been invited personally! Nevertheless, Mgr Peyramale will always be remembered as a devoted priest, full of charity and faith.

PHOTOGRAPHY

Photography's role in the context of the Shrine of Lourdes is an important one and is a precious resource for historians. The first photographs of Bernadette, taken in 1861 by Fr Bernardou (1822-1895), three years after the apparitions, show her, perfectly natural, just as she

was in front of the Virgin. Thanks to research done on the 75 official photographs, eminent scientists have rendered Bernadette an extraordinary homage. A profusion of information on the personalities, the places and the events which, since 1858, have marked the history of Lourdes, has been fully recorded by photography.

In human terms, it plays a great role. Here, photographing pilgrimages is a common ritual for all visitors. In this sacred place, free from commercial activities, the Shrine authorities accredit local photographic societies and authorize them to take photos of groups as requested by leaders of pilgrimages. The photographs taken on the Rosary Esplanade represent a moment of warm contact between the pilgrims and the inhabitants of Lourdes who photograph them. This will remain a moving memory for all. They reinforce in the pilgrims the deep meaning of their visit: 'to live together a strong spiritual and human experience'. Much later, the photographs will have, for future generations, the value of a witness of faith.

PICHENOT, PIERRE-ATHANASE (bishop)

Bishop Pichenot succeeded Bishop Laurence. He played an important role during his short episcopate (1870-1873).

Born in 1816 in Nuits-sous-Rivière, in the Yonne region, he was ordained priest in 1842. He was first curate, and then parish priest at the cathedral of Sens. He became vicar general and wrote practical instruction manuals. Named Bishop of Tarbes on 3 March 1870, he took up his position on the following 15 August and entered his new cathedral on 8 September. He became very quickly aware of the calumnies spread by the writer Henri Lasserre against the Missionaries of the Immaculate Conception and, particularly, against their superior, Fr Sempé. He was able to appreciate their high ideals, the zeal and the spiritual quality of their actions and gave them his complete trust.

The work of construction of the Basilica of the Immaculate Conception, interrupted by the war, was restarted under him and he was to celebrate the first mass there on 15 August 1871. The 'chapel' requested by Our Lady had been born. This place of liturgical celebration was then immediately able to respond to the flood of pilgrims coming from all over the world from 1872. At the end of that year, Bishop Pichenot founded the Confraternity of the Immaculate Conception of Our Lady of Lourdes, which would spread all over the world. Following in the steps of Bishop Laurence, he continued to acquire, for the estate of the Grotto, precious land which became the present *esplanade*, thanks to finance provided by a legacy.

On 18 June 1873, Bishop Pichenot was transferred to Chambéry. He would return several times and was present on 2 and 3 July 1876, at the great celebrations of the coronation of Our Lady of Lourdes.

PILGRIMAGE (theology)

Pilgrimage is a response to a need written in every person's heart, almost an anxiety, a dissatisfaction, which pushes one to go further, in the quest for something greater, more beautiful, more authentic.

During our life we establish milestones on a journey which, for the Christian, has a clear objective: heaven. It was the call of God which sent Abraham on his way and made him a 'wandering

Aramean', looking for the Promised Land. After him, it was the entire people of Israel which went on the move. The exodus from Egypt towards the Holy Land became the symbol of an itinerary which was to lead it from servitude to freedom, from sin to a new life, from earth to heaven. Jesus, who defined himself as 'the way', finally made possible the deliverance of the new people of God. We are here on this earth, as 'strangers and nomads' (1Peter 2:11), 'There is no permanent city for us here; we are looking for the one which is yet to be' (Hebrews 13:14).

The danger, which is always lurking, is that we forget the aim of our journey, that we content ourselves with a life spent allowing this world's contingencies to dominate us and that we settle for human realities as though nothing else was to follow, as though they represented an end in themselves. Pilgrimages are times when we are reawakened; they help us to look towards heaven, to remind us of the meaning of our journey. Scriptures show that the Hebrew people, even after having settled in the Promised Land, remained a travelling people. This was why, every year, the Hebrews had to go up to Jerusalem, to meet God. When Elijah wanted to find the 'original purity' again, he went on pilgrimage to Mount Horeb, where God had met his people and had given them his commandments.

During our pilgrimage on earth, pilgrimages are like a 'sacrament' which remind us of the ephemeral nature of the human condition, the 'perishable' or obsolete and provisional character of what we do. It is a call to live an experience of interior detachment, of asceticism, to acquire the spirit which must never be imprisoned by human realities, a call to start again on a spiritual journey with new enthusiasm and determination. Pilgrimages are not an end in themselves, but moments of grace which then allow us to go back to our everyday life, to get back to our normal activities, to let these moments penetrate and to encourage this ardent desire for heaven which the place of pilgrimage has revived. So we will find once again the good fruits of our nature and enterprise, but free of stain, burnished and transfigured, when Christ hands over to the Father: 'an eternal and universal kingdom' (*Gaudium et spes* 39).

PILGRIMAGES TO LOURDES

Pilgrimages go further back in time than Christianity. They were invented by humanity. When the Virgin Mary, during the 14th apparition, on 2 March, asked: 'that processions be made to this spot' she was no doubt alluding, at least indirectly, to the pilgrimages which are at the root of processions. Processions and pilgrimages would start soon after the official recognition of the apparitions on 18 January 1862.

The first great procession was to be on 4 April 1864, on the occasion of the installation of the statue of Our Lady in the Grotto. The whole town was celebrating and a beautiful procession, which a famous engraving would later immortalize, went down the hairpin bends to the Grotto. Neither Fr Peyramale nor Bernadette were able to be present.

The first pilgrimage took place on 21 July 1864. The village of Loubajac, 8 km from Lourdes, a native of which, Catherine Latapie, had been miraculously cured on 1 March 1858, organized the first official pilgrimage, with mass in the parish church and a procession to the Grotto - humble beginnings, in the style of the apparitions. This example would be followed later by all the French provinces, at the instigation of people such as Fr Marie-Antoine, from Toulouse, one of the greatest preachers of the Shrine.

On 21 May 1866, Bishop Laurence celebrated the first mass at the Grotto and inaugurated the practice of devotion at that place before a considerable crowd, with 300 priests, while Fr Duboe, as chaplain, exhorted the assembly. Bernadette, who was by then 22 years and five months old, was there, hidden among the *Enfants de Marie* (Children of Mary). Two months later, on 4 July 1866, she left Lourdes forever.

On the initiative of Fr Chocarne, parish priest of Beaune, and his brother, a Dominican, the first national pilgrimage was organized under the patronage of leading personalities, from 5 to 8 October 1872. It was hugely successful. This 'Pilgrimage of Banners' left its 250 banners at the Basilica of the Immaculate Conception where they were to remain for more than a century.

At the beginning of July 1876, the coronation of Our Lady of Lourdes, the statue of the esplanade, was the pretext for magnificent celebrations, gathering considerable crowds.

In 1877, the passionate Fr d'Alzon, founder of the Assumptionists, came with thirty sick people. The idea of a national pilgrimage with sick people had just been born. It would give rise to the great pilgrimage of 1878, with 300 sick, led by the Assumptionists, and by the famous Fr Picard, a popular leader and organizer.

The number of pilgrimages continued to increase. Interrupted by the 1914-18 war, they started again from 1919, as a thanksgiving from the land and nautical forces.

The beatification of Bernadette on 14 June 1925, but above all her canonization on 8 December 1933, were the occasion of great gatherings.

In 1934, from 22 to 24 September, the first international army pilgrimage, with veterans from 19 nations, gathering 60,000 persons and under the presidency of Cardinal Lienart, prayed for peace in the name of Christian fraternity.

At the end of April 1935, one of the greatest manifestations of all times, was the closure of the *triduum* of the redemption, presided over by Cardinal Pacelli, the future Pope Pius XII. For three days, some 60 cardinals, archbishops and bishops, more than 4,000 priests and 250,000 pilgrims participated in the celebration. For three days, masses were said at the Grotto without interruption.

After the war there was the pilgrimage of war veterans in 1945. 1958 was the year of the centenary.

The annual military pilgrimages started in 1958. The most original and most festive pilgrimage was organized by the Faith and Light Movement, led by Jean Vanier, from 10 to 12 April 1971: the pilgrimage for those with learning difficulties. Initially this pilgrimage was not understood by the authorities, but eventually it proved to be a miracle of joy, of coming together and of faith.

Innumerable groups of various origins organize pilgrimages. Let us mention, finally, the very beautiful gathering of July 1981, on the occasion of the eucharistic Congress, at which Pope John Paul II was to be present. The attempt on his life on 13 May, however, prevented him from attending. But he was to come in 1983 and again in 2004.

Mosaic of Pius IX on the wall of the Basilica of the Immaculate Conception, made in the Vatican and sent by the pope himself

PIUS IX (1846-78)

Pius IX's time as pope coincided almost exactly with Bernadette's life (1844 – 1879). He had a profound love for Lourdes, stemming from the apparition of 25 March 1858 when Our Lady revealed her name to Bernadette, with the words 'I am the Immaculate Conception.'

Pius IX saw this as direct confirmation of the dogma of the Immaculate Conception, by Our Lady personally, which he had pronounced four years earlier, on 8 December 1854. The Bishop of Lourdes officially declared the authenticity of the apparitions in 1862, and Pius IX gave his own special blessing for the building of the future 'chapel', referring to 'the illuminating evidence of the clement Mother of God'.

In moments of prayer and contemplation he particularly treasured two personal gifts, a small replica of the Grotto, and an image depicting the apparition of 25 March : 'When my soul is desolate,' he said, 'if God remains deaf to my prayers, I will lift up my eyes to Mary Immaculate.'

On 13 March 1874, after greatly praising the work of Fr Sempé and Fr Peyramale, he raised the newly built 'chapel' to the rank of minor basilica, from which moment it became the Basilica of the Immaculate Conception. He also blessed the plans for the next church, the Basilica of the Most Holy Rosary.

On 2 July 1876 great festivities took place in Lourdes to celebrate the consecration of the basilica and at the same time the crowning of the Virgin of the Esplanade. The Holy Father sent Cardinal Guibert, Oblate of Mary Immaculate and archbishop of Paris, as his representative.

The statue of Our Lady of Lourdes was crowned by the papal nuncio Mgr Meglia.

Towards the end of 1876, before leaving for Rome, Bishop Ladoue asked Bernadette to write a letter to the Holy Father. We have three drafts offered by the humble nun. The final version begins with these words: 'I would never have dared to put pen to paper, to write to your Holiness, despite my desire to do so, me, a poor little sister, without the encouragement of our most worthy bishop. It is several years since I made myself, unworthy though I am, your humble servant; my weapons are prayer and sacrifice which I shall guard until my last breath.'

The following year, the pope placed a statue in honour of Our Lady of Lourdes in a great hall in the Vatican. This was followed by a very special gift, taken to Lourdes on his behalf by a pilgrimage from Italy, *la rose d'or*, (the golden rose) which can be seen in the Treasury Museum among the precious gifts offered to the Shrine.

The Holy Father died just a few months before Bernadette.

PIUS X (1903-14)

Pius X wanted to lead an Italian pilgrimage to Lourdes in 1902 while he was still Patriarch of Venice, but poor health prevented him. His deep love for the blessed Virgin left him greatly in awe of the apparitions: 'I consider the apparitions at Lourdes, and all that has resulted from them, so wonderful, timely and healing as to be one of the most significant graces the Church has received following her proclamation of the dogma of the Immaculate Conception.'

On arriving at the Vatican, his first task was to adorn the Grotto set up in the garden by his predecessor, and to entrust himself to Our Lady of Lourdes, through his intermediary Bishop Schoepfer, Bishop of Lourdes.

In 1907, at the request of 24 cardinals and 466 bishops, he extended the 'Office of the Apparition', instituted by his predecessor, Leo XIII, to the universal Church. The following year, 1908, he nominated Cardinal Lécot as his papal legate to represent him at the celebrations of the fiftieth anniversary, and in 1914 Cardinal Granito of Belmonte acted as papal legate during the International Eucharistic Congress, held in Lourdes, 'the most

Mosaic of Pius X, by Facchina, at the entrance to the crypt

glorious of eucharistic thrones in the Catholic world' (July 1914).

He was called to the next life on 18 August, having set in motion the process for Bernadette's beatification and canonisation.

PIUS XI (1922-39)

Cardinal Achille Ratti came to pray at Lourdes in 1893 and again in 1921 whilst leading an Italian pilgrimage from 29 August to 5 September. Six months later he became Pope Pius XI, and continued to treasure the memory of those wonderful days.

With great joy he announced the beatification of Bernadette on 14 June 1925, entering the brilliantly illuminated Basilica of St Peter to venerate the relics of the humble visionary. In 1926 he raised the Church of the Rosary to the rank of minor basilica. Now both churches were basilicas, unique in their proximity to each other.

It is not surprising that the Holy Father chose 11 Feb as the date for signing the famous Lateran Agreement with Mussolini in 1929, ending the long period of separation between Church and State. That was the date Our Lady herself had chosen to begin writing 'one of the most luminous pages, in the history of the Church.'

Pope Pius XI canonised Bernadette on 8 December 1933 with the words: 'O Lourdes! Admire the honour and glory of the Immaculate Virgin Mary, but see also a unique reflection of her holiness in Bernadette Soubirous. See how many people who, having strayed

Bishop Schoepfer with Cardinal Ratti, the future Pius XI

from their Christian path, have returned to their mother, the Church, thanks to Lourdes. How many, whose lives have been stained by many vices, have discovered at Lourdes a new and better life. Still how many more have felt called to follow the way of perfection! How many of the sick and disabled have found healing! We ourselves feel called with all our hearts to enter in spirit the Grotto of the Immaculate Virgin, to pay her homage...'

In 1935, Pope Pius XI chose to conclude the Jubilee of the Redemption at Lourdes, sending Cardinal Pacelli, his secretary of state, and closest confidant to represent him, proof indeed of his special love for Lourdes.

PIUS XII (1939-58)

Cardinal Pacelli first came to Lourdes in 1935 as papal legate to Pius XI, to mark the close of the Jubilee

Year, celebrating 1900 years since the redemption. He was deeply moved. He commented to Bishop Gerlier: 'I have been longing to come and pray at the Grotto, whose walls heard the voice of the Immaculate Conception as she spoke her most blessed name to Bernadette. O Lourdes! What holiness. You repeat the wonder of Nazareth, the sacredness of Bethlehem, and the healing waters of Bethsaida.' As he celebrated the last mass of the triduum, 250,000 pilgrims were present.

Four years later, as Pope Pius XII, he entrusted himself to Our Lady of Lourdes, through his intermediary Bishop Choquet of Lourdes and Tarbes, whom he had received in a private audience on 15 March 1939.

In July 1946, on the death of Bishop Choquet, the pope nominated Bishop Théas, a fervent and apostolic administrator of the diocese, to be the new Bishop of Lourdes. The nomination was met with joyful enthusiasm.

The pilgrimages resumed that same year. Pius XII called for a renewal of faith through the praying of the Rosary. The international situation was still precarious, threatened by a sinister underlying atheism.

In 1948, an exceptional sporting event took place whose echo was felt throughout Europe, including the Vatican: on 7 July 1948, the Tour de France passed through Lourdes. Gino Bartali, stopped at the Grotto to pray, and then went on to win the race. The pope was overjoyed. Bartali was held up as a shining example to the 300,000

Mosaic of Pius XII on the wall of the Rosary Basilica

men of Catholic Action in Italy.

1954 marked the centenary of the dogma of the Immaculate Conception. In his encyclical: *Fulgens Corona*, Pius XII affirmed again how much Mary's words: 'I am the Immaculate Conception', could be recognised as a direct confirmation of the famous dogma proclaimed by Pius IX.

The rector of the Shrine, Mgr Ricaud said the following: 'What an honour for Lourdes to find itself at the heart of all the Shrines of Mary, Mother of God; to be a focal point and a centre of Marian devotion and prayer for all Christians.'

The pope's invitation to pray the Rosary was taken up by all who set out on foot to make their pilgrimage. As a token of gratitude, a mosaic medallion of Pius XII was placed on the façade of the Rosary Basilica.

On 16 January 1956, the Holy Father blessed and approved the plans for the future underground basilica presented by Bishop Théas.

Bishop Théas showing the plans for the underground basilica to Pius XII

The Vatican promised two million francs to complete the project. Work began in March, but by October things had gone badly wrong because the site had filled with water. By December the Vatican had spent three million francs and still only a lake was visible. The project had to be suspended. Fortunately, thanks to the remarkable tenacity of the building contractor (who was sure of his facts), and the faith of Bishop Théas, the project eventually succeeded. This highly original building, superb in technical detail and achievement, was completed in time for the centenary, and the magnificent consecration ceremony by the papal legate, Mgr Roncalli. Pope Pius XII died a few months later on 9 October 1958, whilst the Rosary pilgrimage was taking place in Lourdes.

PLOËRMEL BROTHERS

In 1919, Fr Jean-Marie de la Mennais (1780-1860) founded an institute of brothers in Brittany to serve village schools. They were soon to be called the Ploërmel Brothers. Their institute developed rapidly and was of help to many. The founder was the brother of Felicité de la Mennais, also a priest, author of some famous passionate books which were condemned by Rome in 1832. Felicité left the Church and the affair attracted a lot of attention. Jean-Marie suffered a great deal from his brother's actions and led a saintly life: the cause for his beatification has been opened.

The parish of Lourdes requested the presence of the brothers at the end of 1854. They consequently arrived in 1855 and the local boys' school was put under their management. At the time of the apparitions, the head was Br Leobard Bourgneuf. He deemed it necessary to question Bernadette after the famous apparition of 25 March, which was seared in people's minds. As he did not speak the local language, the only one Bernadette spoke, he asked for Br Cerase's help. Br Cerase was a teacher at the primary school from 29 September 1857 to 25 August 1859.

We are in possession of the letter written by Br Cérase to his family, which follows point by point the interrogation led by Br Leobard Bourgneuf. There is some confusion, and, in part, a lack of precision in this account, but it is faithful to the story; it is a source which should not be neglected.

Br Cérase quoted Mary as saying during the apparition of 25 March, 'Je suis Marie Immaculée' (I am Mary Immaculate). The unequivocal phrase of Our Lady: 'I am the Immaculate Conception' was practically incomprehensible in 1858. Going back on his account in April 1881, the brother declared to Fr Cros, a Jesuit and a great investigator of the Lourdes events, 'I cannot say why I wrote in my letter *je suis Marie Immaculée*. I may have thought that this formula was exactly the same thing as *je suis l'Immaculée Conception*.'

In December 1858, the director of the school wrote a long and very interesting dissertation of twenty-one pages for the benefit of his institute. Unfortunately, we do not have the original copy – all we have is the incomplete draft of an account recounted to fr Cros after 1878. The brother was impressed by the apparitions and the miracles, but he was disconcerted by the humble appearance and the relaxed ways of Bernadette: it did not correspond to his idea of an interlocutor of the Queen of Heaven! The same thing could be said of Mother Marie-Therese Vauzou, in Nevers.

After the apparitions, in 1884, a church school was opened beside the chaplains' house. The two teachers at the school were Ploërmel brothers. In 1893, Fr Cramaussel was asked by the Garaison Fathers to establish a choir school there. In 1894, it became a boarding school.

In 1975, in the context of the reorganisation of Catholic schools, the recruiting of a minimum of 27 children to keep the basic contract with the State was becoming more and more difficult and the Choir School (which provided many priests to the diocese of Tarbes) was closed. A community of brothers remains, however, at the service of the Shrines.

Nowadays, various missions are entrusted to them: organisation (masses, Rosaries, processions) office administration for masses, gifts, correspondence and the distribution of the water. They bring many skills to their work and their presence contributes to the spirit which radiates from the Shrines.

POIRIER, ALEXANDRE (bishop)

After the long reign of Bishop Schoepfer, came the very short one of Bishop Alexandre Poirier (1866-1928). Born in 1866 in Saint-Michel-l'Herm, in the diocese of Luçon, he was ordained priest in 1890. Secretary to the bishop, after a stay in Rome, he soon became vicar general and then prelate of His Holiness. At the same time, he was director of the Vendée pilgrimages and his devotion was such that Bishop Schoepfer named him honorary chaplain of Our Lady of Lourdes. Quite naturally, he was chosen when the time came for naming an auxiliary to Bishop Schoepfer, then aged 82. Eighteen months later, when the bishop died, his successor, who had lived in the chaplains' residence, moved into the bishop's house and took over an administration which he knew well already.

Unfortunately, he did not have time to carry out the projects which he had spent a long time planning. He was only able to restore the tower and the spire of the Basilica of the Immaculate Conception and to have a dwelling built for the caretaker of the bishop's residence. He died on 25 August 1928, after an operation, one year after his predecessor.

In March 1928, just before he died, he obtained permission from the Holy See to establish the all-embracing pious association of Our Lady of Lourdes which brought together all the associations of the same name: thus more than 60 French *hospitalités* and around 20 from abroad were affiliated to Lourdes and were able to benefit from many indulgences and spiritual favours granted by a decree of the 'Sacred Penitentiary'* of 12 May 1928.

* Sometimes known as the 'Apostolic Penitentiary', it is a religious tribunal which is granted the power of absolving certain sins.

POMIAN, BERTRAND-MARIE (priest)

Fr Bertrand-Marie Pomian (1822-1893), confessor of Bernadette, curate in the parish of Lourdes, was the first person to be told of the apparitions. He was 36 at the time.

Born in Aveux, in the Hautes-Pyrénées, in 1822, he was ordained priest on 15 December 1846. Hav-

ing filled the role of curate in Castelnau-Magnoac and Ossun, he was named vicar in Lourdes in 1851. We have a letter from his parish priest, Fr Peyramale, dated 13 February 1857, one year before the apparitions, in which he suggests to Bishop Laurence, that Fr Pomian be chosen as chaplain of the Lourdes hospice. He justified his choice by listing his qualities: his zeal at the time of the cholera epidemic, his dedication and the sober depth of his sermons. Bernadette had not chosen her confessor without care.

Two days after the famous meeting of 11 February, Bernadette went to her confessor to tell him that she had seen 'something white with the shape of a lady' in the Grotto. Intrigued, he asked her permission to speak about it to the parish priest who had not heard anything about it yet. 'We must wait,' was Fr Peyramale's response.

Bernadette returned to the Grotto on 12 February. On that day, her mother had taken her to school to prevent her from going to the Grotto. However, a mysterious force made her go, provoking the fury of policeman Sergeant d'Angla. Disappointment... the Virgin did not appear on that day! Bernadette went to consult her confessor who said: 'No-one has the right to stop you!'

On 1 March, a young priest, Antoine Désirat, was present at the apparition and was filled with wonder, the only priest to go to the Grotto; on that day, a certain Louis Fourcade brought coins left by people to Fr Pomian for a mass to be said on the special date, 4 March, which was to bring to a close the fortnight of the apparitions. People bringing money from the Grotto to the clergy had become a fairly frequent event.

Fr Pomian did not tell Bernadette, on 25 March, the meaning of Mary's words 'I am the Immaculate Conception' which she had reported to him. Like Fr Peyramale, who wept with emotion alone in his room after the departure of Bernadette, he must have been too stunned. It was M Estrade who explained the meaning to Bernadette that afternoon.

A man of great discretion, Fr Pomian never talked about Bernadette, apart from a short oral communication in 1878. When Zola asked for some revelations, in 1891, he had this message for him: 'Tell M Zola that I shall not be able to give him any more information other than that which has already been written; the rest is the concern of the confessor and the confessor does not speak.'

Two years later, Fr Pomian died in Lourdes at the age of 71.

POPULAR RELIGION

Popular religion means the exterior manifestations of faith and piety. It is the way in which Christianity takes root in various environments and how it is lived by people. It is expressed by prayers and rites such as novenas, pilgrimages, feast days, sacred representations, iconography, relics, the blessing of objects and offerings of thanksgiving. By using the various symbols which have been introduced over centuries and which are solidly anchored in popular culture, Christianity is able to express the most profound manifestations of people's hearts: the religious dimension.

Popular religion, which developed in parallel to the official expressions of the liturgy and to the codified norms of Christian life, is not in opposition to them but integrates them. Indeed popular religion calls for spontaneity, intuition, feelings and a sense of festivity. It introduced into devotion an attitude which is less intellectual and less formal, and more spontaneous and appealing to the emotions.

The attitudes it reflects are varied and contradictory in appearance. On the one hand, it underpins strongly the sense of mystery. It exalts for example the prerogatives of Mary by representing her as different from us, sublime, entirely holy. It emphasizes the aspects of wonder and of prodigy of the saints. But, at the same time, it reminds us that the divine is extremely close and makes it more 'human' to us, one might say. The saints become intercessors and advocates for our causes because they have gone through the same trials as us.

When it is the expression of a sincere faith, popular religion opens the way to the sacraments, to an ever deeper understanding of the word of God, to a Christianity which is lived and authentic, felt and personal. However, when it moves away from the source of the Gospel and from the liturgy and is posing as an autonomous expression of religious sentiment, it can degenerate into superstition, or magic, or give birth to sects.

The Apostolic Exhortation *Marialis Cultus* (No.39), recalling the link between devotion to Mary and evangelical life, presents a solid criterion for measuring the value of all expressions of popular religion: 'When the children of the Church unite their voices with the voice of the unknown woman in the Gospel and glorify the mother of Jesus by saying to him: 'Blessed is the womb that bore you and the breasts that you sucked' (Lk.11:27), they will be led to ponder the divine master's serious reply: 'Blessed rather are those who hear the word of God and keep it!' (Lk.11:28).

PRAYER

The events at the Grotto were initiated by the teaching of the sign of the cross, by the unexpected gust

of wind, through the grace of a light which assumed the form of a face. Mary appeared to a child of the poor in a black hole in the rock. She lit up her path and gave meaning to her life by revealing to her the tenderness with which God had always enveloped her, a God who is all love and giving.

The apparitions were to be punctuated by the saying of the Rosary which is a simple meditation on the passage of God among humanity. Bernadette would receive the mission to pray, do penance 'for sinners', thus entering into the passion of Christ for the lost sheep in this world whom he loves so much. 'For sinners' she would readily imitate the gestures of the Virgin. 'For sinners' there would rapidly be processions and a chapel, confessions and eucharistic celebrations, when people nourish themselves anew with the gift of God.

Lourdes would become the capital of prayer. Those wounded by life very soon felt at home there, sure of finding a source of hope and peace. People from all walks of life and from many different nations come here to pray for the world's problems. Lourdes represents the welcome of a mother who never judges her children but gathers them together and shows them God's forgiveness and the way to mutual pardon: Lourdes, place of healing and mercy.

Prayer in Lourdes is the Rosary; it is the Church liturgy which is no longer confined to an enclosed space but deployed in the open, in freedom; it is the prayer for the needs and hopes of the world. Prayer in Lourdes is the secret *rendezvous*, silent and public at the same time, with this God who had been waiting from all time but who was not known or no-one wanted to know. 'It is the first time that I have seen a forty-year old man pray in public,' a young French woman commented. Each person present is alone in private prayer and, at the same time, united with everyone in the same atmosphere of tenderness.

PRESBYTERY

In the town, going up the back street of Boly, one arrives in front of the remains of a garden wall with a little door. An inscription explains its importance: 'Through this door passed Bernadette.'

Behind it is hidden the house of Lavigne. In 1858, the two tenants of that house were M Lannes, a tobacco merchant, and Fr Peyramale. At first, the latter did not pay too much attention to the rumours, and yet he was more troubled than he would admit. Men and women of integrity 'with their heads squarely on their shoulders' spoke seriously and positively about the events which were taking place at the Grotto.

On Tuesday 2 March, such a large crowd was expected that a few people decided to go there during the night. Among them was a group of women of unshakeable faith, but always ready to divulge, in 'strictest' secrecy, what they believed they knew. At the end of the apparition they surrounded Bernadette and urged her to speak. Bernadette did not give in but ended up by saying: '*Aquero* asks for a procession.' At that, the devout women rushed to the presbytery and, on their way, distorted what they had heard: 'The Holy Virgin wants a procession on Thursday!'

Thus, when Bernadette, her aunts Bernarde and Basile at her side, appeared at the door, hardly had she time to say: '*Aquero* asks that processions be made to the Grotto' than the priest flew into a violent rage. Aunt Bernarde, finding

this unbearable, went away silently. As to Basile, she remained, but she was shaking like a leaf. Bernadette tried to recall the exact words of *aquero*, but was unable to do so and was shown the door.

On the way back to the *cachot*, she realized that she had had neither the time nor the opportunity to give the message in its entirety. Since no-one in her family was willing to accompany her, she went to see Dominiquette Cazenave, the sacristan. The latter knew the parish priest well and how to get round him.

At around seven in the evening, terrified but resolute, Bernadette knocked a second time on the little garden door and was able to carry out her mission: 'Father, *aquero* said to me: "Go and tell the priests to have a chapel built here."' Once outside, she found her smile again and returned to the *cachot* with a light step.

PRESS

The press has played a historical and a vital role in communicating the message of Lourdes. From the time of the recognition of the apparitions by the Bishop of Tarbes in 1862, *Le Lavedan*, a literary weekly from the Argelès valley, recounted in a quasi official manner, the events linked to the Shrines of Lourdes, which were then in their early stages. It was succeeded by *Le Journal de Lourdes*, in 1865, followed by *Le Journal de la Grotte de Lourdes* published by the religious in charge of the pastoral services of the Shrines. Further, the *Organe of-*

ficial des pèlerinages et du Bureau de constatations médicales (official organ of pilgrimages and of the bureau for medical reports and findings) was in place as a fortnightly publication. Maximilian Kolbe, according to his writings, had a subscription to the latter in the 1930s, before his departure for Japan.

Parallel to this publication, and designed to go into greater depth with the message of the apparitions of Massabielle, the *Annales de Notre-Dame de Lourdes* was published monthly from 1868 to 1944. The magazine *Recherches sur Lourdes* took over in 1963 on the initiative of the historian René Laurentin and, from 1964, came under the management of Dom Bernard Billet. Its objective was to target a large public, a mission which continued until 1984. The day after the first journey of a pope to Massabielle, a new dynamism emerged with the creation, in 1985, of the magazine *Lourdes*, a quarterly supplement to the *Journal de la Grotte*. This new inspiration found its fulfilment in the *Lourdes Magazine* and its international publications which have existed since 1991.

To give more specific information to the leaders of pilgrimages, the press service of the Shrines published the leaflet *'Allez dire'* ('go and tell'). The *Hospitalité de Notre-Dame de Lourdes* also has a *bulletin de liaison*, a supplement to the *Recherches sur Lourdes* at first, but which is now independent. Fr Henri Joulia, one of the chaplains of the *hospitalité*, was the soul of this publication. Finally, another bulletin linked to the pastoral service of Lourdes is that of the *Association Médicale internationale de Lourdes* (AMIL), *Fons Vitae*, translated into five languages.

PROMINENT WOMEN
(linked to the apparitions)

A number of women played a significant role during the apparitions. The first was a certain Mme Milhet (1813-1892) who, on her own authority, had taken Bernadette to her home, at the very beginning, from 18 to 20 February 1858, as she wanted to obtain information on the events at the Grotto. Bernadette's mother worked for her. She had married M Milhet, in whose house she had worked as a servant, and had inherited a considerable fortune.

On the morning of 18 February she and her friend Antoinette Peynet (1835-1892), daughter of the bailiff, escorted Bernadette, who was anxious to go to the Grotto that day, at five o'clock in the morning, for a third visit, a week after the first apparition. During this visit, Mary spoke for the first time, 'in her fine voice' and asked Bernadette to come for a fortnight, promising to make her happy in the 'other world'. Mlle Peynet had brought a writing case which the Virgin judged unnecessary. Mme Milhet made Bernadette ask if 'their presence was not "unwelcome".' On the way back, Mme Milhet whispered: 'What if it were the Holy Virgin?'

On 21 February, Inspector Jacomet interrogated Bernadette for the first time. He asked her if the 'lady' whom she saw was beautiful:

Madame Pailhasson

'Oh, yes sir, very pretty!' 'Beautiful like who? Like Mme Pailhasson? Like Mlle Dufo?' 'N'y poden pas he' (they cannot compare!).

Mme Pailhasson (1827-86) was a woman of great beauty, very elegant, and mother of five children. As for Mlle Dufo, daughter of the president of the Bar, she had just got engaged to a journalist, Romain Cabdevielle, whom she later married. Recalling these noteworthy women, Fr Laurentin remarked: 'The points of comparison were not mediocre.' We may point out that Marie Dufo's sister was a close friend of Bernadette. She died a nun and Bernadette corresponded with her till the end of her life.

PYRENEES

Lourdes is situated in the heart of the Pyrenees, the mountain chain of south-west Europe which spreads from the Mediterranean Sea to the Atlantic Ocean and constitutes a barrier between the Iberian peninsula, in the south, and continental Europe in the north, forming thus a natural border between France and Spain.

There are three hypotheses on the origin of the name 'Pyrenees':

1. It came from the Greek *Pyrene*, name of the daughter of King *Bebryx*. According to legend, Pyrene was killed by a brown bear and Hercules, whose baby she was carrying, gave her name to these mountains, where she was laid to rest.

2. According to the second hypothesis, the name is derived from the Hispano-Celtic word, *piren*,

which means *mountains*. But it is much more probable that the word Pyrenees, before entering our various languages, would have been introduced to Latin from Greek.

3. A text by Diodore, from Sicily, recounts that the forests, which covered the Pyrenees during a prolonged period, were burnt down by shepherds. Even the earth was burnt, giving birth to pure silver burns. From the ancient Greek, pyr=fire, the name Pyrenees was given to these mountains.

None of these etymologies can be established with certainty, but it is agreeable to think that the events of Lourdes happened in this land of fire and of silver burns.

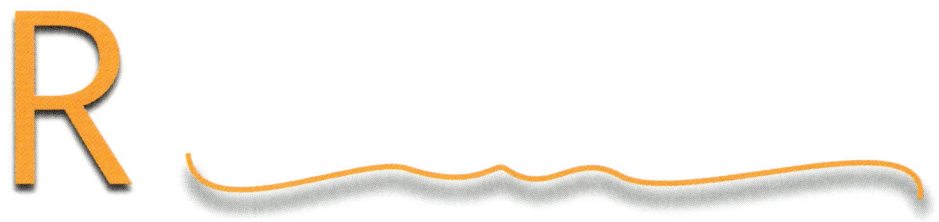

RADIO

Radio Présence Lourdes Pyrénées, the Catholic radio station linked to the Lourdes Shrine, is a diocesan radio station, created in 1993 by Fr Henri Joulia, chaplain of Lourdes (M.I.C.), which covers the Hautes-Pyrénées, the Gers and the Pyrénées Atlantiques. It broadcasts local information, prayers and programmes on the life of the diocese and on the current events of the Shrine.

Since 1999, *Radio Présence LP* constitutes, along with four other Christian radio stations, the first *regional* network of Christian radios. With fourteen frequencies at its disposal, the network covers a large area of two million inhabitants and produces a daily programme of eight hours, fruit of the collaboration of the radio stations.

The national programme, as well as the night programme, is provided by the *Communauté Francophone de Radio Chrétienne* (French-speaking community of Christian radio) which links 60 French language radio stations from all over the world, covered by satellites over France and Africa. The local stations use the COFRAC programmes but also contribute their own. *Radio Présence Lourdes Pyrénées* broadcasts the Rosary from the Grotto, daily at 15h30 and also, punctually, ceremonies of interest to Catholics across the world.

External stations wishing to broadcast from Lourdes have at their disposal a studio and technical facilities. The recording and broadcasting of the high points of pilgrimages are possible thanks to a duplication service.

Finally, *Radio Présence Lourdes Pyrénées*, also offers programmes on the internet: Rosary at the Grotto, prayers, interviews, are all accessible on the website *www.radiopresence.com* and on the wesite of the Shrines:
www.lourdes-france.org.

RAVIER, ANDRÉ

Fr André Ravier (1905-1999), an eminent Jesuit and expert in spirituality, had become famous for his brilliant work on St Francis de Sales, whose works he had published in the collection of the Pleiade* in 1969. He was also very interested in Bernadette: in 1958, for the centenary of the apparitions, he published *Bernadette et son chapelet* (Bernadette and her Rosary) which met with great success and was translated into various languages, like several of his other works.

He wrote more than a dozen books on Bernadette, on her life, her spirituality, her rapport with priests, on what the eucharist meant to her and on the state of her body after her death. But his principal research was *Les Écrits de Sainte Bernadette*, a book published under this title in 1961, republished with corrections in 1980 and in print ever since. It is undoubtedly one of the most interesting and profound books ever written about this engaging saint.

In the introduction to his work, Fr Ravier mentions the great difficulties which he had come up against while working on the texts: were they a true reflection of Bernadette's thoughts, had they been dictated, arranged, reconstituted? How could he get to the originality, the flow of Bernadette's thought, often so personal and so innovative? He states his conviction that, despite Fr Laurentin's and Fr Billet's appeals, there are still many 'notes' and private documents which have remained hidden in private archives.

The mass of documents which are in our possession are divided into eight sections, each one marking a stage in Bernadette's life between the apparitions and her death, on 16 April 1879. To start with, those very precious autobiographical accounts, recounting the apparitions; then the letters and, finally, and most importantly, the precious little notebook *Carnet de notes intimes*, which she kept between 1873 and 1875, one of the most significant documents we have retained. Fr Ravier used it in a masterly fashion to study Bernadette's spirituality.

* *Bibliotheque de la Pleiade* a French collection of books. The entry into the 'Pleiade' is considered a major sign of recognition for an author in France.

RECTORS

The great pilgrimages started at the end of 1871, but before that, it had already been necessary to organize the chaplains and to give them a superior: Fr Sempé, who became superior of the chaplains and would also take the role of rector of the Shrines, with the responsibility of supervising ongoing events. Fr Sempé was named prior of the Missionaries of the Immaculate Conception after the death of their founder, Fr Peydessus and another Garaison Father, Fr Carrère (1883-1891) succeeded him. Below is a list of his successors:

Bordedebat: 1891-1894
Fournou: 1894-1902
Pointis: 1902-1904
Ozon: 1904-1925
Mericq: 1925-1932
Dupont: 1932-1938
Ricaud: 1938-1957
Viscaro: 1957-1972

de Roton:	1972-1978
Bordes:	1978-1993
de Roton:	1993-1998
Jacquin:	1998-2003

As can be seen, Fr Ozon, during the long period starting from the departure of the religious, who were banned in 1903, had to have another organization take over their duties. From then on, the rector would be a priest of the diocese. In 1947, the Garaison Fathers were able to come back and to resume their function as chaplains. The diocesan priests having become fewer, Bishop Perrier launched an appeal, in 1988, for priests outside the diocese, for the first time since the beginning. The rector who succeeded Fr Patrick Jacquin, who became rector of *Notre-Dame de Paris*, is the former rector of the Shrine of Lisieux, Fr Zambelli.

ROCK

The apparitions took place at the Grotto of Massabielle, an old rock. Mountains in the Bible, from Sinai to Mount Tabor, are particular places where God manifests himself, and Grottos are places where man seeks refuge, such as David fleeing Saul, or Elijah, threatened by Queen Jezabel.

Rock contains the idea of solidity, support. Psalms refer to this repeatedly: 'Be for me a rockfastness' (31), 'Blessed be the Lord, my rock' (144). Passing under the Grotto is no longer only an act of veneration for the place where Mary appeared, a simple kiss, but a sign of faith. One can put one's hand on the walls of the Grotto to seek support, with a prayer from the heart:' Lord I lean on you, my refuge, I believe in you.'

Rock also recalls hardness. In this world we can say: 'Take away my heart of stone, give me a heart of flesh' (cf. Ezekiel 11: 19). One can also think of the Church and pray with confidence: 'You are Peter and on this rock I will build my Church and the gates of the underworld can never overpower it' (Mt. 16, 18).

Enlightened by the Bible and by the message, this gesture, which could appear sentimental, superstitious even, becomes a sign of faith which commits humanity: it still continues to live in the life of the pilgrims, after Lourdes, so that they may become living rocks in the Church.

ROSARY

The Rosary, one of the most popular and most used of prayers, has a history dating back nearly a thousand years. It was born in the monasteries, at the beginning of the 12th century, when illiterate monks replaced the 150 psalms with the reciting of 150 Hail Marys. In the 14th century, the Carthusian monk Henri de Kalkar, divided the 'Aves' into fifteen decades and integrated in each the reciting of the Our Father. At the beginning of the 15th century, the prayer started to be divided according to the recalling of some of the events related in the Gospel. In 1569, a Dominican pope, St Pius V, recommended this prayer to the whole Church, at which time it had already acquired its present form. (St Dominic and his order have contributed greatly to the formulation and the circulation of the Rosary). As Pius V said, it is a way of praying which is: 'easy, within everyone's reach, and which consists of honouring the blessed Virgin by the reciting of 150 Hail Marys, in accordance with the number of David's psalms, while adding to each decade the Lord's prayer and very precise meditations illustrating the whole life of Our *Lord Jesus Christ' (Encyclical Consueverunt)*.

The Rosary is a theological prayer through which, with Mary, we turn to God. With her, we pray to the Father, and we give glory to the Holy Trinity - the Our Father at the beginning of each decade and the Gloria at the end.

It is a Marian prayer through which we speak directly to Mary, praising her as she herself invites us to do ('All generations shall call me blessed') and through which we plead with her to pray to God for us.

It is an evangelical prayer, because the three prayers are drawn from the Gospel: it is Jesus who taught us the Our Father, the first part of the Hail Mary is the greeting of the angel and of Elizabeth, and the Gloria recalls the words that Jesus addressed to his disciples before ascending to heaven. It is an evangelical prayer because, before each decade, it recalls the mysteries which present, in the form of a synopsis, the stages of the mystery of Jesus: incarnation (joyous mystery), public life (luminous mysteries, introduced by John Paul II), passion (sorrowful mysteries) and glory (glorious mysteries). The latter also invite us to meditate on the last act accomplished by Christ,

*Over the entrance to the Rosary Basilica:
St Dominic receiving a Rosary from the Virgin*

who takes his mother to heaven and crowns her as queen. It is a meditation with Mary and on the example of Mary, who kept and pondered in her heart the mysteries of her son.

The Rosary is said on a 'crown' of fifty beads, which has its origin in the Muslim crown and, going back further in time, the Buddhist and Hindu crowns. A universal dimension can then be perceived in this prayer.

S

SAHUQUET, JEAN (bishop)

Born in Nîmes on 18 November 1923, Jean Sahuquet went to secondary school at *Sainte-Marie d'Albi*, then studied philosophy and theology at the *Institut Catholique de Toulouse*, where he obtained a degree in theology. He was ordained priest on 29 June 1948 for the Albi diocese. On 16 December 1978, Pope John Paul II named him auxiliary Bishop of Bayonne and he was ordained bishop at the cathedral of Albi on 25 February 1979. In 1985, he was named auxiliary Bishop of Tarbes and Lourdes, and became bishop of that diocese in

1988. He would fill this role until 1998.

As an episcopal delegate to the pastoral council, Bishop Sahuquet was well acquainted with Lourdes and, as chaplain of Catholic Action he had a strong sense of the value of lay people's participation in the apostolate, as members of the people of God: he knew how to listen to them and he trusted them. Very soon therefore, several lay people were placed in posts of responsibility. Through their commitment, Lourdes was modernised: transfer of the printing works freed space for pastoral activities, a bookshop, the general secretariat, the information forum, the Lourdes Magazine and the offices for language co-ordinators.

In parallel, a dialogue allowed, in the name of a common destiny and recognizing the respect due to each partner in this process, the establishment of a town/Shrine co-ordinated project for the development of Lourdes. This included improving traffic, improving facilities for the welcoming of the sick, and for the reception and management of large groups of people and, finally, preservation of the environment and of the architectural heritage.

While it was not possible to achieve everything, this project, underwritten by both the mayor and the bishop, allowed the creation of the 'Societé d'Economie Mixte (SEM) de l'Accueil which was behind the construction, in record time, (11 February 1996-28 March 1997) of the new *Accueil de Notre-Dame* and of the *Accueil Marie Saint-Frai*. Further, the preservation of the architectural heritage project was established. We owe the fact that considerable works could be undertaken for the renovation of the Basilica of the Rosary and of the ramps, to the patient labour of the lay people and to the support of Bishop Sahuquet.

Bishop Sahuquet died on 7 December 2006, at the age of 83.

SAINT-FRAI, MARIE

Marie Saint-Frai (1816-1894) was the foundress of the *Filles de Notre-Dame des Douleurs* (Daughters of Our Lady of Sorrows), a congregation devoted, since 1862, in a most admirable way, to the service of the sick during the Lourdes pilgrimages.

The life of Marie Saint-Frai is simply admirable. A daughter of tanners, at the beginning of the 19th century, she lost both parents in the early part of her life. She opened her house to the unfortunate, both men and women, and gave them shelter. In 1851, aged 35, after the death of her father, she continued her work, attracting a few young girls to help her. Gradually, with the help of a teacher at the seminary of Tarbes, Fr Ribes, and with the blessing of Bishop Laurence, ceaselessly collecting for her poor, she came to found a religious congregation. Thus was born, on 28 March 1866, under the guiding hand of Bishop Laurence, who suggested its name, the congregation of the *Filles de Notre-Dame des Douleurs* under the protection of Our Lady and St Joseph. She became Mother Saint-Jean-Baptiste.

The inspiration for this name came from the particular devotion the foundress had for Our Lady of Sorrows, whom she had started to get to know in her childhood in the small Shrine of Piétat, very near Tarbes, which was maintained by the Garaison Fathers. Bishop Laurence, while still vicar general, wanted to revive Marian fervour in the diocese by the restoration of all the Shrines.

Naturally, the apparitions and the flood of poor pilgrims, of sick people, at the end of the 1870 war, would inspire the sisters to settle in Lourdes where the foundress spent her last years, all the while opening new centres in Bagnères-de-Bigorre, Arles, Avignon, Bastia. The magnificent *Hôpital de Notre-Dame des Douleurs*, started in 1874, receives innumerable pilgrims and remains a witness to the exceptional charity of Marie Saint-Frai and Fr-Ribes. Mother Saint-Jean-Baptiste died on 9 April 1894.

SALUS INFIRMORUM

The *Salus Infirmorum* is a place of welcome for people with a physical disability. It belongs to UNITALSI, the main Italian association of pilgrimages in Lourdes. Situated just at the outside of the Shrine, not far from the Saint-Michel entrance, the structure used to incorporate an old hotel, much appreciated by pilgrims, due to its excellent position.

It used to be called Bethany, in memory of a trip to the Holy Land which had left a deep impression on the owners. Indeed, the guardian of Lazarus' tomb had

made them a gift of a stone, taken from that very tomb, and which is even now still embedded in the sustaining wall. It is said that when the house was acquired by UNITALSI, the owners of the hotel had chosen that particular association remembering the words of the Franciscan guardian: 'I am giving you this stone, but your house must become a house which is always open to those who suffer.'

In 1972, when UNITALSI started its management, SALUS was able to welcome up to 167 people who were ill but relatively self-sufficient, and things developed in the right direction over the next twenty-one years. Then, between 1994 and 1998, important changes were made with a view to welcoming gravely ill pilgrims. The restructuring included an extension of the old building by integrating the Coecilia hotel which is situated a little further up in Pau Street. In 1995, the bed capacity rose to 270, rising to 350 in 1999.

SCHOEPFER, FRANCOIS-XAVIER (bishop)

On the death of Bishop Billère, the pope named a parish priest from Paris, François-Xavier Schoepfer (1843-1927), Bishop of Tarbes, on 14 December 1899. He was to fill this role for more than a quarter of a century. Born in Alsace in 1843, his family had left there after the 1870 war in order to remain French. In Paris, he had met as vicars general, the two future bishops of Tarbes, Jourdan and Langenieux.

On 6 October 1901, the Church of the Rosary was solemnly consecrated. In 1908, an impressive gathering took place to celebrate the fiftieth anniversary of the apparitions and the two turrets were erected at the point of departure of the ramps. In 1912, the title of Lourdes was added to that of Tarbes. On 14 September of that same year, the Stations of the Cross, on the Calvary site, were inaugurated.

The whole world was represented at a great eucharistic congress which took place just before the war, in 1914. The event was presided over by the Cardinal Legate, Granito di Belmonte.

Bernadette was declared venerable in 1923 and beatified in 1925. She was canonised after the death of the bishop, in 1933.

Bishop Schoepfer had to manage the confiscation, by the State, of the Massabielle estate which was handed over to the town of Lourdes in 1903. It was returned, thanks to an arrangement between Bishop Choquet and Marshal Petain, in February 1941.

Fortunately, life on the estate was not affected by the confiscation, and Bishop Schoepfer was able to proceed with a great number of improvements, right up to his death in 1907. The esplanade with the *calvaire breton*, the chapels under the ramps, the steps leading to the Shrines, the passage leading to the Crypt, the old 'Pénitencerie' which is now a Museum, and many other initiatives were all due to his creative zeal. Pius XI paid tribute to him on the occasion of his episcopal silver jubilee on 19 March 1925. In 1926, Mgr Poirier became his auxiliary bishop.

SCIENCE AND LOURDES

The Lourdes healings, which were not anticipated, occurred very soon during the time of the apparitions, and increased rapidly in number. The Church, having the indispensable role of having them officially guaranteed, turned, naturally, to the scientific knowledge of doctors to verify the reality of these healings and to research their origin. After that, when they had been defined as inexplicable in medical terms, some healings could be qualified as 'miraculous'.

In 1883, the *Bureau des Constatations Medicales* (bureau of medical reports and findings) was founded by Dr de Saint-Maclou to proceed with the investigations, with, at its head, a resident doctor, assisted by many other doctors who came from all over the world and who were brought together as the *Association Medicale Internationale de Lourdes* (AMIL), which today numbers around 12,000 doctors from seventy-five different countries.

The medical inquiry must conclude in favour of a 'medically unexplained' healing, with reference to criteria defined by Cardinal Lambertini, in the eighteenth century, for the universal Church and composed of 'seven criteria of exclusion'.

1. The illness must be of a serious character, with an unfavourable diagnosis;
2. The reality and the diagnosis of the illness must be confirmed and precise;
3. The illness must be of an organic nature and tissue related;
4. Any possible treatment must not be at the origin of the healing;
5. The healing must be sudden, immediate and instantaneous;
6. The return of physical function must be complete, without convalescence;
7. It must not be a remission but a long-term healing.

Later, at the beginning of the formidable development of medical science after the war, and on the initiative of Bishop Pierre-Marie Théas, the resident doctor at the time, François Leuret, founded the *Comité Médical International de Lourdes*, a second medical authority, which consisted of a group of medical professors.

The latter study the documents dealing with complete cures which the resident doctor submits to them annually and they then launch an 'expertise'* for the files they retain. Only then is the file transferred to the ecclesial authority, which is the bishop of the diocese of origin of the person in question.

It is evident then that it is not possible to approve a miracle lightly. But, for every case, miracles provide the opportunity for a constructive dialogue between science and faith: Lourdes' vocation is surely also to reconcile two worlds which are not opposed but complementary.

* scrutiny by a team of experts on that subject.

SEMPÉ, RÉMI

Fr Sempé of the Garaison Missionaries was the great architect of the Shrine of Lourdes as can be seen today. When he died, aged 72, on 1 September 1889, Bishop Billère paid him a vibrant tribute as he contemplated the beautiful trees, planted everywhere, the canalised Gave, the magnificent constructions and other marvels: 'Not one of those has been conceived, or realised, without Fr Sempé's input.'

Born into a peasant family near Lourdes in 1818, he was ordained in Notre-Dame de Betham, where he was noted for his Marian devotion. He became secretary to Bishop Laurence who appreciated him greatly for his intelligence and his reliability. A meeting with the great saint, Michel Garicoïts, inspired him to become a Garaison religious. Bishop Laurence asked him to become prefect of studies at the small seminary of Saint-Pé. He heard about the apparitions but did not believe in them. Meanwhile, the father of one of his pupils, Maître Dufo, a lawyer, told him of his emotion when he saw Bernadette making the sign of the cross.

After the famous apparition of 25 March, it was with stupor that he read, in the mail received by his students, of the connection between the Lady of the Grotto and the Immaculate Conception. His judgement changed completely.

Bishop Laurence recognized the apparitions in 1862 and thought of having chaplains for the new Shrine: thus it was that Fr Sempé arrived in Lourdes, on 17 May, 1866, with a few missionaries, just before the inauguration of the first venue for the celebration of liturgy: the Crypt. A great adventure was just starting for him and for the Catholic Church.

Immediately, he launched a small periodical: *Les Annales de Notre-Dame de Lourdes* and assisted the journalist, Henri Lasserre, who was working on a book on the apparitions. Unfortunately, the author, stirred on by the parish priest, who had commissioned the book, would come to resent the chaplains: a wretched rivalry would develop between the parish priest, who had considered himself to be at the centre of the pilgrimage with his parish church, and the new chaplains who were building the new Basilica of the Immaculate Conception in 1872. With a poisoned pen, Henri Lasserre took the part of the parish priest, causing a veritable war of words against Fr Sempé and the chaplains.

Fr Sempé became actively involved in the building of the first great basilica and tried to face the storm unleashed by Henri Lasserre, which would go all the way to Rome. The latter accused the chaplains of involving themselves in vulgar commerce and of killing the spirit of the Shrine. Pius IX himself presided over a meeting of the Holy Office in July 1873 and cleared the chaplains of any blame. Lasserre turned to public opinion with passionate pamphlets while Fr Sempé brought Bishop Pichenot up to date with a very beautiful letter.

It was then that Bishop Langénieux arrived, who was to support Fr Sempé's large-scale plans, which consisted of creating a space in front of the Grotto, designing an esplanade, building a bridge and a new boulevard – which would become the future boulevard of the Grotto – in the direction of the rail station.

These new projects were the subject of fierce criticism by the people of Lourdes and their parish priest, who believed they would be ruined by this direct route from the station to the Shrines. President Mac-Mahon donated 50,000 gold francs for the construction of the new bridge. The town eventually showed its thanks for Fr Sempé's tenacity, by giving their qualified approval in 1878.

Trees had to be planted, the Gave had to be canalised and the piece of land on a hill which would become 'Calvary' had to be bought. There were numerous trials to be faced in terms of the drilling works for the boulevard of the Grotto. In addition, there was the supervision of the construction of the reception facility for the sick, of the new house for the chaplains and, above all, due to the flood of pilgrims, there was the need for a new venue for liturgical celebration. One can imagine this little man, Rosary in hand, circulating among the building sites, taking everything on board. In July 1876, the Virgin was crowned in the presence of the Archbishop of Paris, Cardinal Guibert, O.M.I., a great number of bishops and priests and a considerable crowd.

On the death of Fr Peydessus, the founder of the Garaison Missionaries, in 1882, Fr Sempé was named superior general. His great preoccupation was to have the new Basilica of the Rosary built. Tons of rock had to be moved and there were great difficulties caused by the water which was running everywhere. For ten years the priest surrounded himself with all kinds of advisers, and work finally started on 16 July 1883. Because of all the difficulties this church was to cost an enormous sum, and was completed only on 15 August 1889. Fr Sempé died a fortnight later. 'Ah, how Fr Sempé loved the Virgin of Massabielle! He loved her so much as to become the laughing stock of and a scandal to the world, to the point of suffering persecution and of being anathemised by who knows how many people.' his bishop would say.

Today, the boulevard which runs along the Shrine bears his name.

SERVICE FOR PEOPLE WITH DISABILITIES

There are four very distinct types of disability: physical, mental, sensory (deafness, blindness) and psychological. Disability, therefore, cannot be seen as a single entity. Every type of disability necessitates adaptations which are appropriate to it.

For persons with a disability who arrive in Lourdes alone, or with their families, and not as part of an organised pilgrimage, Bishop Perrier wished, in 2005, to have a specific facility established in the Shrines, at the Saint-Michel entrance: *Le Service des personnes handicapées et de leurs familles*. All will find there a welcome, friendship, the opportunity of meeting others and necessary information for the pilgrimage:

-For persons with reduced mobility: accessible places. Wheelchairs are on loan in two places: at the *Accueil* and at the information forum (Saint-Joseph entrance);

-For persons who are blind or who have impaired vision: the relief model of the Shrines and documents in Braille;

-For persons who are deaf or

have impaired hearing: magnetic loops in certain areas of the Shrines, *rendezvous* with sign language interpreters;

-For persons with a mental disability: persons who offer them a supportive relationship and friendship;

-For persons who have a psychological disorder : persons trained to provide counselling.

It is also a place of information about associations and movements which exist all over the world to support people with a disability and their families and to reduce isolation. The team prays every day for all those they have met.

This service is also a place which raises awareness concerning the various disabilities, through formation and by the witnessing of persons with a disability. It is a school to encourage positive regard for all persons. Bernadette reminds us that here we find what is essential. She said of Mary: 'She looked at me as a person who looks at another person.' This service is the responsibility of OCH (*Office Chrétien des personnes Handicapées*) present in Lourdes since 1972.

SHRINES

Every people, every religion, has its sacred places, its pilgrimage centres; Benares and Mount Kailas for Hinduism, Bodh Gaya and Sarnath, for Buddhism, Ise for Shintoism, Mecca for Islam. The Jewish people also have various Shrines, in the first place the trees, or the altars, and the 'steles' *, erected in the places where God manifested himself. With the Exodus, a Shrine would be God's house in the middle of his people, the tent where the tablets of the Law were kept. It was not a fixed place to visit in pilgrimage. God himself was the traveller, with his people living in him: 'Judah became his sanctuary' (Ps 114:2). After the Jerusalem temple was built, it became the main sanctuary, which God had chosen as his house.

With Jesus the Shrine is himself, God present among his people, transforming people into a temple where God dwells: 'that is what we are – the temple of the living God' (2 Cor: 6:16). The real Christian Shrine is the community of those who are united in the name of Jesus: it reveals his presence among them. (cf Mt 18:20).

Very soon, in the Christian religion, certain places began to acquire a particularly sacred character, namely those where relics of martyrs were kept. All through the first millennium, the word 'Shrine' did not have the same meaning as it does in modern times; it was related solely to martyrs' relics or to their shrouds. The places where the Virgin Mary was venerated were called *domus, ecclesia, memoria, locus...*

In contrast with the Shrines of antiquity prior to Christianity, which are usually linked to specific, cosmic and natural places (mountains, fountains, Grottos), Christian Shrines are associated with historical events: places where martyrdom has occurred or places where relics of saints can be found, where saints or the Virgin have manifested themselves, or where sacred images have been discovered. Jerusalem, and more generally, the Holy Land, remains the main centre of Christian pilgrimage. They are the places of the birth of Jesus and of the 'martyrdom' of Jesus. Then, there is Rome, in memory of the martyrdom of the apostles Peter and Paul, and Compostella, in memory of James.

The idea of a Shrine is linked to that of pilgrimage (the word 'pilgrimage' and its German equivalent *Wallfahrt* means a pilgrimage as a journey, but also as a centre for pilgrimage). The code of Canon Law confirms this in its definition, in paragraph 1230: 'The term Shrine means a church or other sacred place which, with the approval of the local ordinary, is by reason of special devotion frequented by the faithful as pilgrims.' A place therefore becomes a Shrine by popular recognition before ecclesiastical recognition and it is linked to pilgrimage (the faithful must come 'in great numbers').

The communitarian factor, with its coming together of people, is a characteristic of the Shrine. Being with many other people, we rediscover our sense of belonging to a people of believers, and our religious identity is revived. The experience is one of a new fraternity, of a classless social spirit. Sometimes, the Shrine can also reinforce cultural and national identity, as in the case of Guadeloupe in Mexico, or Czestochowa in Poland. Other times, as in Lourdes or Fatima, the supranational character of the pilgrimage reinforces the sense of being a Catholic and the universal sense of the Christian religion.

The Shrine is a place where the human and the divine meet; almost like an icon in the heavenly kingdom. A historical manifestation of the divine occurred and its presence continues to be felt. To reach it one must cross the 'threshold' which marks its boundaries as a sacred place and which separates it from profane places. Entering the Shrine implies purification and reaching sanctification. Coming out of the Shrine, one feels the desire to sanctify the profane environment in which one finds oneself again. The fruit of the road to, and the return from, the Shrine is the unification and the conjugation of the 'sacred' and the 'profane' into a new holiness. It represents a call to divinize each reality and each human activity as well as every earthly place. The Shrine is not therefore the final goal of the pilgrimage but only a stage, from which one draws new strength to resume the journey of life.

The true Shrine, the permanent place of the presence of God is, in effect, the Christian community in which Ezekiel's prophecy comes to fulfilment: 'I shall set my sanctuary among them forever' (Ez 37: 26). In the heavenly Jerusalem there will no longer be any Shrines because: 'I could not see any temple in the city since the Lord God almighty and the Lamb were themselves the temple' (Ap,21:22).

---

* 'Stele' an upright slab of stone with an inscribed or sculptured surface, used as a monument.

SICK PILGRIMS

In Lourdes, one is immediately struck by the presence of the sick and the disabled. It is often a shock to see all these suffering people, happy to have come here, in this blessed place, at the invitation of Our Lady.

Ever since the apparitions, the Shrine of Lourdes has been known for its healing miracles. The Church, therefore, has put in place measures to receive the large number of persons who are sick and to make their pilgrimage easier. To this effect, the *Hospitalité Notre-Dame de Lourdes* was founded to welcome and serve those pilgrims on site in the first instance, and the *Hospitalités d'Accompagnement* (accompanying medical services) to bring the sick to Lourdes. Organised pilgrimages, annual for the most part, were put in place, many diocesan, but also national and international ones, with some organised for specific groups of people (soldiers, gypsies, people involved in sports) or belonging to a specific spirituality e.g. Dominicans, Franciscans, Montfortians. Also, pilgrimages have been established according to specific illnesses affecting people (the Lourdes Cancer Hope being the most developed), but also for the disabled or those suffering from mental illness.

The average annual number of sick people coming to the Shrines is close to a hundred thousand, with an equivalent number of volunteer medical professionals or assistants who work year after year at the service of those suffering in soul, body or mind.

Special pools have been built to allow those pilgrims who so wish to bathe in the water of the spring, an act of humility and purification, dur-

ing which many healings have occurred and continue to take place.

Sleeping accommodation with integral medical facilities have been built and are regularly maintained and renovated for the comfort and security of aged, sick or disabled pilgrims, either in groups or alone. Around 50,000 sick people are received every year in the two *Accueils* (welcoming centres) of the Shrines: *Accueil Notre-Dame* (1,000 beds) and *Accueil Marie Saint-Frai* (400 beds). The remaining patients are provided with accommodation in other units belonging to pilgrimage organisations (*Salus Infirmorum*, Hosanna House) or in hotels.

For people who visit on their own, there is, at the St Michael entrance, the *Pavillon des Handicapés* (pavillion for disabled persons) where individuals can be personally attended to and given information.

Each afternoon during the season (from April to October) the eucharistic procession takes place, with adoration and the blessing of the sick - a very moving moment for them and for the doctors accompanying the prelate who blesses the sick with the Blessed Sacrament.

The anointing of the sick is regularly given throughout the celebrations.

For those persons who are sick but do not appear so, a frequent occurrence, there is a 'carte de malade' (a sick person's badge) so that they are recognized as such. These can be obtained simply by presentation of a certificate from their doctor.

There is also a first aid station which is linked to the emergency services of the Lourdes Hospital and which can deal with any medical problem or accident happening within the Shrines compound. Further, for people suffering from renal problems, there is a dialysis centre.

It is evident that the sick have a privileged place in Lourdes. All sufferers are received with respect, tenderness and love. Here, the Church shows her compassion and also heals through the sacraments of mercy, i.e., the anointing of the sick and the sacrament of reconciliation.

Finally, aren't we all more or less suffering from illness, disability or wounded in our heart or our soul? Are we not all in need of healing?

In the words of Bishop Jacques Perrier: '*Healing* is one of the key words of Lourdes. *Healing* in every sense of the word. Lourdes cannot simply be reduced to a place where miraculous cures occur. Lourdes is a place of peace and reconciliation by the grace of Jesus Christ, under Mary's watchful gaze.

SIGNS

For those who have impaired hearing there exists a language other than words which is called 'sign language'. In the same way, there is a kind of silent language of the fundamental elements of nature: beyond their practical uses, they inspire thought and suggest a deeper, more interior reality. And so it is for the air and the wind, for water, light, rock and mountains.

When one enters the Grotto estate, having come through the tumult of the town and its congestion, one has the feeling of being in a different space, where nature remains, despite all the constructions which were made necessary by the growing flood of pilgrims: walking allows one to see differently, calmly and to discover a whole new world. In this mountain scenery, a dark Grotto, facing north, yet lit by candles which burn night and day... and under the Grotto: a spring. But also, crowds of many nations and languages, people who are ill, put in the front row. One notices gestures: touching the rock, lighting a candle, walking in procession, drinking the water... Seeing this, many ask themselves: is it faith or superstition?

Listening to the message enables one to understand. Indeed the Lady of Massabielle used this language largely to communicate with Bernadette who could neither read nor write. She was her 'catechist'. A catechism of images, teaching her from the beginning, the sign of the cross, asking her to find the spring, showing her gestures of penance: kissing the ground, eating grass, drinking brackish water, before telling her her name.

SISTERS OF NEVERS

In 1676, Jean-Baptiste Delaveyne (1653-1719), a Benedictine monk,

returned to his home town of Saint-Saulge in Nievre, after seven years studying in Paris, which had dazzled him with its wonderful literary and artistic masterpieces of the King Louis XIV era. Attracted by the life of high society, his interests lay with the 'great' and the 'powerful'.

In 1678 a simple remark from a neighbouring curate turned his whole existence upside down: 'It was not at Subiaco that St Benedict found his way.' In that moment Jean-Baptiste made a decision: to search for the true meaning of his life. Moved by the poor conditions in which the peasants lived, he drew close to them in their poverty. As he learned to love them and defend their rights, he discovered in Christ, the supreme witness of God's love, which reached out to all humanity. Speaking to the young women of his home town Saint-Saulge, he encouraged them to follow the same spiritual adventure in their own way: 'Have nothing to do with anything except charity. Have no other interests except those who are in need.' That is how the Congregation of the Sisters of Charity and Christian Instruction of Nevers came about.

It was on 6 August 1834, at the request of the mayor, M Latapie, that the first three Sisters of Nevers arrived in Lourdes to run the hospice. In 1836, a fourth sister arrived to set up free schooling for the local children.

In July 1860, two years after the apparitions, Bernadette was taken in by the nuns. Under their care and supervision, she learned to read and write, and was no longer an object of curiosity in the public eye. These arrangements had been made by Fr Peyramale, with the approval of the mayor, president of the administrative board. In 1866, Bernadette left Lourdes to begin her novitiate in Nevers.

From the beginning of the 20th century the life of the sisters became linked in a special way with the hospice which was soon to become the *Accueil Notre-Dame* (Notre Dame welcome centre). On 8 August 1910, at the request of the bishop, the head of the association of welcome wrote a letter to the mother superior: 'The corporation of the Grotto, is building a hospital with 200 beds, along the bank of the River Gave with the specific aim of caring for sick pilgrims. In memory of Bernadette, the bishop wishes that the running of this hospital be entrusted to your daughters.'

It is here that the sisters have remained ever since, serving the thousands of sick who come to Lourdes. They carried on through the difficult and painful circumstances of two world wars. In 1914, they sheltered and nursed the wounded. In September 1939, when war was declared, there were many sick pilgrims staying at the hospital. Their pilgrimage was cut short and they had to return home within 48 hours. A few days later, the hospital was requisitioned by the military authorities and its 500 beds were quickly filled by as many wounded soldiers.

In 1941-42, still under requisition by the military authorities, in place of the wounded came groups of strong young men and women,

300 at a time, to refresh their souls in the purifying waters of the Grotto.

In 1943, the St Martha, St Therese and Sacred Heart halls, were filled with evacuee children from the occupied regions.

In 1944, the Germans invaded the hospital. Beds were quickly removed to the Hotel Moderne, and those of the Saint-Frai Shelter were moved to the dining room, the tables and chairs having been removed in the twinkling of an eye, to the esplanade. Failing to discover the kitchen on the second floor, the Germans used their own transportable kitchen facilities. Three months later they left the hospital and the region. Their place was quickly taken by nearly 400 young girls from the suburbs of Paris and Marseille, together with an army of lice, against whom the sisters waged a brutal war!

Today the Sisters of Charity and Christian Instruction of Nevers, number 400, living in 67 communities spread out in fifteen different countries, over four continents.

SISTERS OF SAINT-JOSEPH OF TARBES

From 1885, Mother Helene-Marie, superior general of the Sisters of Saint-Joseph of Tarbes, had set up a small community of sisters in Lourdes, in Langelle Street. They cared for the sick and also did the laundry for the parish church.

In 1900, at the request of the bishop, a community of five sisters came to the Shrine. It was the start of a collaboration which is still continuing today. At the time that the Garaison Fathers had to leave Lourdes, the community of the Sisters of Saint-Joseph grew, taking responsibility for the running of the kitchens, the making of altar breads, household duties, the laundry service and the sick-bay for the chaplains.

This congregation had its origins in Cantaous, a small village near Garaison. It is a land where the Revolution, far from eradicating faith, had in fact, reinforced it. In 1842, six peasant women in clogs, with little education, felt a call to a life consecrated to God and, so it would seem, without any outside influence. The life of Carmel was their ideal. Their parents approved this call and the whole village mobilised itself to facilitate the birth of a new congregation.

On 15 August 1843, the date regarded as that of the foundation, the bishop gave them their rule of life. Mgr Laurence, vicar general and future bishop of the apparitions, would appoint a teacher from Ossun to be their superior.

Since 1900, some 90 Sisters of Saint-Joseph have devoted themselves and continue to do so to the service of the Shrine of Lourdes. Their tasks, modest as they may seem, performed in absolute anonymity, far from the pilgrims, have played an invaluable part in the functioning of the Shrine. Today, as in the past, beyond the visible service and work being done, there is always room for a silent apostolate, which some might see as timid and self-effacing, but which every sister tries to mark by simplicity and warmth of contact.

SOCIETY AND LOURDES

It can be said that no-one decreed that pilgrimages should take place at Lourdes, and yet, from the time of the apparitions, the workers of Lourdes descended on the Grotto, singing litanies, without a priest and with no processional cross. The neighbouring villages soon followed their lead and, in the great crisis which shook France after the defeat of 1870 and the death throes of the *Commune de Paris*, a spontaneous impetus propelled crowds of people towards the Shrines of la Salette or the Rue du Bac. In 1872 Lourdes welcomed the great 'manifestation of faith and hope' which brought to the Grotto banners from all the provinces of France, including those, shrouded in black, of Alsace and Lorraine, which had become German.

1872-1873 were the two years which launched Lourdes. While politicians proclaimed: 'Pilgrimages are a thing of the past,' the blind, the deaf and the disabled ran to the desert to find the Good News. After the miraculous medal was made available, according to the revelation made to Catherine Labouré, millions were distributed. Grottos multiplied in all corners of the world and Lourdes water was brought as far as the steppes of Central Asia and the forests of Africa and America. And the crowds continued to come. Not only Catholic youth movements, or diocesan and national pilgrimages, but cyclists, soldiers, gypsies, people suffering from polio, people with mental disabilities, the most diverse social categories, found a rallying point in Lourdes. The Christian and human identities seemed to be reinforced here and those who came as tourists left, in one way or another, as witnesses and observers of a new wonder.

The presence of the sick, who were sustained by the hope of healing, but also by the joy of finding new fraternity, continued to grow, to the point of becoming the distinctive sign of this Shrine: 54 in 1875, with the national French pilgrimage, 492 in 1877, 950 in 1880. Lourdes was becoming an 'institution', according to Paul Claudel, 'a fixation on human misery, immersed here in a pool of prayer'; the healthy felt that they too needed renewal. If, for a long period, healings were used in some way as a challenge to the positivist influence, to 'prove' the reality of the supernatural, gradually, people started coming to receive the grace of a life of giving, sometimes through suffering and illness: 'Do what I do, smile!' proclaimed a sign on an invalid car.

The pilgrims of Lourdes are invited to change their way of seeing things, to abandon the abstraction of general laws and numbers, and to contemplate faces, often faces which are disfigured. In this world, which hides the old and the sick in homes and hospitals, and puts the marginalised in specialist centres, the evocative power of suffering in our streets and in our squares can never be stressed enough. Here we are invited to meet mystery.

Considering this, we can understand the statement by Pius XII, when he recalls in his encyclical *Le Pèlerinage de Lourdes*, the importance of Shrines to attain a 'collective effort of Christian renewal in society'. The Church has wanted to relaunch, in Lourdes, a militant attitude, but Mary, rather, allows everyone here, priests and lay people, the sick and the healthy, the young and the old, the rich and the poor, practising or not, to follow in the way of Bernadette and of the little ones of this world, the way of the Gospel. The encounter of these two young girls with no status in civil or religious society of their time, opens to individuals or groups, a spiritual space, a feminine space, where at last God can make a spring flourish. All God needs is open hearts, because he is the gift. Mary gathers them in a Church that is welcoming and fraternal, united today in the passion of Jesus.

SOUBIROUS, FRANÇOIS

François Soubirous, Bernadette's father, was 'a man of great simplicity, of a gentle disposition and timid character', as depicted by one of his cousins, the schoolteacher Clarens. Bernadette loved her father even more than her mother, and he had a tender love for his eldest daughter. At the age of 34, he had married Louise Castérot, with whom he had fallen in love. He had been expected to marry Bernarde, Louise's sister, because she was the eldest and had the status of 'heir' of a mill which was to be taken over, the mill of Boly, which is visited very frequently nowadays. He only wanted Louise.

The marriage, on 9 January 1843, was the beginning of a family of nine children, of which only four

Bernadette's father with his youngest children

survived. 'There were never any arguments at home; harmony and unity reigned always.' The Soubirous were 'good people, very charitable', but, certainly, uneducated.

On the death of Mme Castérot's mother, things deteriorated. The mill was too old and the flour was of poor quality. The family had to leave the mill and ended up in a lamentable place, called the *cachot*. It was at that point that, to snatch her from the jaws of death, Bernadette was sent to Bartrès, where she was to spend nine months, at the age of 13. Her father visited her often there, walking the three kilometres that separate Lourdes from Bartrès.

A cruel trial was to befall this family. A bag of flour had disappeared and François, suspected because of his great poverty, was remanded in prison for eight days before being released. What shame and what suffering for such dignified people!

This phase, during which the poor parents only managed to survive thanks to odd jobs, corresponded to the time of the apparitions. This period would prove particularly trying for this destitute family, exposed to the curiosity of an ever growing number of people and to the suspicion of the authorities.

Fortunately, Bernadette's exceptional adventure would pull them out of this misery. With remarkable dignity, they refused any gifts. But they were found a better home and life went on. Poor Louise, however, died aged 41, exhausted, in the year of Bernadette's departure from Lourdes, on 8 December 1866. Her beloved father died five years later. Bernadette's childhood world was disappearing. Far away from the family home, she became the head of the family. Her brother Jean-Marie (died 1919), was the only sibling to have children. On the death of her father, Bernadette was to say: 'Do you not know that now my father is Joseph!' Her parents had introduced her to the family of God.

SPRING OF THE GROTTO

On 25 February 1858, the spring of the Grotto was uncovered, under Bernadette's fingers, under memorable circumstances. On that occasion, Bernadette was invited to drink by the apparition, she covered herself with mud and was thought insane by the crowd.

But the water would run for the good of innumerable people. The first healing took place on 1 March for the benefit of Catherine Latapie, from Loubaja. According to the older inhabitants of Lourdes, this spring had probably existed for a long time, but it had never surfaced.

The Mayor of Lourdes, M Lacadé, had the water analysed in May and June 1858. It proved to be of great purity, but with no special properties. It would not rival the mineral water of Couterets and Barèges.

Considering the great demand for the water, particularly during the summer, a great basin of 450,000 litres was built under the Basilica of the Rosary, in order to control the flow. Other reservoirs were put in

place in the park of the episcopal chalet.

In 1948, worried by the diminishing of the flow, Bishop Théas had it measured on 12 August. He decided to try and do something about it. Canon Mailhet, an eminent geologist and hydrologist with two other specialists looked for the origin of the water, and discovered that together with two other important springs, it came from the massif of Béout. This investigation revealed the clogging up of the water flow, which they managed to get resolved.

In 1974, the spring was made visible in the Grotto.

STATIONS OF THE CROSS

Long before becoming the site for the Stations of the Cross of the Shrines, the hill of the Espélugues and the caves which it contains, were known as one of the most beautiful prehistoric sites of the Pyrenees. In 1873 and 1874, important archaeological excavations led to the discovery of important remains, now exhibited in the Pyrenean museum in Lourdes.

It was Bishop Laurence who bought the land of the Espélugues, with a view of having there the Stations of the Cross or a *chemin du rosaire* (way of the Rosary). Already, in 1875, the Diocese of Beauvais had offered an immense wooden cross which was erected at the top of the hill. After falling down several times it was replaced by a reinforced concrete one painted over to imitate wood. The first, provisional Stations of the Cross, marked by simple wooden crosses, made their way up the hill. The initial concept comes from the Montfortians who, at Pontchâteau, not far from Nantes, had constructed monumental Stations of the Cross. The idea appealed to Bishop Billère of Tarbes (who provided the finance for several stations) and it was the same firm from Paris, the house of Raffl, specialists in cast iron sculpture, that

S made the 150 statues of the Lourdes Stations of the Cross, between 1899 and 1912. Dioceses, bishops and pilgrims, often anonymously, financed each one of the stations. From the very beginning of the project, Pope Leo XIII granted the same indulgences to the pilgrims who completed the Stations of the Cross in Lourdes as to those who did the *Scala Santa* in Rome. In 1981, a 15th station, representing the resurrection, was added in a geological fault on a rock on the hill including a large millstone recalling the one which closed the tomb of the Lord at the foot of Golgotha.

A few days before the arrival of Pope John Paul II in 1983, a terrorist attack destroyed the statue of Pontius Pilate at the first station.

Starting in 2004, in the field on the other side of the Gave, a new set of Stations of the Cross has been built, the last stations being set in place in 2008. Constructed from Carrara marble by the Hungarian artist Maria de Faykod, it allows pilgrims of reduced mobility to meditate on the passion of Christ in greener and more gentle surroundings than the hill of the Espélugues.

STATUE OF THE IMMACULATE CONCEPTION

In June 1863, a doctor from the Sorbonne, Fr Alix, visited Lourdes, met Bernadette and went to the Grotto where, overwhelmed by emotion, he shed many tears. He was accompanied by Elfride and Sabine de Lacour who wished to donate a marble statue of Our Lady of Lourdes for the Grotto. After approval by Bishop Laurence, the sculptor Fabisch met Bernadette on 17 September and asked her many questions to find out how the Lady looked like: 'How tall was she? Did she seem young? What colour were her roses? Her dress, belt and veil were made of what kind of material?' It was decided that the inauguration of his work would take place on 4 April 1864, a date to which the feast of the Annunciation had been deferred that year.

In March, Bishop Laurence's advisers began to feel uneasy at how little preparation was taking place for the coming celebration, although they knew that the bishop's silence was due to the sensitivity of the ministers and of the *préfet* with whom he was negotiating. At that time Fr Peyramale became ill and, despite the care of doctors and of prayers, remained confined to his room and, although feeling better, he could not participate in the celebration of 4 April. Bernadette, too, was ill. She was, however, able to attend the unveiling of the work in the presence of Canon Fourcade and of Fabisch, who inquired about the resemblance of the statue to the apparition: 'That's it,' Bernadette said, then a few minutes later, she corrected herself: 'No, that's not it!' On 4 April, the town of Lourdes was in jubilation: its streets and houses were decorated with flags, and structures based on the Arc de Triomphe were erected everywhere. Despite the fact that there had been no publicity in the churches of the diocese, an immense crowd was present. The day started with mass at the parish church, then, Bishop Laurence led the first procession to the Grotto, with 120 priests and 20,000 people. The statue was unveiled in front of the silent crowds, then a voice started singing spontaneously the *Magnificat*, which the multitude joined in before hearing a homily by Fr Alix.

The sculptor Fabisch

T

THANKSGIVING PLAQUES (ex-voto)

When we are in great physical or moral distress, and our trial is then lifted, we often utter a prayer or a promise, like a 'vow', to the Blessed Virgin. Small, engraved plaques of thanksgiving (ex-voto) adorn the walls and pillars of the basilicas as well as the main corridor of the crypt. The inscriptions, in beautiful marble, blend in harmoniously with the background. The Rosary Basilica has nearly 10,000 of them. In the Upper Basilica of the Immaculate Conception there is a whole section from pilgrims of Brittany, Niort and the Vendée who survived a train crash on their way to Lour-

des. At one time, even crutches used to hang from the rock of the Grotto as a testimony to those who no longer needed them.

The inscriptions express supplication, trust, joy, gratitude and promises to Our Lady to repay the graces that have been received. The walls themselves seem to pray, by saying 'Thank you, thank you!' How often do we remember to say thank you in our prayers? We, who often come with petitions, find ourselves moved to express gratitude. Lourdes is a 'school' where we learn to say 'thank you'. We should not be surprised at this because Mary teaches us to sing the marvels the Lord has done in our lives. Holy is his name. It is still possible today, at Lourdes, to offer a plaque of thanksgiving.

THÉAS, PIERRE-MARIE (bishop)

Born in Bazzun, very near Lourdes, in 1894, into a peasant family, Pierre-Marie Théas became as a young priest lecturer in ethics at the seminary of Bayonne. Later he became Bishop of Montauban, where he showed his courage, during the war, facing the occupiers. He was interned in Compiègne and threatened with concentration camp imprisonment before his liberation in August 1944. He was named Bishop of Tarbes and Lourdes on 17 February 1947, and an important period was about to start for the Shrine.

A very spiritual person, the bishop was also a great builder: the Saint-Michel shelter, the new baths with the great reservoir for the management of the water of the spring and, added to this, the improvement of the Grotto, cleared of its railings and of its extended constructions, the church of Saint-Joseph, the two bridges on the Gave and other numerous developments were his accomplishments.

His major building work was the Basilica of Saint-Pius X. For a long time the need had been felt for a place where major celebrations could be held, particularly as the celebration of the hundredth anniversary of the apparitions was nearing. Fortunately, Bishop Théas worked with a well-known architect, Pierre Vago, and, especially, with a first class engineer, M Freyssinet, the inventor of prestressed, high quality concrete. The latter made possible the construction of that vault of 200 metres, which is without support, a veritable *tour de force*.

Approved by the assembly of cardinals and archbishops of France in January 1956, work started on 30 May, with the blessing of Cardinal Gerlier. The finances needed were enormous, and was aggravated by the fact that the building site, encircled by the Gave, filled up with water, creating panic and sending shock waves through the episcopate. The Holy See ordered work to be stopped on 10 December. One can understand the anguish of the bishop as he dropped medals of the Virgin into the foundations.

Salvation would come from the unfailing faith of the bishop and from the wonderful spirit of the entrepreneur, M Campenon who uttered the words, later judged by the bishop as 'historic': 'Me, I will go on!' on that same 10 December. An ingenious system of long metal sheets, forming a provisional dam to dry out the worksite, would hermetically surround the building site and the water would be pumped out. The work could continue and would finish gloriously with a splendid ceremony on 25 March 1958, presided over by Cardinal Roncalli, the papal legate.

Rome had imposed an auxiliary bishop and, above all, a religious association called the Cenacle, founded by Cardinal Tisserand, to manage the financing. But as confidence returned, Bishop Théas was freed providentially from those cumbersome supervisors.

In 1970, Bishop Théas left his post with the warm congratulations of Paul VI, on the occasion of his jubilee. He retired to Betharam, where he died on 3 April 1977.

TOWN

Many legends and hypotheses make up the history of the foundation of the town of Lourdes. One such legend is that *Tarbis*, Queen of Ethiopia, fleeing unrequited love, came to settle in the Bigorre with her sister Lorda. Tarbis would found Tarbes and Lorda founded Lourdes.

Over the centuries, the Gauls, the Romans, the Barbarians and the Moors, fortified the rock of Lourdes. The Moors, beaten in Poitiers, and withdrawing to Spain, besieged the castle of Lourdes, which became, in 778, the territory of the Saracen, Mirat. To dislodge him, Charlemagne undertook a siege of several months. One morning, as famine was raging, an eagle flew over the castle, dropping a trout it had in its beak. Mirat snatched the fish and threw it back over the battlements. Deceived by this ruse, Turpi, the besieger and companion of Charlemagne, concluded that the besieged still had supplies. He negotiated with Mirat who surrendered and converted to Christianity, taking for his Christian baptism the name of Lorus, from which Lourdes would come. This episode is depicted on the town's coat of arms.

On 8 May 1360, through the Treaty of Brétigny, the dungeon passed to English ownership. It resisted the Duke of Anjou, but the town was sacked. It was devastated again on 8 June 1573 by the

The town hall

Huguenots of the Baron of Arros, lieutenant of Jeanne de Navarre. In the 17th century, the unification of the Bigorre with France brought peace to the town.

In 1858, the apparitions of the Virgin were to change the destiny of this modest town of 4,200 souls. A few years later, due to the flood of pilgrims, important works changed the face of the town: widening of the Grotto street and of the *Pont-Vieux*, the constructions of the boulevard of the Grotto, of the *Palais de Justice* and of the new parish church... To have accommodation in Lourdes, to live one's faith there, to move around, find help, shelter and comfort, such are the bricks which have been building the town for the last 150 years.

It was especially around the *Accueils* for the sick and persons with disabilities that the dynamics of the Lourdes pilgrimages developed. In 1997 and 1998, two modern and functional buildings, the *Accueils Notre-Dame* and *Saint-Frai*, with a total of 1,400 beds, replaced the former secular *Accueils*, which had become obsolete.

Transport: The railway plays an essential role in the transportation of pilgrims. The airport of Lourdes-Tarbes-Pyrenees, modern and well adapted, has been greatly developed while cars, because of their flexibility, are being used more and more.

Hotels: Lourdes is ranked second in France for the hotel industry. Its accommodation infrastructure is constantly being developed and its 223 hotels constitute a reception system which is modern and well adapted to persons with a disability.

With the accommodation facilities for visitors becoming insufficient for the increasing number of pilgrimages, the town and the Shrine became aware over the years of the need to work together. Concerted, rapid and energetic action was essential. In 1994, a joint operational structure, the *Société d'Économie Mixte* (SEM) *de l'Accueil* was created to put into force a *Projet d'A-*

The gardens

menagement Concerte (planned development project), the priorities of which were: improving traffic and parking, the renovation of the *Accueils* for the sick, the reception and management of large crowds, the preservation of the environment and architectural heritage.

This collaboration, which has already proved to be of immense benefit, is now in full operation. It is, in fact, being extended further by the various initiatives undertaken by the *SEM de l'Accueil*, such as the recent renovation of the Basilica of the Rosary. It also highlights what is still needed for Lourdes to constantly adapt to new demands and to be anchored at the heart of world pilgrimage.

Beside the 'lower town', where the Shrine and most of the hotels are situated, the traditional town sits in the higher part, on the same level as the castle. The resident population is 17,500, which increases with the arrival of the seasonal workers.

Situated at the conversion of several major roads, at the heart of a splendid region which attracts many tourists, Lourdes is an important centre in its own right, independently of the religious aspect. It is a very busy commercial centre. Within a magnificently renovated covered structure, a lively and picturesque daily market and a great variety of shops attract customers from the region and also visitors who come from all over the world.

On the industrial side, there are some forty industrial enterprises employing more than 1200 people. In collaboration with international enterprises commercial activities have been set up in several areas of expertise: in the field of plastics, electrical goods, aeronautical assembly, mechanical engineering, biomedical products and industrial electronics.

VEUILLOT, LOUIS (journalist)

At the time of the events of Lourdes, Louis Veuillot (1813-1883) had been an established and well-respected Catholic journalist for more than 20 years.

In July 1858 he was parish priest at Bagnères and Mgr Salinis, who also lived there, insisted that he went with him to live with the widow Beauregard. He complained about this in a letter to his brother Eugene dated 23 July. He had heard of Lourdes and went there on 28 of that month. He spoke at length with the parish priest, deeply convinced by the apparitions. He found himself in noble company, because the governess of the imperial prince, her three daughters, a religious sister and a priest were there as well. It was forbidden at that time to visit the Grotto, but our tourists, pilgrims in their own way, went there all the same. They were charged by the gendarme Callet, who found himself in an interesting position when the whole saga became known to the authorities, the mayor, the police inspector and the *préfet*.

Louis Veuillot, who had already studied the facts around la Salette, was convinced of the truth of the apparitions and publishes the article of M Estrade who had been an astonished witness of the apparition of 3 March, in his newspaper *L'Univers*. And on 28 August 1858 he published in the same paper a five column article about the facts of Lourdes. Several passages of it were directly taken from the writings of M Estrade. Two copies of the newspaper were sent to the parish priest and to Mlle Pailhasson, so that the whole town could read them.

Louis Veuillot had a personal meeting with Bernadette during which his convictions about the supernatural reality of the apparitions will be enforced. As one can imagine, the taking of position of a man of his stature triggered a real storm in the press. The declaration of Bishop Laurence of 18 January 1862 will finally put a full-stop to the Catholic interrogations.

VIPs

Innumerable VIPs have visited the Grotto. They were not long in coming: on the day after the last apparition, on 17 July 1858, the parade started already with the Bishop of Montpellier, coming from Cauterets, and wishing to meet Bernadette. A carriage arrived discreetly at around one o'clock in the afternoon, near the presbytery: a young priest, a vicar general and Bishop Thibault descended. Dr Douzou and M Estrade took it upon themselves to bring Bernadette. The latter, true to herself, spoke with simplicity, declined to participate in a small meal and brushed aside the Rosary, set in gold, which was offered to her. She called the bishop Monsieur le Curé, as she had never seen a bishop before. Bishop Thibault was dumbfounded by the exchange, overwhelmed, and could not understand the reticence of Bishop Laurence who would meet Bernadette only two years later. It was thanks to him that eleven days later Bishop Laurence, methodical and prudent as he was, would set up a commission to study the events of Lourdes.

The next day, another important visitor, Bishop de Garsignies of Soissons, arrived, followed by Archbishop de Salinis of Auch. The *Préfet* Massy became curious and wrote to his minister on 23 July. He didn't know what was awaiting him.

On 28 July Lady Admirale Bruat, governess of the imperial prince, her three daughters and a religious sister, came to the presbytery to see Bernadette and to go to the Grotto, which had been closed by legal action. Bernadette refused to accompany them: 'It is forbidden!' Another very well known person joined them: the great journalist Louis Veuillot.

All this was the preamble to an uninterrupted sequence of visitors. Nowadays, the Order of Malta has made the presence in Lourdes of the princes and princesses of Gotha a regular feature; Europe's greatest doctors have come to Lourdes after Alexis Carrel, a Nobel prize winner, had been witness to an astonishing miracle in 1902; and also heads of State and personalities from the world of entertainment.

Of course, some of these did not pass unnoticed, such as Emile Zola, in 1892. His short stay of two weeks caused a veritable shock wave as it led to the publication of his polemical book, *Lourdes*, which was the first direct attack against the supernatural character of the apparitions and healings. Twelve years later, Huysmans gave his reply with his famous book, *Les Foules de Lourdes.*

Certain facts of apparently minor importance had a huge impact: on 7 July 1948, the Tour de France passed through Lourdes with its great winner, Gino Bartali. Pius XII was enthusiastic and commended the cyclist as an example to the 300,000 members of the Italian Catholic Action, while Bishop Théas invoked 'Our Lady of the Tour de France'!

How many foreign ambassadors, Hindu, Muslim and, particularly, Buddhist personalities have felt at ease with the universal symbols of Lourdes. The Dalai-Lama visited Massabielle officially, in the context of a service of prayer for peace, on 15 November 1993.

Orthodox and Anglican dignitaries have been happy to celebrate liturgies in Lourdes. The Patriarch of Constantinople, Bartholomew, came to visit the Grotto in 1996.

The greatest visitors have been, without doubt, Pope John XXIII, who inaugurated the Basilica of Saint Pius X, just before his election, and Pope John Paul II. He had planned to come in July 1981 for the International Eucharistic Congress. The attempt on his life of 13 May prevented his visit. His first great encounter with the Grotto took place on 15 August 1983. He would return, already ill and almost without power of speech, in that painful and splendid pilgrimage of 2004, to pray to this Virgin whom he loved so much, to whom he wanted to fully belong: *totus tuus.*

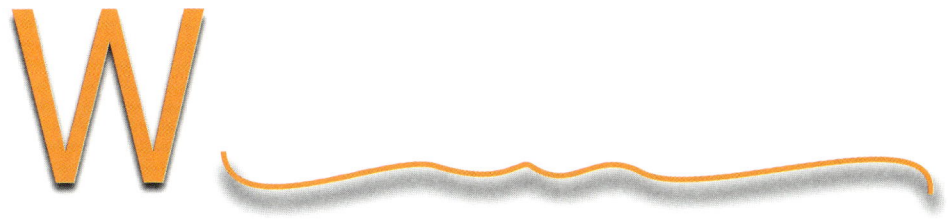

WATER

Water is imbued with many and varied symbolic meanings. It is the source of life – without water, there is only death and desert. Water quenches our thirst, it is invigorating, it purifies. Water also, sometimes, signifies death: the water of the floods which engulfs everything in its passage, the tsunami, the tidal waves. Water: sepulchral and maternal.

In the light of the Scriptures
'They have abandoned me, the fountain of living water, and dug water-tanks for themselves, cracked water-tanks that hold no water at all' (Jeremiah, 2: 13). 'My soul is thirsting for the living God' (Ps 63, 2). 'Let anyone who is thirsty come to me ... and drink,' Jesus says to us (John 7: 37-38). 'Sir, give me some of that living water,' said the Samaritan woman to Jesus (John 4,15). And Jesus said to Nicodemus: 'No one can enter the kingdom of God without being born through water and the Spirit' (John 3,5). And so we are invited to re-visit our baptism.

Water of Lourdes
In Lourdes, the Virgin Mary announces only the Gospel. In the 'penance apparitions', the eighth on 24 February and those which followed, the Lady, her face marked with sadness, asked Bernadette to make gestures of penance 'for sinners' such as: walking on her knees, kissing the ground, eating grass and, above all, praying: 'Pray for sinners.' And she added: 'Go and drink at the spring and wash.'

'Go': It is an invitation to start on one's way; to be a pilgrim is to walk towards God. I am invited to go on the 'water of Lourdes trail'.

'To the spring': the spring existed but it was hidden, buried. We are required to search for it, as Bernadette had to do, guided by God from within, then to free it from all that encumbers it, to purify it'.

'Drink': to quench our thirst in the midst of the consumer civilization. Mary bids us to ask for living water, to drink from God's word, to go towards Jesus, the source of eternal life.' '...but whoever drinks the water that I will give him will never be thirsty again. The water

W

that I will give him will become in him a spring which will provide life-giving water and give him eternal life' (John 4, 14).

'**And wash yourself in it**': a call to revive the grace of our baptism when we were immersed in God; a call, under Mary's gaze, to recognize what is unclear inside ourselves, to let God wash us, purify us, give us the joy of being forgiven.

And so, all our actions, when we drink the Grotto water, wash our faces in it, immerse ourselves in it by bathing in the pools, when we receive the sacrament of reconciliation, will be gestures of faith, of a new life.

Water is an archetypal symbol within most religions: the water of the Ganges as well as the water of the Jordan. So what is this Lourdes water which pilgrims take home in bucketfuls, and which is despatched all over the world?

The term 'Grotto water' should be used at all times as it must always be linked to the apparitions. Otherwise, there is a great risk of making it a 'miraculous', 'magical' kind of water, a pot of gold for the 'souvenirs' merchants.

Already, during Bernadette's lifetime, Mayor Lacadé dreamed of making Lourdes a thermal resort. To this end, he had the water analysed. The result was always the same: 'Drinking water, of good quality.' So the water of the Grotto is neither thermal, nor radioactive – it is ordinary. And yet, sick people were cured by it. Bishop Laurence, in his pastoral letter on the apparitions, extracted as examples, seven cures which he recognized as the 'work of God', stating: 'These cures were the result of the use of water which has no natural healing qualities, as reported by reputed chemists who subjected it to rigorous analysis... These cures are the work of God. They are linked to the apparition... It is she who inspired the sick persons' trust.'

And so, it is clear, the Grotto water is not in itself miraculous. It is faith which saves, as Bernadette would say, when she was a nurse in Nevers: 'We should give him/her some Lourdes water and pray to the Holy Virgin to bring him/her some relief.' She never separated water from prayer: 'This water is not medicine... one must have faith and pray... this water would have no special quality without faith.'

It is important always to safeguard:

- its authenticity: it is the Grotto water, as it can be seen under a glass protection, always connected with the message which gives it its meaning;

- its gift status: sign of a gift from God, it is not sold, no trade can ever take place.

- its truth – it is neither an amulet nor a talisman; it contains nothing 'magical'.

The Grotto water supports our prayer and is a symbol of our trust in Mary. It comes as a particular gift from God who wishes our healing through this vital sign. Near the fountains there is an inscription which reminds us of this fact: 'Wash your face and ask God to purify your heart.'

YOUNG PEOPLE

Between Lourdes and young people there has been a relationship that has existed since the very first apparition. Bernadette herself was no more than a young girl of 14. Young people feel drawn to Lourdes as though someone is waiting there for them - Mary.

Every year around 400,000 young people visit Lourdes. The majority come with their diocese or other organisations, movements and associations. Some come on special youth pilgrimages, others as helpers for the sick. Many come out of curiosity: they wish to see and to discover what it is like, but they are also searching for answers to the great existential questions of life.

The Christian experience they

Young people's village

Village chapel

Y live at Lourdes focuses on 4 main principles which are characteristic of young people:

1) Young people feel a strong need to meet and celebrate with other young people. They are happy to live alongside each other. Lourdes offers them this possibility with an international dimension. They meet young people of other nationalities who share the same faith in Jesus and the same desire to be of service. This brings them together and leads to mutual discovery of one another.

2) Young people feel the deep need to serve others. They know they can do this at Lourdes, freely giving up their time and energy to help others. By taking on new responsibilities in this way they grow in maturity and some of them find their vocation, to which they commit themselves for the rest of their lives.

3) Lourdes is a place of catechesis. At Lourdes young people can take advantage of time for reflection in which to contemplate the beauty of the Gospel. They are being offered Bernadette's own experience, that of being taught the Catechism by Our Lady herself. Often an unexpected grace invades their soul leaving a lasting impression on them. In the presence of the Shrine they do not feel judged, but rather set free, free to express their faith. They experience their own 'transfiguration'; thinking they are a certain type of person, they suddenly discover that they are different, made new by the waters of the spring with hearts that are healed by God's mercy in the sacrament of reconciliation which they

may not have received for a long time.

4) The Liturgy, which is so often inaccessible to young people, in Lourdes touches their hearts. Every year an international mass for young people is celebrated, especially adapted for them, rich in symbolism and language they can relate to. Their mass reveals the youthful face of the universal Church which prays and celebrates with joy. The monthly prayer vigil; the liturgy of water which invites them to renew their baptismal promises; the sacrament of reconciliation preceded by a special time of preparation and the Way of the Cross, all of these enable young people to gradually discover Christ and the Church, and worship the Lord in their own way.

At Lourdes, young people are given great importance. They bring change to the Shrine, such as the creation of the young people's village (*le village des jeunes*), which is approximately 15 hectares in size, providing accommodation for up to 350 people, in various buildings, as well as providing camping facilities for a further 3,000 young people. These camping facilities are more than just a campsite; they are places full of life, communion and prayer.

We can conclude by saying that this world of young people is 'missionary territory', on which a new evangelisation is being carried out which in its own time will bear many fruits.

Map

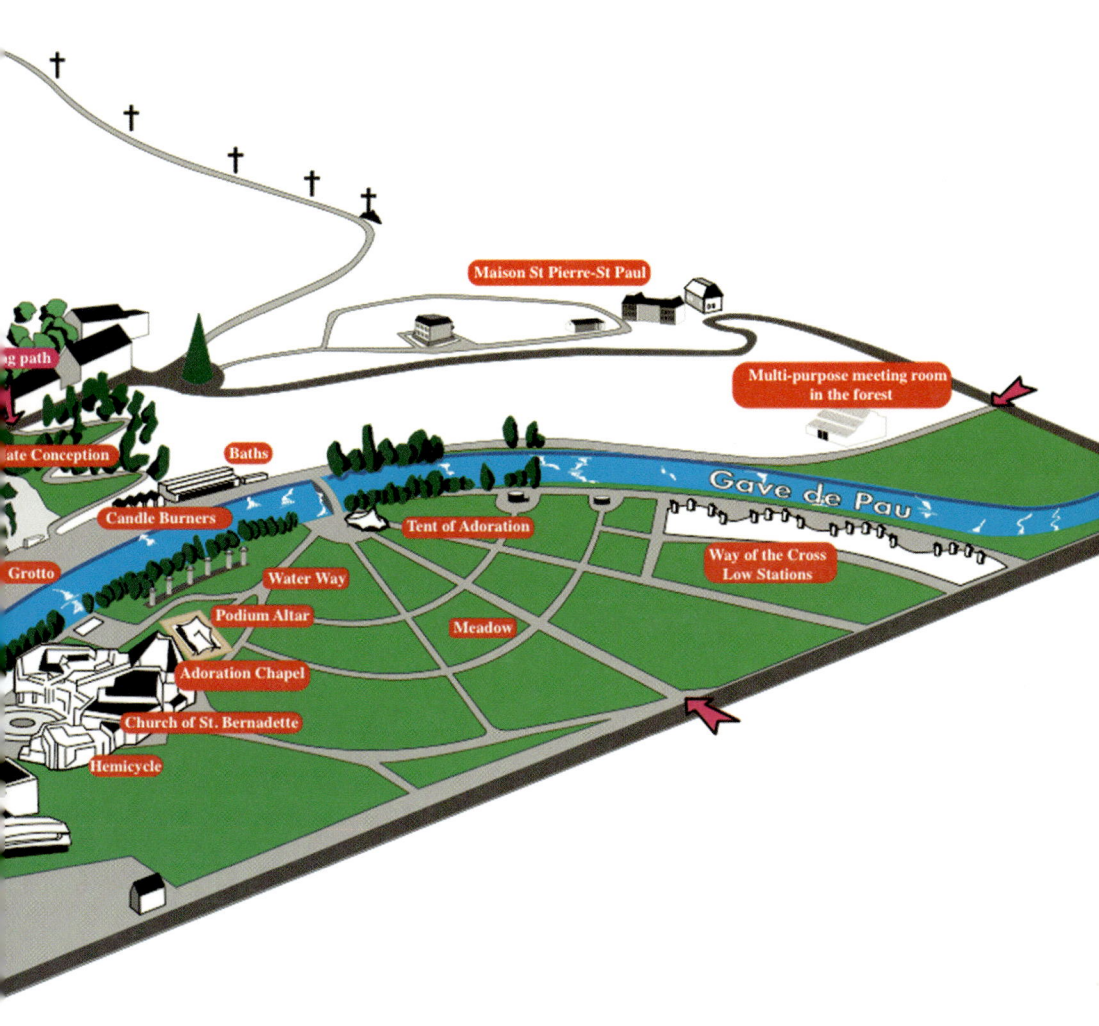

CREDITS

Pierre Adias
Media

Gérard Altuzarra
Accueil Notre-Dame, Baths, Grotto Estate, Photography, Sisters of St Joseph of Tarbes

Nino Bucca
Dance Theatre, Eucharist, Hospice, Museum of Bernadette, Nevers, Oblates of Mary Immaculate, Parish Church, Penance, Presbytery, Pyrenees, *Salus Infirmorum*, Sisters of Nevers

André Cabes
Cachot, Ecumenism, Immaculate Conception, Mary, Mariology of Lourdes, Mill of Boly, Prayer, Society and Lourdes

Fabio Ciardi
Apparitions, Church, Miracles, Pilgrimage, Popular Religion, Rosary, Shrines

Denis Crampe
Town

Régis-Marie de la Teyssonière
Chaplains, *Hospitalité*, Internationality, Outreach of Lourdes in the World

Michel de Roton
Apparitions of Lourdes, Bernadette, Donze - Henri, Light, Message of Lourdes, Thanksgiving Plaques, Rock, Sahuquet - Jean, Signs, Water

Francis Dias
Information Forum

André Doze
Accueil Marie Saint-Frai, Annals of Our Lady of Lourdes, *Aquero*, Bartrès, Bétharram, Bigorre, Billère - Prosper-Marie, Billet - Bernard, Boissarie - Gustave, Castérot - Louise, Castle, Centenary, Choquet - Georges, Cohen - Hermann, Courtin - Jean-Baptiste, Cros - Léonard-Marie, Désirat - Antoine, Diary of Bernadette, Dozous - Pierre-Romain, Dufo - Brice, de Saint-Maclou - Dunot, Dutour Vital, Enfants de Marie, Espélugues, Estrade - Jean-Baptiste, Garicoïts - Michel, Gave, Gerlier - Pierre Paul-Marie, Grotto, Images, Jacomet - Dominique, John XXXIII, John Paul II, Jourdan - César-Victor, Lacadé - Anselme, Laguës - Marie, Langénieux - Benoît, Lasserre - Henri, Laurence - Bertrand-Sévère, Laurentin - René, Leo XIII, Literature, Marie-Antoine, Massy - Oscar, Napoleon III, Paul VI, Peyramale - Dominique, Pichenot - Pierre-Athanase, Pilgrimages to Lourdes, Pius IX, Pius X, Pius XI, Pius XII, Ploërmel Brothers, Poirier - Alexandre, Pomian - Bertrand-Marie, Prominent Women, Ravier - André, Rectors, Saint-Frai - Marie, Schoepfer - François-Xavier, Sempé - Rémi, Soubirous - François, Spring, Théas - Pierre-Marie, Veuillot - Louis, VIPs

Chelo Feral
Pavilions

Vittorio Giacci
Cinema

Martine Guénard
Service for People with Disabilities

Laurent Jarneau
Internet

Jean-Claude Lebrun
Cité Saint-Pierre

Jean-Paul Lecot
Ave Maria, Festival of Sacred Music, Liturgical Music, Organs

Jean-François Monnory
Eucharistic Procession, Liturgy, Marian Procession, Museum (Treasure), Stations of the Cross

Bishop Jacques Perrier
Diocese, Pastoral Ministry, European Marian Network

René Point
Garaison, Missionaries of the Immaculate Conception

Mathias Terrier
Radio

Patrick Theillier
Bureau Medical, Miracles of Lourdes, Science and Lourdes, Sick Pilgrims

Chantal Touvet
Architecture, Archives, Basilica of the Immaculate Conception, Basilica of the Rosary, Basilica of St Pius X, Branthomme - Henri, Crypt, Church of St Bernadette, Crowned Virgin, Statue of the Immaculate Conception

François Vayne
Bookshop, Lourdes Magazine, Press

Saverio Zampa
Young People

PHOTOGRAPHS

Sanctuaires Notre-Dame de Lourdes / EURL Basilique Rosaire:
* 11, 14, 19, 23, 29, 30, 33, 34, 35, 41, 46, 49, 56, 59, 61, 62, 63, 67, 70, 75, 76, 78, 79, 85, 86, 92, 95, 97, 98, 99, 101, 103, 110, 113, 119, 126, 141, 143, 149, 151, 156, 158, 160, 161, 167, 175, 178, 180, 191, 193, 194, 195, 198, 203.

Nino Bucca
** 13, 24, 25, 26, 27, 36, 39, 40, 42, 45, 55, 67, 77, 81, 83, 87, 104, 105, 111, 116, 123, 128, 129, 137, 147, 150, 154, 155, 157, 163, 164, 165, 168, 171, 175, 177, 182, 185, 187, 200, 201, 207, 211, 212

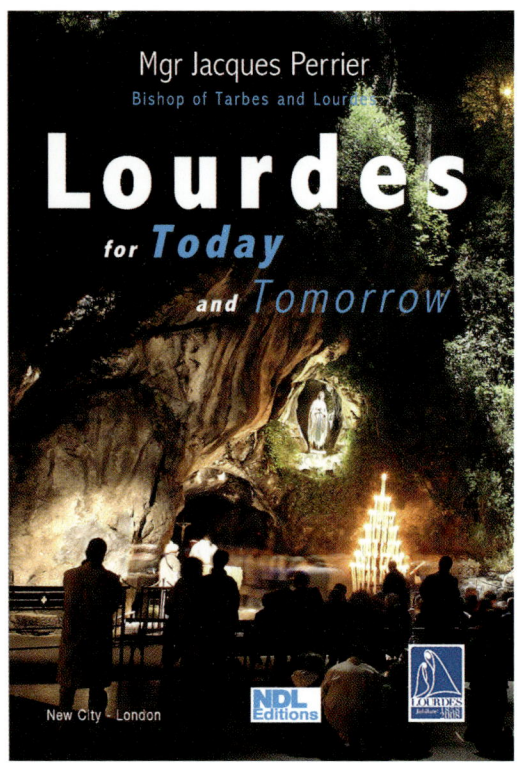

ISBN: 978-1-905039-05-0   174 pp   £11.95

2008 marked the 150th anniversary of the apparitions of the Virgin Mary to Bernadette Soubirous. Over the last century and a half Lourdes has grown and developed as a centre for pilgrims from all over the world, from every walk of life, from various Christian traditions and from other faiths.

In this special anniversary book, Jacques Perrier, the Bishop of Tarbes and Lourdes, looks to the future and sets out what he sees as the 12 'missions' of Lourdes. These include the mission to the sick, and the disabled, but also to the young and the marginalised. Each chapter is followed by a personal experience relating to the particular theme.

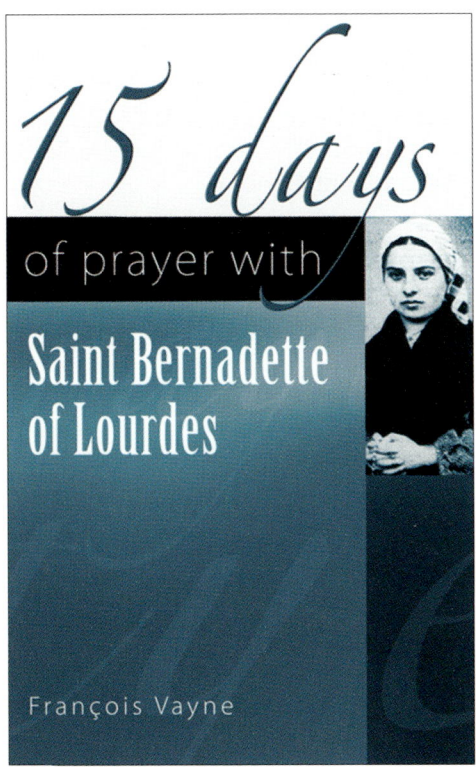

ISBN: 978-1-56548-314-9   136 pp   £8.95

Bernadette became a saint, not because the Virgin Mary appeared to her, but because of her willingness to do God's will and to love those around her.

Born into a humble family which fell into extreme poverty, Bernadette was only fourteen when the Virgin Mary appeared to her for the first of eighteen visits near Lourdes, in southern France. A woman of faith and purity, Bernadette maintained a state of childlike innocence throughout her short life believing that God is Love and that he never stops calling us away from sin. Although Bernadette endured the painful disease of tuberculosis of the bone she continued to live a life of service faithfully as a Sister of Charity until her death in 1879.

Enjoy your time with Saint Bernadette of Lourdes and be prepared to be surprised as you journey with one of the most engaging spiritual figures of our time.

This book studies an often neglected strand of Anglican theological thought, but one which will speak to Christians of all traditions.
It shows how issues to do with Mary and her place in salvation history are highly relevant to contemporary concerns.

ISBN: 0-904287-48-3   218 pp   £9.95

The pages of this beautiful reflection on Mary offer the reader a new vision of the mother of Jesus, and a new understanding of her role as a model for the Church and for individual Christians.

ISBN: 0-904287-86-6
107 pp   £6.50

Megan McKenna is a storyteller with a passion for justice and in this book looks at Mary as a sign of contradiction. Written in marvelous prose it offers an excellent choice for reflection on Marian celebrations throughout the year.

ISBN: 978-1-56548-260
191 pp   £10.95

Rooted in mariological teaching and making constant references to Scripture, tradition and the magisterium, this work describes Mary as an 'enchanting creature, the most beautiful one that ever bloomed in the garden of humanity, who sprang from the very heart of the Trinity'.

ISBN: 978-1-56548-292-0 344 pp   £21.50

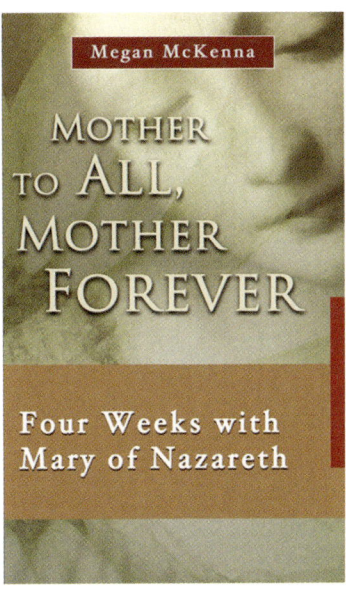

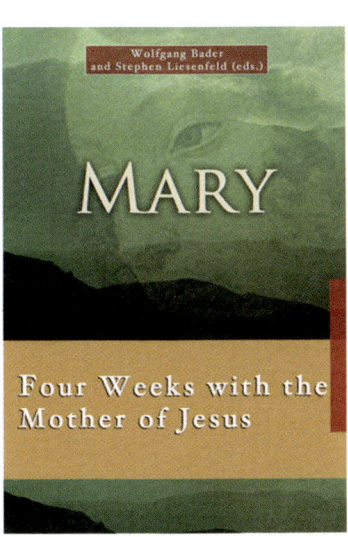

In this meditative work we are given a four week period pondering Mary's relationship with God, with her son, with others and with us.

Using as a title an expression of John Paul II in referring to Mary, this book is an invitation to take Mary into our own homes and so show the world the fruitfulness of love and the authentic meaning of life.

ISBN: 978-1-56548-316-3
71 pp   £5.95

ISBN: 978-1-56548-281-4
72 pp   £5.95